"*Unraveling Assumptions* opens the door to seeing your place in the world in a new way. Suyemoto, Donovan, and Kim lead their readers to a nuanced understanding of oppression and privilege, supported by concrete tools to deepen engagement with one's own learning process. The clear examples and personal reflection prompts encourage self-reflection and meaningful conversations."

    – **Sofya Aptekar**, *Associate Professor, School of Labor and Urban Studies, City University of New York*

"Conversations about privilege, oppression, racism, social class, disability, sexuality, gender, and culture can be like walking amid land mines. How, therefore, do we resist together while we hold ourselves accountable and stay in relationship? Suyemoto, Donovan, and Kim offer much more than a clear conceptual map for having these conversations, offering resources and stories that can help us transverse these land mines without losing our souls or the other. This is a must book in courses related to social justice, multicultural education, human services, psychology, and almost any professional field that hopes to incorporate dialogue across difference and the pervasive injustice that has been part of each of us."

    – **Gonzalo Bacigalupe**, *Professor, Department of Counseling and School Psychology, University of Massachusetts*

"Suyemoto, Donovan, and Kim's *Unraveling Assumptions: A Primer for Understanding Oppression and Privilege* is the book I have been looking for since I started teaching multicultural psychology over 10 years ago. It provides excellent descriptions of important constructs while also engaging the reader to reflect on their assumptions, experiences, and emotional reactions with reflection prompts. The authors both challenge and encourage the reader throughout the book and also provide ideas on how to continue the work of resisting oppression."

    – **Nadine Nakamura**, *Professor, California School of Professional Psychology, Alliant International University*

Unraveling Assumptions

Unraveling Assumptions: A Primer for Understanding Oppression and Privilege offers fundamental understandings of concepts and frameworks related to diversity and social justice. Aimed at university and community audiences, it offers an introductory exploration of power, privilege, and oppression as foundations of systems of inequity, and examines complexities within meanings and lived experiences of race, ethnicity, gender, sexuality, disability, and social class.

After considering why it is so difficult to engage these issues, the authors explore meanings and impacts of power, privilege, and oppression as a primary lens of analysis. Subsequent chapters offer definitions of race, ethnicity, gender, sexuality, disability, and social class, identifying erroneous assumptions and challenging the tendency to oversimplify and decontextualize. Meanings, identities, and effects of oppression and privilege are central foci within each chapter. The book ends with a chapter examining ways that individuals may take action as allies and advocates to resist oppression. Throughout the book, *Unraveling Assumptions* makes connections among individual, interpersonal, and systemic levels of inequity, while focusing on relational and psychological implications for lived experience—including the reader's lived experience.

By integrating social science research with concrete examples and personal reflection, this concise, introductory level text invites the reader to consider the costs of systemic hierarchies for all people and envision possible alternatives to participating in oppressive hierarchy.

Karen L. Suyemoto is Professor of Psychology with affiliations in Asian American Studies and Critical Ethnic and Community Studies at the University of Massachusetts Boston.

Roxanne A. Donovan is a licensed psychologist and Professor of Psychological Sciences jointly appointed in Interdisciplinary Studies at Kennesaw State University.

Grace S. Kim is Clinical Associate Professor in the department of Counseling Psychology & Applied Human Development at Boston University.

Unraveling Assumptions

A Primer for Understanding Oppression
and Privilege

Karen L. Suyemoto
Roxanne A. Donovan
Grace S. Kim

Routledge
Taylor & Francis Group

NEW YORK AND LONDON

Cover image: Getty Images

First published 2022
by Routledge
605 Third Avenue, New York, NY 10158

and by Routledge
4 Park Square, Milton Park, Abingdon, Oxon OX14 4RN

Routledge is an imprint of the Taylor & Francis Group, an informa business

Library of Congress Cataloging-in-Publication Data
A catalog record for this title has been requested

ISBN: 978-0-367-18120-8 (hbk)
ISBN: 978-0-367-18121-5 (pbk)
ISBN: 978-0-429-05959-9 (ebk)

DOI: 10.4324/9780429059599

Typeset in Baskerville
by Taylor & Francis Books

For those who seek to unravel assumptions and challenge impositions, who hold our hopes for a more liberated future.

For Eric, who asked for this book over a decade ago, and who has journeyed with me and dared to change.

(**KLS**)

For Jonah and Micah, there is no greater inspiration for the work I do than you.

(**RAD**)

For Yohan and Yuri, who sustain me in the present and give me hope for the future.

(**GSK**)

Contents

Figures

Tables

Acknowledgements

With thanks to those who provided thorough and thoughtful feedback on chapter drafts, many of whom have also shaped our understanding and growth: Sofya Aptekar, Lou Felipe, Elliot Marrow, Robert McCully, Michelle Nario-Redmond, David Pantalone, Jae Puckett, Rebecca Toporek. Thanks to folks who clarified points or guided us in identifying resources, including Chris Bobel, Erik Blaser, Zsuzsa Kaldy, and Gloria Wong-Padoongpatt. Big appreciation to Thanh Nguyen for artwork and figures. Thanks to Grace's graduate research assistants who identified, checked, and formatted our references and resources: Tanvi Shah, Tanya Songtachalert, Lauren Wong, and Leah Rosenzweig.

With appreciation to the family and friends who supported and sustained us through the writing process:

- Roxanne: Andy Pieper, Micah and Jonah Pieper, Yvonne Donovan, Jackie Donovan, Joseph Donovan, Nichole Guillory, Grace Kim, and Karen Suyemoto.
- Karen: Eric Parker, Alice Frye, Liz Roemer, Grace Kim, Roxanne Donovan, Tiffany Donaldson, Stephanie Day, and Tahirah Abdullah.
- Grace: Min Hyoung Song, Yohan Song, Yuri Song, Tina Durand, Kathy McDonough, Stephanie Day, Julie AhnAllen, Karen Suyemoto, and Roxanne Donovan.

Introduction

What This Book Is about

This primer introduces readers to core concepts and frameworks related to understanding diversity and social justice, with a relative focus on race and racism. Our overall aims in writing this book are to:

- Provide an introductory understanding of power, privilege, and oppression as foundations of social systems of inequity.
- Provide basic definitions and introductory discussion of several major social systems of inequity: race, ethnicity, gender, sexuality, disability, and social class.
- Encourage readers to make connections among individual, interpersonal, and systemic levels of inequality and consider their personal experiences within these systems of inequity.

Throughout the text, we integrate social science (e.g., psychology, sociology, anthropology, ethnic studies) understandings and research on these concepts, with a focus on relational and psychological meanings, responses, and implications for lived experience—including the reader's lived experience. Following an introductory chapter, the book consists of three sections:

- *Section One: Foundations: Social Construction, Culture, Power, Oppression, and Privilege*. In this section, we provide an introductory understanding of power, privilege, and oppression as foundations of social systems of inequity.
- *Section Two: Understanding Hierarchies of Oppression and Privilege: Race, Ethnicity, Sex and Gender, Sexuality, Disability, and Social Class*. In the chapters in this section, we provide basic definitions of each of these major social systems of inequity; describe erroneous assumptions; explore complexities of each category as social construct and identity; and examine associated dynamics of oppression.
- *Section Three: Resisting Oppression*. In the final chapter of the book, we focus on understanding and enacting resistance to oppression, considering how people can act in ways that reflect values of equity and justice.

Throughout the book, we consider how readers (particularly readers who are new to this material) might respond, especially given the socialization

DOI: 10.4324/9780429059599-1

available in the United States. This approach begins in Chapter 1: "Preparing for Learning," which explicitly invites readers to consider how and why they might respond to this content and offers some basic strategies to encourage an openness to engagement. Chapters throughout the rest of the text include reflection exercises that explicitly invite readers to apply the concepts to their own experiences, perspectives, and interactions. We also include "pull-outs" that focus on issues of language ("How Do I Say?") and expanding complexities of some basic concepts ("It's Complicated"). Each chapter concludes with "Resources for Learning More," a list of resources for further engagement.

Our intention is for this book to serve as an *introduction*. The concepts we discuss here are complicated, and there are thousands of books and articles that have been written about these topics that examine things like historical development, social and political dynamics, cross-cultural differences, language, psychological effects, identity, representations in literature and media, and many more. Each discipline area has books or articles that relate to these issues. And understandings and language for these ideas are constantly growing and changing. Our hope is that what we present here will provide a foundation for readers to reflect on and pique their curiosity for further exploration.

1 Preparing for Learning about Oppression and Privilege

Dear Reader,

Welcome! Whatever your reason for reading our book—whether for a class you're taking or personal interest—we're excited you're here. Embarking on any new journey of learning can be challenging. How challenging partly depends on the path you're taking and your preparation. According to our students, learning about diversity[1] is not an easy path and students often feel apprehensive about this material. We understand. As psychologists, we get how it can be uncomfortable, even upsetting, to engage learning that asks you to take a critical look at how you think about yourself, others, and the world. These realities are why this first chapter focuses on preparing you for what's to come. Specifically, we address what makes talking about diversity hard, the difficult reactions you might have to the topics explored in this book, and the psychological principles that can help you interpret and best respond to these reactions.

Our intention in writing this book is to open possibilities. We are inviting you to consider the possibility that you may have assumptions that you haven't yet critically examined. Most people do. We seek to explore these assumptions: where they come from and why they matter. Because such explorations can bring up difficult emotions, we also invite you to pay attention to your own reactions to learning, and to consider these reactions in light of the social dynamics surrounding ideas about diversity.

At the same time, learning about diversity isn't only about challenge. There are many rewards and opportunities for growth. The remainder of this letter is about those possibilities, about what might open for you internally and inter-personally through your learning (and afterward). We hope sharing these possibilities and the potential of diversity education brings you motivation and excitement for the learning ahead.

One possibility of learning to challenge assumptions can be expanded insight and agency (the feeling and ability to take action). We often hear things like "This is how things have always been and will always be" and "There's

---

1   By diversity, we mean issues such as race, ethnicity, social class, sexuality, disability, and intersectionality among these that affect individual experiences, as well as access to resources and opportunities, because of the ways that these issues are related to social hierarchies of power, privilege, and oppression.

DOI: 10.4324/9780429059599-2

nothing I can do to make a difference" from students new to the study of diversity. What you read in this book may challenge these beliefs (if you have them) by bringing understanding about the origins and perpetuation of bias, clarity as to why different groups may perceive the world differently, and, most importantly, hope around your ability to acknowledge and embrace differences while also challenging unwanted bias. This hope is especially important in our present moment when issues like racism, sexism, and heterosexism seem intractable. In this divisive environment, it's easy to forget that you have agency to effect positive change. Even if your actions seem small, the ripples they create can extend beyond your imagining.

Another possibility relates to developing deeper and more authentic inter-personal connections. Humans are a social species. Like food, water, and shelter, interpersonal connection is necessary to our health and well-being. Connecting across difference, though, isn't easy. We tend to favor those who are like us and disfavor those who aren't. This *ingroup bias* means that it's easier to see, hear, or value those who share our race, class, or nationality, for instance, and easier to misrecognize, devalue, or discriminate against those who don't (i.e., outgroup members). At its foundation, diversity education opens the possibility of widening our circles to include those previously viewed as outgroup members. We believe this perception shift provides great opportunities for personal growth and for societal healing. Our students agree. At the end of our classes, many report a sense of connection with those who are similar to *and* different from them, without having to erase or ignore important differences. They also describe a deeper sense of purpose for and commitment to advancing well-being for all.

A third possibility is expanding your engagement in valued action, which is action that aligns with your values and the person you want to be. We assume that you and the rest of our readers value fairness, that you are good people who don't want to be biased or hurt others. Bias, though, is tricky because you can hold biases and not know it, which is called *implicit bias.* Research in social psychology shows that implicit bias is quite common and affects our beliefs about social groups. Moreover, we may act from these hidden biases, causing uninten-tional harm to others. However, if we develop greater awareness, we can be more effective at enacting our intentions for equity. The learning offered throughout this book is an opportunity to make these biases visible. As a result, you may discover avenues for greater alignment between your own values and your actions.

As you start this journey of possibilities, you may want to know what lies at the end. We have no answers because diversity learning has no endpoint, no location that you arrive at where you now know all, understand all. The learning is *in* the journey. It's in the understanding, the connection, the clarity you discover along the way. It is even in the struggle to understand and the process of questioning both old and new understandings. Unfortunately, we know that every reader won't want to engage in this learning. How you approach the material matters. You may have to face questions for yourself such as, "do I persevere when obstacles or doubts arise, do I stop, do I turn back?" This chapter is about tipping the scales toward perseverance, because there is beauty in the struggle even when that beauty is hard to see.

In peace and solidarity,

Karen, Roxanne, and Grace

Why Is Talking (and Learning) about Diversity So Hard?

If you've ever tried to talk about diversity topics like racism or sexism or classism with someone who didn't share your viewpoint, you already know how uncomfortable and contentious these conversations can be. More likely than not, one or both of you felt frustrated or unheard, distressed or angry. Maybe little was resolved at the end other than agreeing to disagree. You might have wondered why the other person didn't share your perspective or why you couldn't find common ground. How we see ourselves and the world is influenced by intersecting and oftentimes hidden factors that can support or hinder our ability to engage diversity issues. We introduce several of these factors in this section and explore them in more detail throughout the book, because knowing what might be impacting your perspective and reactions, and the reactions of others with whom you are interacting, can go a long way toward helping you choose how you'd like to show up to these conversations and engage the learning in this book.

Early Lessons That Some Topics Are Taboo

Talking about diversity in ways that emphasize distinctions among groups is so uncomfortable you were probably taught to avoid it. You're not alone. In the United States, most of us learn early on from family, teachers, and/or others not to talk openly about our experiences with race and racism, or other kinds of diversity and "isms." Even when we do talk about these things, it's rarely with those we don't know well or with those who don't share our background. Think for a minute about your own experience, and your friends and family. How often do you talk with others about race or ethnicity? How often do you talk about gender or sexuality? Social class or disabilities? To whom do you talk about these things? Are there kinds of people with whom you are more or less likely to talk about each of these issues? We go into socialization in more detail in Chapters 2 and 3, but our point here is that engaging "taboo" topics can feel dangerous and uncomfortable because you are not used to it, and you're challenging notions of what is and isn't okay to talk about.

[handwritten margin note: -not often -hispanics - never gender sexuality]

Limited Educational Preparation

Adding to the challenge of conversing about diversity is the U.S. K-12 education system which typically does not prepare students to grapple with the complications of social difference. You might have been taught about race and gender and maybe even sexuality, social class, and ability but were likely not taught as much or as in depth about these topics as you might have been, or as others were. Even when history that directly relates to social differences is addressed in K-12 education, these events are rarely connected to present day challenges. This means, for example, you probably learned about slavery without also learning about the many post-slavery policies and practices that continue to negatively affect financial security in Black communities (e.g., redlining, job discrimination, mortgage discrimination, community displacement, gerrymandering). The oversimplification and decontextualization around social differences leave many of us under- or mis-educated about the topics covered in this book. And without the shared understanding and clear meanings as a starting point, it is no wonder that talking to each other constructively about differences is fraught with discomfort and difficulties.

Cultural Belief in Meritocracy

Learning about power, privilege, and oppression can also be difficult because it challenges widely accepted and unquestioned cultural beliefs in meritocracy and a just world. Meritocracy is the belief that success results solely or primarily from an individual's personal skills and hard work. Meritocracy is a compelling narrative because it creates the soothing impression that you are the sole architect of your future, that where you end up in life is mostly under your control. If you believe in meritocracy and the idea of a just world, you tend to believe that people get what they deserve. So, if people are successful and have a lot of "goodies," it is because they deserve that success. And if people don't have success and related goodies, it is because they haven't earned them and don't deserve them. "Goodies" here includes many positive things such as money and resources, respect, positive assumptions and judgments from others, feelings of belonging and safety, representation in media or institutions (e.g., seeing people who are like you on TV shows or in movies, as teachers in your schools or officials in your government). It also includes the experiences related to earning the goodies, such as access to a good education or good jobs.

Under a true meritocracy, the answer to the question "who gets to have the goodies?" would be "the people who deserve the goodies." In some cases, this might be all people (as in human rights), in other cases, this might be the people who work hard or are talented or use their skills who will get to have the goodies. Either way, the goodies are being distributed fairly, on the basis of shared entitlement and earned merit: this is what we are taught to believe, that we live in a meritocracy. However, behind the self-determinism of meritocracy is an unspoken assumption that everyone has equal opportunities to have the goodies, that we all start on a level playing field. Learning about power, privilege, and oppression challenges this assumption by calling our attention to observations of U.S. society and research in many disciplines that show the U.S. context is not a level playing field: not everyone has the same opportunities to earn the goodies, no matter how hard they try. Confronting this reality can be disorienting and raise questions about your own deservingness. However, rejecting a simple and absolute idea of meritocracy doesn't mean that you haven't worked hard, or that you are not deserving of your success, only that actually achieving success is not just about what you (or others) do to earn it. In sum, holding too strongly to the idea of meritocracy can undermine our ability to appreciate the limits of individual effort and the complicated ways social differences like race and gender, sexuality, class, and ability can impact life outcomes. But because the notion of meritocracy is so widespread, you may find learning about power, privilege, and oppression in this book to be challenging.

Invisible Influence of Social Hierarchies

Some students find it difficult to engage learning about power, privilege, and oppression because they feel or believe the social differences that are talked about such as race, gender, or disability, are not what is most important to them. Given all of the ways two people might differ—hair color, athletic ability, hand preference, political affiliation, and height—you might wonder why we focus this book on the social differences of race, ethnicity, gender, sexuality, social class, and ability. Why do these differences matter so much? While we provide a detailed answer in Chapter 2, the short answer for now is that race, ethnicity, gender, sexuality, social class, and ability all have considerable meaning and organizing power in society. Unlike other human differences like hair color and political affiliation, these categories and related statuses have outsized influence on our access to "the goodies," as well as our self-views and worldviews. However, the emphasis within the U.S. on individual experience sometimes makes it harder for some students to see how these categories are important, particularly if they have not seemed important to your life. It might be helpful to think about it this way: would your life—your access to education, your access to healthcare, your access to financial, food, housing security, your relationships—change fundamentally if [insert difference here] were to change? If the answer is an emphatic "yes," you've probably inserted a status that has particular social meaning, and not only individual meaning.

Alternatively, you may be very tuned in to the impact of these hierarchies and the effects on your life. But you might still experience engaging this material as tricky, difficult, or emotional. You may find it challenging to engage this material because you feel it so intensely. Or you may find it challenging to learn new things about areas that you thought you knew about, or that are really important to you. Even when students are aware of the influence of social hierarchies, they often have internalized erroneous assumptions about themselves and others.

In our experience, students know that other students might have different views and experiences. Students who haven't experienced these issues as personally relevant, or who have little knowledge about them are often aware that other students in a class find these issues very salient, feel very passionately about them, or have more knowledge. And vice versa. Sometimes, students coming from different backgrounds can also have prior negative experiences of trying to talk across these differences. Apprehension about engaging these social differences with your peers can also make it harder to engage the material in this book, both as you read and in related discussions. In sum how hard it is to talk about diversity can depend on how the topic relates to your status locations and the status locations of those you are talking to.

Unraveling Assumptions through Increasing Understanding and Awareness

Taken together, our early learning, cultural and educational influences, and status locations are like blinders on a horse, working together to constrict or expand what we can see. Not being aware of these blinders can make us confident that what we perceive, our worldview, is accurate. But this is an assumption that is often challenged by others or by later experience, as we confront the things we didn't know we didn't know. The good news is that none of us is stuck with the blinders we currently have. We can work to acknowledge that there are things we can't perceive (known unknowns) and seek out learning and experiences that widen our perception.

When people have or seek the opportunity to learn more about the world, interact with those who are different, and reflect on their own experiences, they often begin to question ideas of categorization and the established hierarchies within social systems of inequality. As they question, they seek out more information and experiences, and turn a more focused attention to questioning where these ideas come from and whether these ideas make sense to them personally. Sometimes, this means that they also make changes in the ways they see themselves and others. When people learn about diversity in more depth, they can develop more conscious or deliberate ideas about themselves in relation to hierarchies and groups. They may move from acceptance of assumptions to immersing themselves in learning and social experiences that actively challenge preexisting worldviews in order to explore possible alternatives. From here, people often move to work out their own balanced approach.

As you begin your learning journey, we want to underscore that you aren't bound by your previous lessons and experiences. Growth is possible and education, like your reading of this book, is one pathway. It is also important to understand that you are the creator of your worldview. So, our goal in this book is not to *make* you think or believe certain things, but (again) to invite you to consider possibilities, and bring your own skills in critical thinking and personal reflection to the learning. As you learn more—as you open yourself to more experiences, get to know what were once your unknown unknowns, and make more conscious choices about your own views—your ability to engage constructively with others around topics of diversity also improves. As a result, difficult dialogues about diversity don't have to end in frustration and disagreement. Empathy and understanding become possible, and it is in that space of empathy and understanding that true connection lies.

What Might Come Up for You while Reading This Book

Because of the aforementioned convergence of individual and cultural factors that lead to a general lack of preparedness to have conversations about diversity and a social context that conveys diversity topics are "taboo," many of us come into conversations about diversity in a state of heightened emotions that can cloud our ability to engage constructively with others even if that is our wish. You probably know this already, having likely experienced how conversations tend to fall apart when you try to have them when very angry or anxious. This means that understanding what makes talking about diversity hard is only the first step toward preparing yourself for this learning journey. The next step is to understand what emotions might come up for you while reading this book, and why some reactions are more likely than others.

Psychologists use the term *cognitive dissonance* to describe the discomfort that arises when faced with contradictions to our worldview or sense of self. Although this discomfort can manifest in a variety of ways, some common reactions we've seen among students in our diversity classes include:

- Fear or apprehension at being judged, at offending, at being called out, at being misunderstood
- Confusion or anxiety as you explore understandings of privilege and the ways that these understandings challenge simple ideas of meritocracy
- Anger or distress at not having learned the material before, at inequitable access to resources based on social hierarchies, at others who you may see as racist or sexist or classist, heterosexist or ableist
- Guilt or shame at past actions or inaction; and
- Despair or helplessness at the scope of the problem.

We'd like to pause here to note that cognitive dissonance is common, not inevitable. Some of our students experience positive emotions like relief at having diversity issues named, described, and validated; reassurance at having the language to talk about what they have felt or experienced; excitement at having new understanding; and empowerment from the possibility of breaking down isolation and promoting personal values. Furthermore, the level of dissonance or discomfort you experience throughout this book can range from nonexistent to mild to intense, depending on how challenging it is to fit the new learning into your existing experiences and understandings of the world.

Dissonance, and the active experience of related emotions, is actually an encouraging sign because it doesn't happen when we patently reject or fully agree with a perspective. Dissonance only occurs when we're faced with a perspective that is compelling *and* feels threatening because it is different from what we are used to, at the same time. Dissonance is a signal that you're on your growing edge, that place where growth and learning and breakthroughs are possible, if only you can hang on long enough. For those students who do hang on, usually by turning toward the emotions, initial dissonance can give way over time to greater understanding and a sense of empowerment and agency.

Turning toward difficult emotions, however, can be so challenging many of us unconsciously do the opposite. The tendency to turn away from, to defend ourselves against unpleasant emotions doesn't make us bad or broken, it makes us human. The survival of our species required an ability to distance ourselves from potentially harmful things, whether dangerous animals, poisonous foods, or unsafe environments. Similarly, the emotional upheaval that comes with cognitive dissonance can pull readers toward defending against the learning and pushing it away without even considering the ideas.

In psychology, this defending is called *resistance* and it often happens outside of awareness. Someone who deeply values fairness and self-determinism, for example, might experience significant dissonance after learning the extent to which privilege and status influence life outcomes through differential access to education, healthcare, generational wealth, and job opportunities, as well as the negative psychological effects of discrimination. Unlike their ancestors who might have run away in the face of physical danger, their resistance may reveal itself more subtly as asserting that racism is not a problem because it's better now than in the past (minimization) or racism doesn't impact most people (denial) or there is nothing anyone can do to change the current system (rationalization) or gender is the real problem in society (recentering) or that we, the authors, don't know what we're talking about (justification for dismissing possibilities). Just as avoidance of danger helped our ancestors stay physically safe, resistance helps us feel psychologically safe, as we turn away from uncomfortable emotions that feel threatening, including emotions that are related to being uncertain or ambivalent. But new ideas are not the same as life-threatening danger. And the cost of turning away is lost opportunity for growth in our understanding and our ability to choose what we want to believe, who we want to be, and how we want to act and relate to others.

At this point, you might have questions like: Is there anything I can do to enhance the possibilities this book opens up when the cards are stacked against me? Can I turn toward difficult emotions if my human tendency is to turn away? We assure you the answer to both questions is "yes." Just because something is hard doesn't make it impossible. Behavioral tendency isn't behavioral destiny. We all have the ability to move from unconsciously reacting to difficult emotions to responding with intention and making active choices. This next section is about those responses, the practices that make regulating and tolerating difficult emotions easier.

Practices That Enhance Learning

Curiosity

We've found learners who engage the material with curiosity—a desire for new knowledge—are less reactive than those who engage the material with skepticism. This is not unexpected given curiosity is associated with personal growth, problem-solving, and social competence. Asking yourself these questions throughout the reading can help you tap into your curiosity: What surprised me; what new information did I learn; what do I want to know more about; what might be behind the reactions I am having?

Intellectual Humility

Along the lines of curiosity, engaging the material with intellectual humility enhances learning and reduces reactionary responses. Intellectual humility involves recognizing the limits of our current knowledge and being open to new ideas and to the possibility that viewpoints contrary to our own may hold validity. This isn't an easy ask for many learners. You may feel you know the subject well, especially if it relates to your own experiences; however, as we mentioned, your perspective may have been narrowed by having limited access to information or limited opportunities to explore meanings through discussion. Exploring the basis of your knowledge when you encounter information that contradicts your beliefs helps with intellectual humility. Where did I learn my belief? How do I know my belief is true? What evidence do I have to support my belief; is this evidence trustworthy? What evidence do I have to counter my belief; is this evidence trustworthy? What would change for me if I were wrong?

Self-compassion

Meeting difficult emotions with compassion and gentleness is another key to tolerance and therefore getting the most out of your learning. Self-compassion can entail speaking to yourself in a kind, loving manner ("I am feeling bad now and that's okay"); forgiving yourself for past actions/inactions while committing to behaving differently ("now that I know better, I will do better"); accepting that suffering is a sign of empathy ("my pain signals I care"); reminding yourself that learning new ways of interpreting the world and unlearning old ones is hard for everyone ("I'm only human"). Whatever form of self-compassion you choose, the aim is to recognize your reactions without amplifying them by being upset about what you're experiencing or defending yourself against them in an effort to make them go away.

Mindfulness

Mindfulness also combats the amplification of suffering that results when we time-travel from our current pain to past hurts or to future worries. Mindfulness is the act of bringing your attention without judgment to the here and now, to the emotional and bodily experiences that are unfolding for you in the present moment. Attending to the experiences you are currently having versus ignoring or avoiding them has the paradoxical effect of helping you regulate those experiences. You can practice mindfulness in the reading of this book by naming any emotions that come up for you ("I'm feeling angry, sad, overwhelmed") and noting where in the body the emotion is manifesting ("there is heaviness in my chest," "my throat feels tight," "my stomach is upset"). Taking several deep, slow breaths if your feelings are intense can also ground you in the present moment, as can journaling about your reactions and talking about what you're going through with empathic friends or family.

Where We Are Coming from

Before we end this chapter, we want to tell you a bit about us. Throughout this book, we assert that who you are affects how you engage this material. In some ways, this seems pretty common sensical—our worldview is affected by the experiences we have and don't have, the ideas we have been exposed to, the views of the people who have raised and educated us. But even though this can seem pretty obvious, people don't often consider *how* their view of a concept—or an experience, a theory, a fact, a research finding, or anything else—is affected by who they are. In the coming chapters, we will be actively inviting you to this consideration. Relatedly, we are aware that our (the authors') experiences, identities, and **positionalities** affect how we engage this material, so we want to share some of that with you.

> *How Do I Say?* Positionality is about the ways that your status within social categories and hierarchies affect your experience. Positionality is not only about identity and how you see yourself, but also about how your experiences of power, privilege, and oppression related to social categories affect your experiences, worldview, and actions.

We are three psychology professors who have been thinking, discussing, teaching, and researching about the kinds of social hierarchies and inequities discussed in this book for over two decades. Here is a bit about each of us:

KAREN: I am a professor at UMass Boston, which is a public, urban, mostly commuter research-intensive university with a large (now majority) proportion of students of color. I teach undergraduate and graduate classes in psychology and ethnic studies.

I identify as Asian American and am multiracial. My father's parents were immigrants from Japan and my father was born in the United States as the youngest of 11 children. His family had limited income and resources, even before they were incarcerated in the Japanese American concentration camps during World War II. My mother was White European American, from rural Texas with a strong Southern Baptist background. Her family had very limited income and resources, but her older sister helped her afford nursing school (after Bible college). My mother struggled with a major mental illness throughout her adult life, experiencing more or less intense disability, which had a big effect on my becoming a psychologist and also interacted with my racial and ethnic experiences in terms of how I negotiated my emotional responses and reality. Depression and anxiety are central parts of my family and personal development in other ways as well. My stepmother is White and Jewish, raised in New England, and also college educated. I was born in the United States and raised in the greater Boston area in a primarily White, affluent suburb. Although my parents both came from working-class backgrounds with limited income and resources, they both went to college (my father went on to get a doctorate), and I grew up in a middle-class background with a lot of privileges that were harder to see because I was not as relatively affluent as most of my peers growing up. My access to educational opportunities was a big privilege that shaped so many future outcomes for me.

Like Grace, I negotiate the complicated racial position of Asian Americans: I am generally "coded" as a person of color by others (although they don't always know what kind) and my sense of who I am has been shaped by direct personal and intergenerational experiences of interpersonal and systemic racism as an Asian American from White and non-White people. At the same time, as an Asian American, my experiences of racism are often minimized or invisibilized. I have come to understand this in relation to a divide and conquer strategy that maintains oppression, and how I need to work to resist my own and others' internalization of this. Being a multiracial person, who can be racially ambiguous to some people, has also led to experiences of discrimination and exclusion, including from other Asian Americans, and to relative privilege because White people are often more comfortable with me.

I identify as a queer woman. My gender and sexuality have led to questions, assumptions, and sometimes hostile discrimination from others including assumptions about my partner, behavior, or political views; microaggressions or silencing about sexuality injustice; and name calling or discriminatory comments (e.g., being called "butch" by strangers). I am heterosexually married and therefore have privilege in relation to day-to-day experiences of my sexuality when I am with my partner, but this can also clash with these other experiences I have when I am not with him. I also have privilege as a U.S. born citizen who never faced the challenges of immigration and as someone who is not disabled. Both of these statuses have opened many doors from me and protected me from harm and pain in many ways.

I grew up in a time where there was less dialogue and acceptance of people who didn't fit into pre-defined boxes within social categories of race, gender, sexuality, and disability. All of this has meant that I have had to spend time figuring out what it means to be "in between" spaces, and to negotiate assumptions from others about who I am or am not, including others whom I hoped or expected would be more accepting. These experiences have shaped me to emphasize solidarity and relational connection. My process of (un)learning about privilege and oppression has unfolded largely in the context of connecting ethnic studies and psychology, working and learning with students to challenge socialized assumptions and negotiate the pain of being caught in oppressive systems.

ROXANNE: I'm a licensed clinical psychologist in Georgia and Professor of Psychology dually appointed in the departments of Psychological Science and Interdisciplinary Studies at Kennesaw State University, a large research university in metro-Atlanta with a considerable student of color population (currently 52%). I teach undergraduate courses in psychology, Black studies, and gender and women's studies.

I am an immigrant who moved to New York City (NYC) with my family at eight years old from Guyana, a small English-speaking country on the northern tip of South America whose culture is similar to other Caribbean nations colonized by the British (e.g., Jamaica, Trinidad, Barbados). Both my parents are multiracial (Black, Asian, and White). Race was not a topic my family discussed in Guyana, making the racialized nature of the United States initially confusing for me—everyone from teachers to neighbors wanted to know my race. When I asked my father how to answer the racial questions, he let me know that I'm considered Black in the States because I have African ancestry. His explanation of hypodescent influenced my initially ascribed and later internalized identity as a Black woman. This identity is complicated because I'm not always coded as Black but have had experiences of racism that are clearly about my Blackness, such as being called the N word by strangers. At the same time, I am granted relative privilege in White spaces because I'm a light-skinned straight-haired English-speaking immigrant with access to White ancestry. The recent acceptance of multiracial as a social category has added to this complication. I reconcile my internal sense of self with the shifting racial boundaries by identifying as a Black woman of multiracial descent, a messy compromise I remain ambivalent about and acknowledge may shift over time.

In relation to my intersecting identities, I'm cisgender with current middle-class privilege and a history of financially vulnerable periods while growing up in NYC. I am mostly nondisabled physically and psychologically, although serious mental illness is a significant part of my family history. I am exclusively heterosexual in my behavior but experience varying levels of attraction for individuals across the gender spectrum. Heterosexual marriage, U.S. citizenship, education, and Christian upbringing convey additional societal privileges.

The aspects of my identity that opened me to oppression were more present for me than those aspects that conveyed privilege. Being a student (and teacher) of Black Feminist Theory, particularly its focus on intersectionality, helped in my (un)learning process along with having a diverse community of women of color and White allies willing to lovingly (and sometimes not so lovingly) call me on my privilege, including the complex and contextual nature of relative racial privilege among people of color. All of this learning has by no means brought me to some "woke" destination, nor do I believe such an endpoint exists. What I do believe in is being continuously open to feedback and to seek knowledge about the ways I may inadvertently uphold systems of privilege and a commitment to, as Maya Angelou says, "Do the best you can until you know better. Then when you know better, do better."

GRACE: I am a Clinical Associate Professor at Boston University, a large urban research university. I teach undergraduate and graduate courses in psychology.

I am an Asian American, and an immigrant. I was born and raised in Seoul, South Korea, moved to the U.S. at the age of 14, and grew up in the East Coast. I also identify as a parachute kid, whose parents returned to Korea a couple of years after my family's initial relocation; so, for a few years after that my sister and I lived in the United States with family friends. Both my parents identify themselves as mono-racial Korean, and they were both children when they experienced the Korean War. As my parents and I have lived in different countries for decades, my bicultural and bilingual experiences and experiences of international family separation add to my cultural and ethnic identity as a 1.5-generation immigrant who navigates both worlds. Issues of identities and belonging are things I frequently think about.

My racial identity as an Asian American has developed over time, as I acculturated further into the U.S. culture and started noticing racialized experiences. Coming from a country where race is not often discussed, and the most immediate reference groups were other Asian ethnic groups (especially other East Asian people), I had to quickly learn about the race relations in the United States, and how I was perceived here, and what that meant to my identity. Since then, I have contended with the complexities in being an Asian American, in which I am simultaneously visible and invisible in inter-racial contexts, both in primarily White and also in people of color interpersonal spaces. That is, I am clearly visible because of my racial features, but at the same time I am sometimes not considered a person of color by both White and other people of color, and my racialized experiences are often not recognized. Being an Asian American woman in the East Coast, where the racial dialogues continue to focus on Black and White relations, there are a lot of times others perceive me in racially stereotyped ways (e.g., a hard-working and quiet woman who may be a great team member but perhaps not a natural leader), and I have to resist being stereotyped and discriminated by forging my own identities. The impact of these experiences has been quite draining. At the same time, I learned that the false ideas about racial hierarchy had a global reach, often through popular media that is distributed worldwide, and that even as an immigrant, I was socialized into the racist global society. Hence, I need to continue to work on myself to see how socialization has affected me about my knowledge and assumptions about other people.

In relation to intersecting identities, I am also aware that I have lived with many privileges as a straight, cisgender, middle-class, mono-racial, nondisabled individual, who was raised in Christianity, one of the dominant religions in both in Korea and the U.S. Being bilingual and English-speaking, and having had access to educational opportunities are other things that I reflect on as clear privileges. I am aware that in the areas in which I have privilege, I am less likely to notice things, and it takes a lot of work to be aware, and pursue ally actions in support of others who do not share these privileges. It took me a lot of time to heal from experiences of racism and discrimination, in everyday life and in schools. Hence, noticing privileges took more time and effort to recognize, to really sit with the discomfort of having these privileges, and to actively work to unlearn things I had previously learned. I still have a lot of new things to learn and to grow in, and at times holding the intersections of privileges and pain from oppression feels overwhelming. However, I am reminded to keep learning and keep trying, because my ultimate goal is to contribute toward creating a more just world for my two children, who are children of color, and their peers.

Where Do You Go from Here?

The purpose of this chapter was to invite you to consider how you might approach and experience the material in this book. One of our primary hopes is that you will choose to be open to exploring and unraveling assumptions, so we have also tried to prepare you for the reading of this book and for your diversity education journey generally. We've tried to walk the line between articulating the difficulties *and* the joy you might find along the way. Now it's up to you to step onto the path and keep moving forward.

Resources for Learning More

This section offers additional readings and resources, acknowledging that this text is a primer and therefore only a springboard to the need to learn more.

Goodman, D. (2011). *Promoting diversity and social justice: Educating people from privileged groups* (2nd edition). Routledge.

Kim, A. S., & del Prado, A. (2019). *It's time to talk (and listen): How to have constructive conversations about race, class, sexuality, ability, and gender in a polarized world.* New Harbinger Publications.

Loewen, J. W. (2018). *Lies my teacher told me: Everything your American history textbook got wrong.* New Press.

Sue, D. W. (2010). *Microaggressions in everyday life: Race, gender, and sexual orientation.* Wiley.

Section One

Foundations: Social Construction, Power, Privilege, and Oppression

In this section, we focus on understanding how we create meanings (social constructs), and how these meanings are embedded in our cultural worldview. Chapter 2 ("Understanding Social Construction and Culture as Foundations of Meaning Making") describes the ways that culture is a foundation for creating worldviews and meanings and explores how people may not be aware of the influences of the cultures in which they live. We discuss the process of making differences into distinctions that relate to privilege and oppression. We also introduce the central idea that social constructs and our personally experienced identity are not the same thing, although they influence each other. This differentiation is one that we will explore in each of the chapters in Section Two. Chapter 3 ("Understanding Power, Privilege, and Oppression") explores the meanings of privilege, the multiple facets of oppression, and the ways that hierarchies of privilege and oppression affect experiences at multiple levels: individual, interpersonal, and institutional. We also briefly consider the complexities of relative, ascribed, contextual, and intersectional privilege.

One of our major goals in this book is to demonstrate how everyday concepts connected to diversity (e.g., culture, privilege, race, and racism) are more complex than people often think, and to encourage you to think more deeply and critically about your own meanings, where these meanings come from, and how these meanings and the assumptions they relate to may be shaping how you see the world and interact with other people. We know that some readers might not agree with the definitions and explorations presented in this book. You don't have to agree, but we hope you will be open to engaging these meanings, rather than letting your disagreement lead to complete disconnection. We have approached these definitions and exploration with the goal of having a shared starting place from which to explore. If we agree with these definitions, we can know that we are agreeing about the same thing. If we disagree, we can more clearly describe how and why we disagree as we engage in conversations about these challenging topics.

DOI: 10.4324/9780429059599-3

2 Understanding Social Construction and Culture as Foundations of Meaning Making

When we talk about "diversity," people often think we are talking about simple differences in things like culture, race, gender, sexuality, social class, ability, and so forth. For example, you may think about differences in race as things like whether your skin is pale or dark, or whether your eyes are rounder and hooded or narrower with an epicanthic fold. Many of us want to believe these "diversity" differences no longer matter—who doesn't love Beyonce, and didn't Barack Obama and Kamala Harris get elected? Unfortunately, considerable evidence shows these differences are still not value neutral in our society. The color of your skin doesn't simply mean that some clothing colors look better on you than others. Skin color and other "diversity" differences are connected to *distinctions* we make between people with these different characteristics. So, in one way, the exact color of your skin doesn't (or shouldn't) inherently matter, but in another way, the color of your skin is associated with others' ideas about your experiences and personal characteristics. Ideas that you may also believe.

These ideas don't just stay in our heads—they influence our behavior. We use the differences we perceive to create categories of people that we arrange in hierarchies related to what we assume about their experiences and characteristics. The result: some people are seen more positively and worthy of good things (privileged), while others are seen more negatively and less worthy of good things (less privileged, or oppressed). It is therefore the distinctions—the hierarchies of power and privilege—that make "diversity" categories meaningful and particularly important in our society.

In this chapter, we first discuss the meaning of culture, because all our thoughts and behaviors develop within cultured relationships and societies. Being embedded within our own culture(s) can make it difficult to see the effect of culture unless we step back and define culture more explicitly. We then talk about how culture is the foundation of social constructs such as race, ethnicity, gender, sexuality, ability, and social class. People often assume that these social categories and the status hierarchies within them are "natural," "real," or inherent (sometimes biologically inherent). These assumptions persist even though people will often also say that these things are "social constructs." So, we seek to unravel these assumptions by examining what "social

DOI: 10.4324/9780429059599-4

construct" means and explore the ways that culture relates to determining how certain categories and statuses matter.

Defining Culture and Social Construct

Culture: a learned and variable (changing) system of meanings that represent a way of living which is shared and transmitted by an identifiable group of people.

Social Construct: an idea or concept that exists because people believe it exists and maintain its existence through acting as if the idea has consequence.

Some Possible Responses to the Material in This Chapter

There was a lot of information packed into the previous paragraphs about how culture shapes our (mis)perceptions that social categories/hierarchies are real or inherent. Some of this information might be quite familiar to you, some might be quite new. Take a moment to check-in with yourself about how you experienced what you just read.

- Are you feeling surprised or intrigued that culture shapes what you see and believe?
- In a state of disbelief or anger or frustration that we're saying your perceptions of what you experience as real differences may be inaccurate?
- Happy or bored to revisit material you were introduced to previously?
- Something else?

Noticing and naming what's coming up for you now can prepare you for what might come up as you go deeper in the chapter. Moreover, if you are experiencing strong emotions that suggest what we're saying here is new to you, is questionable, or is PC nonsense or liberal brainwashing, that reaction is itself a sign that cultural socialization is influential because challenges to our socialization make us uncomfortable. We invite you to keep this in mind as you engage in reading the chapter.

Before we go on, we want to address something that tends to trip up our students. We're not saying here that there are no differences among social groups or that everyone is exactly the same. That's untrue. For example, cis women do tend to be smaller and have more estrogen and less testosterone on average than cis men. And many Black people do have darker skin than people of other races. What we are pointing to is that these biological differences do not by themselves relate to more complex aspects of who we are such as our personality traits, preferences, and abilities. Because humans have higher brain functioning and agency than many other species, our culture and socialization play an outsized role in our development, meaning who we are goes beyond biological determinants. Keeping this in mind might also help in your remaining open to the learning that follows.

Culture as a Foundation of Meaning

Questions: In the United States—

- If you want to speak in class, why do you raise your hand rather than stand up?
- Why do you sit in a chair versus on pillows laid on the floor or directly on the ground?
- Why do men typically shake hands or fist bump versus greet each other with a kiss?

Answer: Culture.

A formal definition of **culture** is a learned and variable (changing) system of meanings that represent a way of living which is shared and transmitted by an identifiable group of people. A "system of meanings" includes social norms, values, beliefs, and behaviors, as well as more concrete things like food, art, music, architecture/buildings, and so forth.

It's Complicated: There is much discussion in the social sciences about what culture is because it encompasses so many aspects and variables. In this book, we are focusing more on the internal aspects of culture as experienced by individuals rather than "objective" aspects of culture like artifacts and architecture. Understanding culture can also be complicated because experiences within a culture vary and many cultures contain various subcultures. For example, if you attempt to describe "American" culture, you might end up highlighting what is actually the dominant culture in the United States—meaning the culture most aligned with White, Judeo-Christian middle-class, straight, cismen living in the U.S. mainland—which leaves out the numerous other cultures that make up the U.S. landscape and those of other countries in the Americas. So, when we think about a given culture, we need to remember that there may be identifiable shared or "modal" experiences, but there is also variability. We talk more about this in Chapter 5, when we talk about ethnicity and ethnocultures.

There are many different kinds of culture, because there are many different kinds of identifiable groups. Some examples of cultures include youth culture, regional culture (e.g., Southern culture, New England culture), gay or lesbian cultures, Deaf culture, and national or ethnic culture (e.g., American culture, Japanese culture).

How Do I Say? Deaf versus deaf. Labels are important and can mean different things depending on context. On the one hand, a label can be a simple descriptor of the inability to hear, as in deaf with a lower case "d" or of a color, as in black with a lower case "b." On the other hand, a label can be related to a deeply held part of one's identity that is connected to a collective experience among those who share that identity, as in Deaf with an upper case "D" and Black with an upper case "B." Intentionally capitalizing in these ways acknowledges and honors a cultural and racial group's identity, history, and experience. This relates to whether we are using language as an adjectival description (small "d" in deaf) or as an identity with shared experience and group meaning (large "D" as in Deaf).

As you can see from the list of examples above, some cultures are experienced or shared by a very large group of people (such as American culture) while others are experienced or shared by a smaller or more specific group of people (such as Deaf culture).

We are embedded in our cultures and our cultures are embedded in our understanding of ourselves and others. The definition of culture above points out that cultural meanings, values, norms, and so forth are "transmitted": this means that we teach our cultural meanings to our children and to newcomers to our group or societies. We socialize our children and new members of our society (e.g., immigrants) to behave and think in certain ways. Some of this teaching is intentional and conscious, but much of it happens without our conscious intention—just by being who we are and communicating what is the "normal" or usual way we do things within our culture. One way we do this is through our relationships and interpersonal interactions. For example, when a parent teaches a child to wave goodbye when guests are leaving, or when a teacher tells a student to "look at me when I am speaking," we are transmitting cultural norms and practices. We also incorporate these meanings, values, norms, and expectations into our histories and into our stories and art, such as books, movies, and television. Cultural meanings are also integrated into our institutions, such as the legal system (police, courts, and prisons), education (schools), and health care (policies, judgments of what is healthy, and practices to promote health). In this way, we build and maintain our cultures. However, the definition of culture above also indicates that this system of meanings is not set in stone and absolute, but is instead continuously changing.

Part of what makes culture so hard to see from within is that *everything* is cultured (where "cultured" means affected by culture). Look around you—the shape of the room, the material it is made of, the kind and shape of furniture in that room: all of that is cultured. But we usually don't think about that. If we have grown up deeply embedded in a culture it is harder to see because we see our own experiences as "normal," "typical," or "natural." We think that the way our culture does things is the way that *people in general* think and feel and behave. We take it for granted that this is just the way it is and perhaps the way it should be. For example, you probably haven't actively noticed that this book is cultured: it is written in English (language is one aspect of ethnic culture), sentences progress from left to right, and pages turn from right to left. If you have only been exposed to this kind of book, you may not even know that the structure of the book, the writing, and your expectations about that structure and writing is cultured.

The fact that everything is cultured becomes more obvious to us when something steps outside familiar cultural rules.

For

example,

if

we

write

like

this,

you

notice

that

you

do

have

expectations

about

books

(which

are

cultured).

In fact, you might feel a bit annoyed with us now, because we have "broken" the cultural rules for writing in English textbook prose.

This is an example of how the ways in which we are cultured become more visible when there is a contrast. Another example is the experience of college students from the United States who visit other countries and see differences between how they live in the United States, and how people live elsewhere around the world. They often become much more aware of how they have been cultured to be "American," and what things they do that are cultured.

How Do I Say? The use of "American" to mean "United States" is somewhat controversial. Some people protest that there are two continents of "Americans" that contain multiple countries, so that using "American" is both incorrect and marginalizing to the many people who are also "Americans" but who don't live in the United States. We could, more accurately, speak about the United States versus America, or "United Statesian" culture versus "American" culture. What would be the pros and cons of doing this? What objections might be raised? How are your views or the views of others on this issue part of a cultural lens?

Some aspects of culture are more obvious: students traveling abroad often enjoy exploring new foods, music, art, and language. But other aspects of culture are harder to see, such as values about time, communication styles, or assumptions about how people should act in different relationships. Students may be frustrated by interactions with others without even realizing why; they don't necessarily see that they don't know the cultural rules that others in the new country take for granted. We often don't know what we don't know. This can be especially true about less visible or concrete aspects of culture.

Culture is more complex than we often think. Think about culture as an iceberg: the majority of the iceberg is hidden below the water (see Figure 2.1). We can go diving and become aware of the things below the waterline, but it takes more effort. Although the parts below the waterline are less obvious, they are major influences on our worldviews, interactions, and ideas about what is "normal".

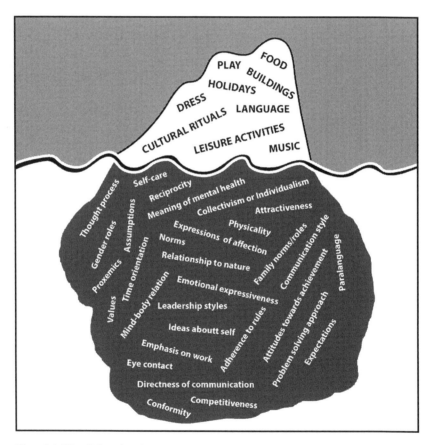

Figure 2.1 The Cultural Iceberg: Visible and Invisible Culture
Source: Developed by Thanh Nguyen and authors. This work is licensed under a Creative Commons Attribution-NonCommercial-ShareAlike 4.0 International License. Used by permission.

Understanding that everything is cultured helps us consider how the meaning of concepts such as race or gender, and the relation of these concepts to privilege and oppression, have been shaped by our own culture and how our views of those categories have been shaped by our own socialization into that culture. For example, in the mainstream U.S. culture, what kinds of differences or statuses are related to gender? Can you think of a culture outside of the United States, a historical period, or a particular context or subculture where the gender hierarchy has been different or even just more or less extreme? Can you imagine ways that the United States might have developed so that gender status really doesn't matter? If you could change historical events, laws, policies, or practices, what might you do to decrease the ways that gender (or race or social class) is less related to privilege or oppression?

Reflection Questions

Consider the cultures that you belong to. These may include ethnic culture, regional culture, or cultures related to other identities such as queer culture or Republican culture or Buddhist culture.

- What are some of the values, behavioral norms, traditions, or ways of relating to others depicted in Figure 2.1 that are associated with those cultures?
- What are some ways those cultures have shaped your worldview, including how you understand yourself and how you perceive and relate to others? Are there things you disagree with?
- What ways have those cultures shaped your view of which social categories, statuses, or identities matter and which do not? Or of how people who have different identities or statuses are expected to think, act, or be? of machismo

---

Culture and Social Constructs: Why Diversity Statuses Matter

Can you explain exactly what a social construct is? We bet it's a bit hard to do beyond the definition we provide that a **social construct** is an idea or concept that exists because people believe it exists and maintain its existence through acting as if the idea has consequence. Although you may have heard the statement "Race (or gender, or sexuality, or social class) is a social construct," you may not have thought much about what this *really* means. Understanding that something is a social construct means understanding that concepts like race cannot be inherently or definitively identified outside of social context. Instead, the meanings of these concepts, the boundaries of the categories that we create through these concepts, and the ways these concepts impact people and relationships are *created* by people within cultured societies.

A common example of a social construct is the idea of money. Money doesn't have inherent value. It is valuable because we agree that it is valuable.

Social constructs don't have "objective" reality or inherent meaning. And our social meanings of diversity concepts are frequently changing. We can say that a square always has four equal and straight sides, but we cannot say that a Black person is always X in all contexts and all places, and therefore X defines what it means to be racially Black. Our history and research indicate we aren't even consistent across time and people in our meaning within the U.S. society. There is widespread and consistent agreement that "blue" is the color of the sky, but much less agreement about the meaning of race, or about who is Black, and what kinds of experiences are or should be associated with being Black. We will talk much more about the complicated meanings of race in Chapter 4.

So, if there is no definitive meaning or agreement about these concepts, then where does our understanding of them come from? As social constructs, the meanings of concepts such as ethnicity, race, or gender in the United States are created, maintained, and changed by people: people who are influenced by their cultures. So, when race or ethnicity, gender or sexuality, social class or disability is talked about within the United States, it's important to consider the U.S. culture with its particular histories and diverse and changing populations. That societies change over time and different societies have different cultures with different histories and current experiences relates to why the meanings of these concepts are so complex, and are not consistent across cultural contexts. The meanings of the concepts we present in this book have been developed within the culture of the United States. Many of these meanings have similarities to meanings in other cultures and countries (particularly European cultures), but there are also cultural differences.

The determination of which social categories or differences relate to hierarchies of power, privilege, and oppression is cultured. How the statuses within these categories relate to power, privilege, and oppression is also cultured. In other words, *what* status matters and *how* it matters are both cultural meanings. Try thinking about it this way: People vary in myriad ways. Some of these are visible, but many are not. Think about someone you know: what are some of the ways the two of you are different from each other? Which of these differences matter a lot and which are less important?

As discussed in Chapter 1, people can differ in many ways, but some kinds of difference matter more than others in shaping our personal development and view of ourselves and the world more generally (worldview), our relationships and the ways we are treated by others, and our interactions with social institutions such as media, schools, or laws. For example, do you know whether you have attached earlobes or detached earlobes? This is a difference between people that is visible, where the bottom of the earlobe curves up before connecting to the head (detached) or doesn't (attached). But we usually don't even think to look (in fact, you might have been surprised to learn that this is a difference, or you might have had to reach up to feel your own ears to answer the question). What kind of earlobes you have doesn't really matter. It doesn't affect how you see yourself, how others treat you and the assumptions they make about you, or what kinds of legal rights you or your parents have or had. But the color of your skin *does* matter. And this mattering is evident not only in the ways other people treat us but, as decades of research shows, in tangible access to resources. What makes this so?

The meanings we socially assign to particular things are what shape how those things matter at individual, interpersonal, and systemic levels. These meanings are part of the social construction of the concept. Let's begin by using race as an example to expand this.[1] Many people think that race is simply differences in skin color or physical features. If this were true, then being categorized as racially Asian or Asian American could be just as meaningless to life as detached earlobes. But, instead, being categorized as racially Asian impacts so many experiences. If you are categorized as Asian in the United States, it affects people's assumptions of where you come from, whether you belong, how smart you are, how well you drive, how much of a leader you can be, how you communicate, and much more. Thus, the meaning of race for our lives is primarily about the associations of characteristics and behaviors that we have been taught to connect to racial categories (e.g., see AAA statement on race [American Anthropological Association, 1998]; Smedley & Smedley, 2012). The meanings associated to race and different racial categories have become part of our culture. Because they are part of our culture, we share and transmit these meanings within our society, and these meanings continue across generations. This means we have been socialized into how we should think about race and racial categorization, how and why race is (or is not) important, how we should categorize ourselves racially, how we should act or think given our racial categorization, and how we should treat people who we perceive as being of different races. If we had been brought up in a different culture (e.g., in Brazil, or Japan, or Sweden), our thinking about these issues would be different in some ways, although there would also be similarities.

How we get socialized about race and racism starts very early. Although some people assume that children don't notice racial differences and are free of stereotyped and prejudicial thinking, research on child development illustrates the opposite. Many researchers (e.g., Katz, 2003) have demonstrated that infants as young as six months old react to racial differences (i.e., they can discriminate or notice racial differences), and by ages three or four, children can identify, differentiate, and articulate racial differences. In these early

---

1   Within these initial foundational chapters that focus on the processes of creating meaning in relation to diversity hierarchies, we will have a relatively greater focus on race. This focus on race does not mean that race is the primary or most important distinction. We agree with Audre Lorde (1983) that "there is no hierarchy of oppression." At the same time, we feel that it can be helpful to be able to have examples within one category to be able to illustrate more fully how complex all of these issues are, how many misunderstandings we have, and how pervasive are the effects of the hierarchies we create as a society.

years, children are noticing *differences*, but they are not yet making *distinctions* about what kinds of people are better or more desirable. They are not necessarily aware that these differences have particular and important social meaning. But by the time children are five to six years old, many children already have notions about how people of different races are perceived by others in the society, and they start connecting different adjectives or qualities to people of different races (Katz, 2003; Ramsey, 2008). Children of color who are in the targeted or low-status group become aware of the stereotypes earlier than those who are White and in the majority or higher status group. As developmental psychologists Bigler and Wright (2014) suggest, children hold stereotyped and prejudicial beliefs "on the basis of many human traits, including race, gender, age, and attractiveness" (p. 18). Bullying and victimization of others even in early ages are clear indications of how children can hold stereotypes and discriminate against others.

Children receive conflicting messages about the importance of racial differences and simultaneous messages that noticing these differences (particularly in others) is not okay. You see this happen when, for example, a White child asks their parents in public about why an Asian person they just passed has "squinty" eyes or whether the dark skin of a Black child can be washed away, causing said parent to become flustered or quick to apologize for the attention their child is causing, and hush the child from asking more questions. After experiencing repeated versions of this interaction from various adults, children learn that these differences that are associated with the concept "race" are not a topic that should be discussed because it makes people, including their parents, uncomfortable. The taboo about race simultaneously communicates the significance of race.

It is, however, more common for the taboo to be more strongly communicated to White children. Because of the impact of racism, some non-White families actually do discuss race and racism on regular basis. For instance, Black parents often discuss having to have conversations about racism with their children, in order to provide support and prepare children about potential bias they may face (Umaña-Taylor & Hill, 2020). However, other than such racial socializations within families, in our society talking about race has, until recently, been pretty unusual.

As children age they start to segregate more, while holding on to intergroup bias and stereotyped beliefs about others. Beliefs about others' race often remain unconscious and unchecked because they are typically not reflected on and made conscious (Aboud et al., 2003; Katz, 2003). Simultaneously, while racial socialization prepares children for bias, it may also contribute to protective social distance. Unfortunately, research studies suggest that by the time adults think White children may be "ready" to talk about race or other differences (e.g., in third or fourth grade), children have already segregated themselves by groups and learned the lesson that talking about differences associated with race is taboo, making it challenging to meaningfully discuss any issue of differences.

Reflection Questions

- What is one of your earliest memories of awareness of racial difference? What happened? How did the adults around you respond? What messages did you take from that response?
- In general, what messages did you receive as a child from your family members about race, racism, or people from other races? What messages did you receive from teachers? From other adults? From friends?
- Are you comfortable talking about race and racism with others? How might your answers to the previous questions influence your answer to this one?

In sum, as a society, we develop meanings about things like race, ethnicity, or ability. These meanings become part of our culture, which means we transmit them to children and others who enter the culture. And we transmit them in ways that convey their significance and their emotional import. Once meanings become embedded in our culture, it is difficult for any single individual or group to change those meanings or the associations that have been developed. If you personally wanted to say that individuals with your kind of earlobes should be treated better because they are smarter, stronger, more moral, more capable, and generally better, it would be pretty challenging to suddenly get everyone to agree with you and treat you that way. Similarly, a single Asian American person can't simply say the assumptions are wrong and have the stereotypes and assumptions magically go away. We will talk more about the meanings of race (and gender, social class, and other diversity categories) and the development of these meanings in future chapters, but the point we want to make here is that our meanings of race and other diversity categories is shaped by our culture. Furthermore, these categories are so impactful on people's lives because of the cultured connections we make between what *could* be simple physical differences but have instead become hierarchical categories of privilege and oppression with significant social meaning. These connections are also created within our culture as part of our process of creating meanings of race, gender, and so forth.

Understanding Social Categories Related to Oppression and Privilege

What do we mean by "significant social meaning?" Why do things like race and gender matter while things like earlobes don't? Everett Hughes (1945) coined the term "master status" which relates to the status or identity that is most meaningful and impactful for an individual, that serves to organize the individual's sense of self. Similarly, some **social categories** have particular meaning in terms of how a given society or culture organizes relationships and capital. We might think of these categories as "master statuses" for a society, which, of course, then has implications for their importance for the individual.

> *How Do I Say?* "Social categories" can refer to a really wide range of differences and distinctions. For example, "athletes" may refer to a social category, meaning a category of people who define themselves by some shared culture or experience. But we are, here, talking about particular kinds of social categories that relate to oppression, privilege, and hierarchy. Some people use the general language "social category" when referring to these kinds of categories (e.g., Cole, 2009). Others talk about social identities to mean a social category that structures people's identities because of social meanings, and distinguish this from social identifications referring to an individual's particular personal meaning (Warner et al., 2018). Still others specifically refer to "social systems" or **"systems of inequity."** We use the words **"social category"** or **"social hierarchy"** to refer to the social construct, the category as it is given meaning by shared understanding and agreement. We use the word "status" to refer to one's position within sub-categories within a hierarchy.

Within these social categories we, as a society, have created the idea of a dominant group and at least one subordinate group with differences in access to power, decision making, capital, social acceptance and positive regard, stigma and stereotypes, segregation and social distance, and prejudice and discrimination. In sum, what makes specific social categories particularly meaningful is their relation to power, privilege, and oppression, and the ways that statuses or positions within those categories are organized in hierarchies.

Race, ethnicity, gender, sexuality, social class, and ability are some of these social hierarchical categories, and are the ones we focus on in this book. You might be thinking "what if these categories aren't important to me?" This question brings up the issue of how one's personal identity is not necessarily the biggest influence on what is *socially* meaningful. Categories that are socially meaningful are not necessarily the identity or status that you *personally* most identify with (e.g., athlete), but the one(s) that shape your worldviews, self-concepts, relationships, opportunities, and other aspects of life because of their *social* meaning. Some questions to consider in order to weigh whether a social category or related status is socially meaningful are: "How important is it to others to know my status?" "How much does it affect how I am treated when other people know my status?" and "How much does being in this category or status affect the opportunities I have had (or will have), the resources I have access to, and my ability to influence or control what happens to me?"

There are other social categories we don't address that nonetheless influence access to power and unearned privilege, including age, religion, nationality, or immigration and citizenship status, to name a few. Our choice of focus is not an attempt to minimize the impact of these other categories as much as it reflects the difficult decisions we had to make due to the primer nature of this text.

Because the foundations of the social categories we discuss in this book are power, privilege, and oppression, we must first understand those concepts before we can consider the particularities of each social category. Understanding power, privilege, and oppression is the focus of the next chapter (Chapter 3). But before we move on, let's consider some of the other similarities and foundational factors of these centrally meaningful social categories.

The social categories associated with privilege and oppression are complex partly because they operate and have influences on people at multiple ecological levels. "Ecological levels" is a term we borrow from Bronfenbrenner (1979), who emphasized that our experiences and development are affected by our environments. Applying an ecological model to social categories related to privilege and oppression includes considering how statuses within these categories are conceptualized and have social meanings and implications beyond individual intentions and experiences, how these statuses create group experiences and group identities, how they affect our worldviews and relationships, and how they interact with the way we have structured our society. Simultaneously, it's important to consider how these categories and statuses *are* individually experienced in relation to identity, personal worldview and ideologies, and psychological experiences. In the definitions presented in Section Two of the book, we therefore present foundational meanings of the categories as social constructs. We do so while also considering the more personal and interpersonal aspects that affect how we (as individual people and social/cultural groups) develop *and* maintain these social constructs; how the social constructs shape our psychological perspectives about the world, ourselves, and other people; and how these perspectives then shape our interpersonal interactions and behaviors and the culture we collaboratively create. However, we first want to unravel the common assumption that these categories and the statuses within them are *mostly* about personal identity choices.

Differentiating Influences of Social Categories and Status from Personal Identity

When we think about diversity, we need to actively consider how personal identity differs from social categories and status within those categories. Personal identity is what you think about or how you label yourself: it reflects what you think is important, the choices you make about who and how you want to be, and the ways you communicate these choices to others. Simultaneously, categories like race or gender are *socially* created, so there is a shared meaning and consequences that are not about your personal choice or the identity you personally claim or choose. For example, an individual might not identify as a man, but people might see that person as a man; regardless of their personal identity, they will need to negotiate the social meaning of the imposed status and make choices about asserting their personal identity in the face of the identity imposed by others because of the social construct of gender. As another example, transracial Asian American adoptees adopted by White parents may not experience their race as salient or may even identify racially as "American" or White like their families when they are younger, but research suggests that a major task for these children is negotiating their meaning of race given that others categorize them and impose ideas from the social construct of race (Kim et al., 2010).

Social identity focuses on identity in relation to social groups and categories, such as racial identity, ethnic identity, and so forth. Social identities are shaped by personal experiences and viewpoints *and* by experiences of affinity, belonging, or exclusion with social groups, as well as impositions of group categorization. There is a good amount of social science research that explores how people create social groups and how people develop personal identity meanings in relation to those groups. Some of this research focuses on group formation and related identity generally, while some focuses on group formation and identities around categories that have particular social meaning in relation to privilege and oppression, such as those we discuss in this book (Schwartz et al., 2011). This latter research often focuses on the developmental process of negotiating power, privilege, and oppression that we will talk more about in Chapter 3, and the ways people engage meanings of hierarchical social constructs as we describe in Chapters 4 through 9. Social identity is therefore about how you, as an individual, understand yourself in relation to the social categories and statuses that exist in the dominant culture.

Differentiating the social construct and category from identity is important because it helps highlight how these concepts have social meaning *and* individual meaning. Considering both is important because they may not always match up. For example, Jan may be a Black person who believes skin color doesn't really matter and feels that claims of racism by people of color are overblown. Similarly, Lark may be a disabled person who feels being "differently abled" is a personal experience of overcoming individual challenges and is unrelated to oppression or privilege or a shared experience within a group. Jan and Lark's individual perspectives don't negate the considerable evidence showing discrimination related to race and disability is widespread (e.g., stereotypes about limitations and characteristics that contribute to job discrimination, social exclusion, etc.). And it's likely Jan and Lark have experienced and been affected by such discrimination although they may not have recognized it or understood it as a shared experience that connects them to other people of color (in Jan's case) and people with disabilities in (Lark's case).

Social identity models see identity as a process, because the ways that people relate to their own status within hierarchies change over time. We describe this identity process in more depth using race as an example in

Chapter 4. Some of the most significant developmental changes within social identity over time relate to the ways in which people develop a more critical analysis of social categories, privilege, and oppression, a process that also affects their view of other people and groups.

Our point here is that an individual's personal experience or identity is not what defines the social category or the statuses within the category, the group experience, or the social implications. And an individual's personal experience or identity may not even be the most influential factor in how their status within a category affects them. As we talk about the meanings of social categories and hierarchies in Section Two, remember that all of these concepts are simultaneously social constructs operating at a group or societal levels *and* individual identity or interpersonal experiences. Your own individual experiences, identity, or viewpoint might not line up with the definition we provide and the associated experiences, but you can learn from considering the different perspectives, connections, and disconnections.

Common Factors among Categories Related to Oppression and Privilege

The social categories that carry the most social significance are centrally important in our society because of how they relate to power, privilege, and oppression. These categories also have similarities that relate to how they are created, how statuses within the categories become more or less differentiated, and how individual characteristics become connected to these categories. The following foundations apply to our understanding of all the social categories that are our focus in this book:

- Within social categories, *statuses (subcategories) are created as distinct and boundaried (binary or distinctly categorical)* although they are, in lived reality, much more fluid or continuous than our categorical schema and hierarchy suggest. These subcategories are placed in a hierarchy and associated with power, privilege, or oppression. The category gender, for example, is often viewed as binary, with (cis) men above (cis) women in the hierarchy.
- *Cultures emerge in association with statuses* within the social category, as people develop a collective identity and values, norms, and behaviors are shaped by shared experiences. For example, sexual and gender minority communities have specific cultural humor, slang, events, and so forth. Some or many aspects of the cultural differences that distinguish statuses relate to the shared experience of oppression, and the need to develop strategies for survival and well-being given these experiences of oppression. For example, "cultural mistrust" in African Americans relates to a realistic approach to coping with oppression (Whaley, 2001).

How Do I Say: Language reflects our cultural understandings. Cultural mistrust used to be referred to as "cultural paranoia". The language of "paranoia" is criticized and no longer used because "paranoia" implies that Black Americans' justifiable skepticism is akin to experiences of mental illness and judged as excessive, not normative (Whaley, 2001). The language of "cultural mistrust" is more accurate and less pathologizing.

Given experiences of racism, the tendency to be skeptical, guarded, or distrusting can be adaptive, and preparing for discrimination (including promoting mistrust) may be psychologically protective given the current realities (Hughes et al., 2006). Thus, it is not *being* Black or African American that creates the characteristic, but the experience of discrimination as a Black person that does so.

- *Personality characteristics, abilities, and skills are associated* with specific categories and often treated as if they are inherent and essential.
- *Categories are hierarchical and "lower" status categories are associated with negative characteristics* (e.g., laziness, lack of intelligence), while higher status categories are associated with positive characteristics.

Sometimes characteristics are not inherently negative or positive. But characteristics can be devalued *because* they are associated with subordinate positions and more valued if associated with privileged positions. Characteristics are framed negatively when they are associated with lower status categories versus with higher status categories. Thus, characteristics that could reflect simple variabilty among people (e.g., nurturing, deference, interdependence) lose their contextual functionality as simple differences and become about how we use those characteristics to judge or determine people's place on the hierarchy, or constrain what they can do or receive. For example, women have been assumed to be more nurturing and stereotyped as "belonging in the home" and lacking good leadership abilities, such as being goal focused and relationally assertive to promote the goals they seek to advance. This stereotype has been supported by citing research that shows that women are more "context dependent" and "less assertive." However, this same research could be interpreted as women being more context *responsive* and better at considering multiple peoples' perspectives, which could be important skills for a leader. Indeed, these characteristics are clearly emerging as strengths in the current emphasis on "soft skills" and more collaborative leadership models.

Negative or positive characteristics are attributed to the individual and the category as inherent and related to meritocracy of the individual. Consideration of variability, and of the effect of the context and the hierarchy is minimized. People who display the characteristics or culture associated with lower status categories are judged negatively. And people who are known to be in a lower status category are judged negatively and assumed to have those characteristics. Sticking with the example of nurturance and gender, straight men who display considerable care for their partners or are deferential to women are derided as "whipped" or "gay," in direct contrast to expectations of straight women.

Thus, we continually create the meanings of the categories in ways that ensure that those in higher status categories are viewed more positively and their privileged position is protected. Remember, one major privilege of those in higher status positions is more power to determine the cultural norms and narrative.

The next chapter focuses on power, privilege, and oppression, which we have said is the foundation of why the social categories of race, ethnicity, gender, sexuality, disability, and social class matter so much in our society. Understanding power, privilege, and oppression can help us further understand how these social categories function in similar ways in our society, and have similar dynamics as we describe above. But most of this book focuses on specific social categories, and on unraveling the assumptions and confusions associated with their unique histories and meanings. Defining each social hierarchy separately helps us understand the specific errors we have been taught, and how these assumptions might affect our thinking and interacting. Simultaneously, although looking at a given status separately is important, these categorical social hierarchies are complex, contextual, and intersectional. **Intersectionality** means that social categories are experienced in interaction with each other. For example, the meaning and experience of being Latine or Latinx is different for a cisgender woman living in poverty than it is for a trans, affluent Asian American woman. And this example only includes race, ethnicity, gender, and social class, while sexuality and ability also affect the experience.

How Do I Say? Why use "Latine" or "Latinx" rather than "Latino/a"? Latinx reflects an inclusive, gender-neutral alternative to the gender-binary construction reflected in the terms Latino and Latina. As with all new terms, there is some debate about the appropriateness of using Latinx, including among people from "Hispanic" and/or "Latin American" background. In addition, there is an emerging critique that Latinx reflects an anglicization or cultural imposition of language because it was not made by and for Spanish speakers and is difficult to pronounce and conjugate in Spanish. This critique advances *Latine* as the preferred gender-neutral word, which is the word we will use throughout this book.

Considering intersectionality means that whenever we discuss the definition of a concept and the people it affects, we need to simultaneously consider how this discussion is likely incomplete because it doesn't fully address the variability and complexities *within* the group. We therefore invite you to consider how the explorations we present in future chapters (especially those in Section Two) may themselves reflect power and privilege because the experience of some folks in the group is not fully described.

Resources for Learning More about Culture and History

Guest, K. J. (2020). *Essentials of cultural anthropology: A toolkit for a global age* (3rd edition). W. W. Norton.

Jones, J. M., Dovidio, J. F., & Vietze, D. L. (2014). *The psychology of diversity: Beyond prejudice and racism*. Wiley.

Zinn, H. (2015). *A people's history of the United States: 1492–present* (3rd edition). HarperCollins.

3 Understanding Power, Privilege, and Oppression

To learn about diversity and to apprehend social justice we need to understand power, privilege, and oppression. People often assume that "power" means power *over* and that power is related to being harmful or oppressive to others. Alternatively, people may assume that everyone has power, or that the power one has is related to personal merit or effort. This idea is challenged in the current moment, when there are active discussions about social inequities and privilege. We also have erroneous assumptions about privilege. Some people may not believe in the idea of privilege, while others may view privilege as a personal choice and think that equity will be achieved if individual people would choose to give up their privileges. Similarly, some people may believe that oppression is only about experiences that are caused by individuals with bad intentions such as name calling or hate crimes. Many of these assumptions relate to seeing power, privilege, and oppression as primarily about individual choice and intention. In this chapter, we unravel these assumptions by exploring how these constructs are embedded in cultural worldviews and institutions that then have effects on individuals and interpersonal interactions. After considering the foundations of meaning for these concepts, we explore how they work in more depth, considering things like positive and negative advantages within privilege, relative and ascribed privilege, and intersectionality.

Defining Power, Privilege, and Oppression

Power is the ability to influence an outcome in a desired direction, including outcomes that relate to another person's actions, feelings, or thoughts (e.g., social or relational power).

Privilege is unearned power and benefits, based on identities, status, or background variables.

Oppression is the harmful experiences related to having identities, status, or backgrounds that have been constructed (currently or historically with current legacies) as less deserving, less worthy, or less human.

DOI: 10.4324/9780429059599-5

Some Possible Responses to the Material in This Chapter

Let's pause here to talk a bit about how you might respond to the material in the coming sections. Unpacking the more complicated meanings of power, privilege, and oppression can put into sharp focus how much these issues affect our lives and how much the effects of systemic hierarchies of power, privilege, and oppression can't be controlled by individual intentions, desires, or actions. These ideas might make you pretty uncomfortable and many of the emotional responses that we discussed in Chapter 1 may arise, such as reticence or guilt or frustration or anger. We want you to know such responses are normal, even expected. They reflect how loaded and controversial these concepts have become, particularly privilege. The word alone can spark complicated reactions in people from rage on the one extreme (that such a falsehood is taught in schools) to celebration on the other (that experiences of the dominant group that connect to oppression for marginalized people are finally being examined). Central to your learning of this material is being able to sit with whatever comes up for you (versus turning away from it) while still interacting with others who are learning alongside you. The challenge is figuring out how to interact without re-enacting the dynamics of privilege and oppression that you are learning about. This is a big challenge, one that we experience as a lifelong process. So we hope you will be compassionate with yourself and each other as you engage this material.

We have also found that students' reactions to engaging issues about privilege and oppression relate to how much their personal identity or self-view is connected to statuses that are privileged versus statuses that are oppressed. And how much emphasis there is in a given moment on understanding privilege and oppression in relation to specific social categories. For example, if a discussion is primarily focused on race, a White student sees themselves in relation to the discussion of privilege and a student of color sees themselves in relation to the discussion of oppression. Students then react internally and interpersonally from that positioning. That is, White students may feel resistance and guilt about privilege; in discussions, they may deny that they feel privileged, or feel like they shouldn't talk because they are privileged. Students of color may feel pain or anger as their experiences of oppression become more salient, or feel relieved that their experiences and perspectives are being validated; in discussions, they may be angry at privileged students who are struggling with defensiveness, feel frustrated that privileged students may be ignorant about these issues, resent having to educate their peers or feel empowered by doing so, or feel that White students *should* be feeling guilt, anxiety, and silencing. All of these feelings (and more) are well documented and justifiable given the ways that oppression and privilege affect us as individuals and inevitably play out in our relationships (Sue, 2015).

Furthermore, intersectionality reminds us that people are complicated with multiple social categories and statuses. The White student we mention above may also identify as a lesbian from a working-class status, and the student of color may be from a middle-class background and identify as heterosexual. For students who have many privileged statuses, we invite you to consider how your privilege may have protected you from having to know about some of these issues (more on this below). For students who have oppressed statuses, we invite you to consider how you, too, may have blind spots in relation to statuses where you are privileged, because most students have some statuses where they hold relative privilege.

Meanings of Power and Privilege

Understanding Power

Simply put, **power** is the ability to influence an outcome in a desired direction, including outcomes that relate to another person's actions, feelings, or thoughts (e.g., social or relational power). Some people consider power to be always a negative thing, because the word "power" often conjures ideas about misuse or abuse of power, and because we often talk about power in relation to privilege (see below). However, power is a good thing to have—we all want to be able to reach our goals and to have our actions matter.

At a very basic level, you can see power in an infant who is reaching for a sippy cup when they are thirsty. This seems pretty straightforward: the goal is to quench the thirst and the infant is using their power to achieve that goal. If the cup is outside of their reach, they might cry or bang on the table, using their power of communication to get others to respond. Things get more complicated when you start to think about what it means to influence a complex outcome that takes many tasks and considerable time to achieve. For example, the power to reach the desired outcome of a financially secure life that is personally rewarding is much more complex: the trajectory toward this outcome involves a long-term duration, involving multiple actions and the ability to influence many people and circumstances.

In the United States, we often assume that the power a person has is *earned* power, or merit. Our society is invested in the idea that individuals determine their own destinies based on their hard work—a.k.a. bootstrap mentality or work ethic or meritocracy. However, hard work is much more likely to lead to success when one starts out ahead, with privilege; that is, success is not only about earned power but also about privilege that is afforded to some statuses and not others.

Understanding Privilege

Privilege is unearned power and benefits. It is power and benefits that we have because of our identities, status, or background variables. You haven't done anything to earn this power if you have it, and you haven't done anything to *not* deserve to have it if you don't. This contributes to the ways that thinking about ourselves as privileged is uncomfortable (more on this later).

Privilege is created when societies develop hierarchies that categorize people into those who are assumed to be inherently more deserving and those who are inherently less deserving. "Inherently" is important here, because it means that it is not about what you have done or how hard you have worked. Privilege, as we discuss it here, is not a personal choice, it is not something you can work to have. It is not even something you can refuse to have or choose to give up. In fact, you may not even see that you have this unearned power that is privilege; you may not *feel* that you are powerful. This is because privilege isn't about power that you or others seek to have or choose to develop, instead this kind of power is systemic, rather than individual. Privilege is something that you get because of the way the culture and society you live in has created hierarchies that affect *all* the people in that society.

Which groups are privileged or oppressed is determined culturally over time and embedded in our cultural understandings and worldviews as described above. Think about the core concepts that this book focuses upon: race, ethnicity, gender, sexuality, social class, disability.

How Do I Say? The language of "sexuality" is currently used instead of "sexual orientation" to encompass a wider range of experiences, expressions, and identity. Sexuality includes sexual feelings, interests, needs, desires, values, and fantasies; sexual experiences, acts, and expressions; and sexual orientation. Sexual orientation is a deep rooted orientation of one's erotic feelings towards particular people in one's sexuality, so is a more specific term. See Chapter 7 for much more discussion about sexuality and sexual orientation.

Within each of these social categories, which group (status) is dominant and most privileged? Which groups are oppressed? Is there a hierarchy among the oppressed groups? What determines the "ordering" of groups?

Although privilege as a system is part of shared cultural understandings and institutions, privilege also affects individuals and relationships. Said another way, privilege shapes how you view and interact with the world and how the world views and interacts with you. Thus, each of us, as individuals, participates in this system. But that participation can be very hard to recognize because we take our experiences for granted. Stepping back from being within our experiences so we can examine them from a distance helps begin the process of understanding the impact of privilege in our lives. This distancing requires recognizing that other people may have experiences very different from yours and questioning whether your positive experiences are the result of merit. Peggy McIntosh (1988) did just that. In her groundbreaking paper, she effortfully focuses her attention to see the privileges she has because she is White. Her list includes many things, including the following examples, most of which could also be applied to social hierarchies other than race:

- I can, if I wish, arrange to be in the company of people of my race most of the time.
- I can turn on the television or open to the front page of the paper and see people of my race widely represented.
- I can arrange to protect my children most of the time from people who might not like them.
- I am never asked to speak for all the people of my racial group.
- If my day, week or year is going badly, I need not ask of each negative episode or situation whether it has racial overtones.

A number of other authors have developed similar lists of privileges in relation to other social categories, such as gender, sexuality, social class, and ability (see "Resources for learning more" at the end of this chapter). The goal of these privilege lists is to make what is often invisible more visible. Can you think about some examples of privileges related to statuses in social hierarchies other than race? A couple of examples might include being safer walking alone at night if you are a cisgender male, being able to afford to travel for vacation if you are middle or upper class, being able to easily find cards that depict couples like yours for Valentine's Day or anniversaries if you are heterosexual, or not having to check specifically about the coverage for mental health benefits if you have the option to choose your health insurance.

> *How Do I Say?* Cisgender is the term used when a person's gender identity is consistent with their sex ascribed at birth. Although there have been multiple ways to write the term, consensus is building that it should be written as one word without hyphenation and should definitely not have an "ed" at the end (e.g., the language should not be cisgen-*dered* or trangender*ed*) because it is an identity and status, not something that "happened" to someone. Try an internet search of "why transgender and not transgendered" for more information.

People sometimes think that having privilege always means that you are personally oppressing someone else who doesn't have privilege. And that people who are privileged should try to give up all their privileges. But privilege is more complicated than that. McIntosh (1988) talks about how privilege consists of positive advantages and negative advantages. **Positive advantages** are things that all people should have. Examples of positive advantages include:

- Basic respect: for example, all people should be able to go into a store and be treated respectfully. Currently, however, some people such as White people or middle- or upper-class people are treated respectfully while others such as Black people or limited income people are looked at with suspicion and may be followed or harassed.

- Safety: for example, all people should be able to walk down the street and feel safe from harassment or assault from other people or authority figures. Currently, however, people of color and sexual and gender minority people often encounter slurs, harassment or attacks, and profiling and assumptions about their characteristics or abilities from teachers, police, and other officials.
- Representation: for example, people of all backgrounds should be able to see their own experiences reflected in movies, books, magazines, toys, and so forth, and to have positive examples of people like them. Currently, however, White, middle- and upper-class, cisgender, nondisabled men are overrepresented in media.

Positive advantages are things that most people agree need to be shared. This means we should work to make sure that *everyone* has those advantages, rather than having only some people have them while others do not. It also means that if we have these advantages, we shouldn't feel guilty that we enjoy them, because the problem isn't that we have them: the problem is that other people should *also* have them but don't. Some additional examples of positive advantages are respect from others, shelter, food, education, and health care.

> *It's Complicated:* Positive advantages are related to human rights, as things that people should have because they are people and entitled to some basic things such as life and liberty, freedom from slavery and torture, freedom to think as one wishes and to express those thoughts, the right to work and education. These are some of the things that the United Nations describes as human rights. Not everyone will agree on all the details of what should be shared or how it should be shared, but our point here is that some things should be shared by all. And that positive advantages should be spread rather than eradicated. We shouldn't, for example, try to create equality by giving up our freedom of expression, or taking it from others.

In contrast, **negative advantages** are things that one *only* has when someone else is experiencing something negative—one group's benefit is possible only because of another group's loss or burden. A historical example of a negative advantage is the wealth amassed by slave owners: this wealth would not have been possible without slavery. One of the most insidious negative advantages currently is the advantage of not having to think about issues of diversity or oppression. People who are financially secure, for example, don't have to think about where their next meal is coming from or how they'll pay their rent or utilities. Similarly, heterosexual people don't have to think about whether it's safe to share information about their romantic partners with those they don't know well or show affection in public. Having enough money to pay for the meal or the rent or utilities is something that should be shared (a positive advantage). But the ability to not consider that others can't access those things as easily (or at all) maintains the system that reserves those goodies for only some people. This relates to our earlier discussion of culture, and how some things become so "normal" to us that we don't even see them. In this instance, the cultured norm is that some people (privileged people) are more entitled to the goodies (as we discussed in Chapter 1). Privileged people often don't see this cultural norm (social construct), while those who are not in privileged groups tend to see it clearly, because of the negative effects it has.

The idea that you can have privilege but not see or feel it can be hard to understand, so let's pause here to explore this idea a bit more. In some ways, our inability to see privilege is evolutionary. Humans are primed to focus on threat. It's part of our survival mechanism. This means that without prompting, we don't usually focus on aspects of ourselves that aren't stressful to us or make us vulnerable to pain (i.e., areas of privilege). Let's take this idea a step further by looking at racial privilege. Because being White is privileged in U.S. society, White Americans don't typically have to worry about how their race will negatively influence how the police, potential employers, teachers, and strangers will perceive them. There is less social or physical threat related to being White. As a result, White people are unlikely to consider what it means to be White, to think about how being White has shaped their experiences, or to perceive themselves as raced. Dominant societal norms create and reinforce this view by, for example, making Whiteness invisible through practices like naming race when identifying a non-White person ("an Asian man was here looking for you") and being silent on race when it relates to a White person ("a man was here looking for you"). People of color, in contrast, are regularly reminded of their race through naming and "othering" practices and through experiences of racism.

In sum, privilege is the power and related advantages one holds as a result of belonging to a dominant group or a group that is of higher status within the social system.

Reflection Questions

- Consider your own identities and statuses in relation to race, ethnicity, gender, sexuality, disability, and social class.
- Which of your identities are privileged?
- Within these, what are some of the privileges that you, personally, have? How much do you think about these privileges?
- How much do you think about the experiences of people who don't have those privileges?
- Which of these are positive advantages that would benefit everyone and should be shared? Are there things you do to try to spread them or make sure that these experiences are available to everyone?

Meanings of Prejudice and Oppression

Oppression consists of the harmful experiences that come with having identities or backgrounds that are seen as not deserving. The word "seen" is important here because it calls our attention to the fact that people with these backgrounds or identities are not *actually* less deserving.

Oppression and privilege are two sides of the same coin: one exists because of and in relation to the other. When we talk about privilege, we often name privileges we might have without considering that those privileges may be maintaining or creating oppression for others. Similarly, when we talk about the experience of oppression, we are often talking about the difficult experiences of people who are the "targets" of oppression, without simultaneously addressing the fact that oppression is enacted or maintained by people with privilege, even if this is unintentional, and even if this results from all people being caught within a hierarchical system. The existence of oppression requires the existence of privilege, and vice versa. So, if there are targets of oppression, there are inevitably agents of oppression.

Often, students feel defensive at this point—they think that we are saying that people who are privileged are inherently and intentionally oppressive to others, meaning they don't value equity or inclusion. So, we want to be clear that naming those who are privileged as "agents" does *not* mean that those who are privileged are intentionally and consciously setting out to oppress others. Agent status means that one has privilege, and that this privilege has effects on your experience and actions. People with privilege have the power to choose how to use (or not use) their power and privilege within the overall system to address oppression. White people can work to resist and undo racism, men can work to resist and undo sexism, and so forth. This is what is meant by striving to be an ally, or accomplice, which we discuss in Chapter 10. If you want to not be an *active* agent, you can work to dismantle the system of oppression.

Our point here is that lack of attention to the interaction and interdependence of privilege and oppression is one of the things that contributes to our difficulty in apprehending the complex meaning of social justice and effectively communicating across differences. Furthermore, when we don't consider oppression and privilege as interactive and co-dependent, we decrease our power to challenge these hierarchies—you can't effectively address one without addressing the other. So, we hope you will bear with us through any discomfort as we try to unpack these complexities in the following pages.

Understanding Prejudice and Stereotyping

Human beings are cognitively hard wired to create categories, so that we can organize our perceptions and experiences to avoid being overwhelmed. Categorizing our experiences helps us make sense of them and generalize our learning and understanding to other experiences. A simple example that is clearly necessary for our survival is categorizing things into "food" and "not food." We begin to categorize our experiences and things in our world from a very young age. For example, you may have watched young children sort blocks by color (red or blue blocks) or shape (circles or squares) and begin to learn words for these categories. This categorizing is about noticing and learning about similarities and differences. Furthermore, children (and adults) may have preferences within these differences, say a favorite color. A preference for one color doesn't necessarily mean a person thinks other colors are bad. However, preferences for one thing *can* relate to viewing other things as less positive. And this process of making associations and connecting them to what is seen as good or bad differentiates simple categorizing from bias, prejudice, and stereotyping.

Prejudice is bias that consists of negative attitudes toward a group or favoring one group over another. There are many theories about how and why prejudice develops and how it can be reduced that you can explore further through the resources provided at the end of this chapter. For now, it's important to know that prejudice is fed by the creation of social **stereotypes**— simplified and rigid overgeneralizations about a group of people or a single person because of their relation to a group. Stereotyping is not the same as applying knowledge about group differences. We all hold beliefs about group differences, and many of these beliefs have some kernel of "truth," meaning that many people in the group *do* behave in a certain way. For example, the statement "Most Asian Americans are less emotionally expressive ..." holds some truth is supported by research (e.g., Ip et al., 2021; Park & Kim, 2008): the cultural norms and modal experience within many Asian countries are less emotionally expressive than the cultural norms within the United States. So we might want to consider this possibility when we interact with people from Asian heritages. However, the meaning of the statement "Most Asian Americans are less emotionally expressive ..." needs to be considered more fully: less emotionally expressive *than whom in what context?* And what do we mean by "Asian American"—does the research we have to support this statement include the wide range of ethnic groups within this umbrella term (e.g., Indians, Filipinx, Hmong)? Are we including Asian Americans whose families have been here in the United States for centuries and who may be more "American" than "Asian" in their cultural exposure or practices? Are we including Asian Americans who have been adopted and raised within European American families and cultural norms? Without considering these questions, we are oversimplifying. Furthermore, if we assume that *all* Asian Americans *will* be less emotionally expressive or if we meet an Asian American person and automatically expect them to be less emotionally expressive, then we are moving from applying our knowledge to stereotyping. We have changed our statement to be "[All] Asian Americans are not emotionally expressive," even if we are not acknowledging the change to ourselves. This is what we mean by "rigid" and "overgeneralized."

Anyone can be prejudiced. And anyone can hold stereotypes of groups that they over-apply to all individuals in that group. These dynamics relate to ingroup and outgroup biases that apply to many kinds of group criteria. For examples, many White people have negative views of people of color and people of color can have negative views of White people (Dovidio et al., 2010). Many Asian people have negative views of Black people, and many Black people have negative views of Asian people (Tawa et al., 2013). These are all examples of racial prejudice. And we can easily think of the stereotypes that are likely part of those negative views.

Understanding Oppression

Being the target of prejudice or stereotyping is not the same thing as being the target of oppression. The nature and impact of prejudice and stereotyping is different when the prejudice supports systemic privilege and oppression. In relation to our example above, stereotyping Asian Americans as less emotionally expressive is particularly problematic because this cultural characteristic is associated with views of Asian Americans as less empathic, inscrutable, and sneaky that have been used to justify oppression.

It's Complicated: Often, our racial associations are related to "forgotten" history, even as that history continues to affect our social worldviews. During World War II, for example, racialized ideas about Japanese Americans as *inherently* sneaky, traitorous, and unAmerican justified the unconstitutional incarceration of over 100,000 people of Japanese descent, the vast majority of whom were American citizens. But there was no evidence at all for these views. And yet, these racialized ideas continue to shape our stereotypes of Asian Americans, interacting with ideas of Asian Americans as "forever foreigners" and leading to tragedies such as the death of Vincent Chin, who was beaten to death by two White men due to his race, and the persecution of Wen Ho Lee, a scientist in the United States who was accused of espionage by the U.S. government without evidence, also due to his race and cultural heritage.

This connection of prejudice with power/privilege is one of the most difficult things to understand about privilege and oppression and it requires fully understanding that oppression is not about specific instances of interpersonal discrimination at the individual level. And that even when there are specific instances or examples, these need to be understood as related to, informed by, and inherently embedded in systemic hierarchies.

Let's try to explore a new example. Imagine a Black person, Morgan, who believes that White people are less intelligent. Morgan is endorsing personal racial prejudice. A White person, Chris, who interacts with Morgan may feel really hurt and offended by Morgan's discrimination. But while Morgan's belief is interpersonally painful for Chris, it doesn't have much effect on Chris's life opportunities or even Chris's self-view. Chris is not surrounded by social and media messages that White people are less intelligent. There is not a widely held social belief that White people are less intelligent that affects how Chris was treated by teachers or the level of math class Chris was placed in as a child. Chris is not affected by intergenerational consequences of anti-White policies. For example, it has not been illegal to teach White people to read, and Chris's White grandparents were not shut out of colleges and higher education. Chris receives lots of messages that the White group that Chris belongs to is normal, and positive, and powerful. Chris has not had to endure lots of explicit and implicit messages from other people that indicate White people are less intelligent, or to repeatedly produce the scientific evidence that intelligence is not related to race. Chris's interaction with Morgan is most likely a "one-off" experience, because the belief that White people are less intelligent is not reflected in shared sociohistorical meaning and social and institutional practices. So, while Morgan is, indeed, enacting racial prejudice and Chris is, indeed, the target of that prejudice, this doesn't mean that Chris, as a White person, is oppressed. But if Chris believed that Morgan was less intelligent because Chris believed that Black people were less intelligent, then it would be a different experience and effect for Morgan. And Chris would also be supporting the racialized hierarchy that privileges White people in our general society.

It's Complicated: The ways that people are affected by having or not having power associated with their statuses within hierarchies (structural power) can be complicated by power associated with one's role. For example, if Morgan is Chris's boss, then Morgan's prejudice against White people like Chris could have considerable effect for Chris, individually. So, we need to look at the interactions of individuals with context and institutional power. Some things to think about in this example include: it is more often the case that Chris (the White person) will be the boss; Chris may experience prejudice with detrimental effects in this one instance with Morgan but is much less likely to experience it repeatedly, while detrimental effects of prejudice from White people with role power towards Black people are widespread. In sum, what makes racial prejudice oppression is not about individual examples or interactions but is instead about widespread and institutional patterns.

When prejudice and stereotypes connect to the negative network of associations we have because of social hierarchies, they contribute to maintaining inequities and justifications for treating some people better than others simply because of their group. This is what we mean by the "**-isms.**" You may have heard someone say something like "Racism (or sexism, or classism, etc.) is prejudice plus power." This statement is emphasizing that the nature and effects of prejudice that are used to maintain hierarchies of privilege and oppression are different from the nature and effects of prejudice that are not connected to those hierarchies, or that are reacting to those hierarchies. Hopefully, you can see this difference in our example of Chris and Morgan. Another example is when limited income people stereotype rich people as cold or uncaring. Such stereotyping has different effects than when rich people stereotype limited income and economically marginalized people as lazy or undeserving. The latter is much more damaging because rich people have the power to affect the lives of limited income people with that judgment. Because of the different implications of stereotyping, it's important to think carefully about how prejudice, privilege, and oppression interact, to consider the social power that is held by the person who is enacting prejudice, and the nature and effects of that prejudice in relation to the damaging hierarchies of inequity in our society.

In sum, an oppression "-ism" is different from a prejudice. An oppression -ism is defined as a *system* of judgments, beliefs, actions, norms, and social/institutional practices that protects institutional privilege and hierarchy. This means that for something to be oppression, rather than prejudice, it interacts with the systemic hierarchies of our socially constructed categories: it is problematic because it maintains those hierarchies and the privilege and oppression that are related to them. This is different from a given individual's personal belief or behavior, although it is certainly true that individuals are affected by such systemic privilege, and that oppression can and is enacted interpersonally. But the experience of oppression is much more than hurtful and deliberate interpersonal interactions.

The experience of oppression therefore goes beyond an experience of interpersonal prejudice or stereotyping. Young (1990) expands on the difference between discrimination and oppression, emphasizing how oppression can occur even without a specific individual enacting overt discrimination or prejudice. She describes five "faces" or categories of experience that characterize oppression: marginalization, powerlessness, exploitation, cultural imperialism (the dominance of one culture and the power to determine the dominant culture), and violence (including psychological, verbal, repressive, or physical violence). These five faces can be enacted and experienced at various ecological levels.

Expanding and Complicating Meanings of Oppression and Privilege

Levels of Oppression and Privilege

Hierarchies of inequity are maintained and experienced ideologically, intrapsychically, interpersonally, and institutionally. And the endorsement of biased attitudes and enactment of privilege and oppression as an agent do not have to be active, intentional, or explicit; they can be passive, unintentional, and microaggressive. Also, one can also be both an agent and a target of oppression simultaneously.

In Chapter 2, we discussed **ideological oppression and privilege** when we discussed the meaning of social construct and how our worldview is shaped by ideologies of hierarchy. Ideologies of oppression and privilege permeate and interact with all other levels, as they are the foundations of our understandings of ourselves, others, and the world around us.

Intrapsychic oppression and associated privilege relate to the attitudes and beliefs we have personally internalized about categorical groups and people who belong to these groups, including ourselves. Because hierarchical systems of oppression and privilege are systemic and embedded in our cultural socialization, we develop oppressive attitudes and beliefs even when we don't want to. Many of us may not even be aware of these attitudes or may even think that we don't endorse them or are not affected by them. However, research suggests that even if we don't want to have these attitudes, many people do have unconscious discriminatory attitudes, often referred to as **implicit bias or aversive racism**, that actively affects their choices and behavior (more on this later in the chapter).

How Do I Say? Implicit bias versus aversive racism. As stated, implicit bias refers to unconscious and automatic stereotypes and beliefs about a categorical group (e.g., women, gay men, SWANA [South West Asian North African] people) that can influence behavior outside of our awareness. Aversive racism is an experience where implicit bias is held by an individual who also has overt, conscious beliefs in equality. Aversive racism is "aversive" to the person who enacts it: The term aversive points to the strong negative reaction someone who believes they value justice and equality would have if they became aware they were acting in ways that were oppressive and prejudicial. Numerous studies with White participants who are asked to make judgments or interact with people of color support the existence of aversive racism, particularly in cases where biased behavior can be attributed to unbiased motives (e.g., helping strangers and hiring decisions). See below for more discussion of this term and the associated research.

For example, implicit bias about social class is widespread, and it is closely tied with one's privilege around this area. In university settings, people sometimes make assumptions about others' access and availability of resources for course-related activities (e.g., purchasing textbooks, attending course-related activities) or social activities (e.g., going out to eat with friends). While those who have resources to easily pursue these activities may not think much of it, this privilege can lead people to easily overlook the needs of others who do not share in this privilege. Furthermore, people's attitudes about social class do not stop at tangible activities, but also relate to the unconscious assumptions people make about others' abilities and intelligence based on assumptions about social class (e.g., rich people are better spoken and intelligent: Durante & Fiske, 2017).

Internalized oppression is a specific type of intrapsychic oppression, where people who belong to a target marginalized group have accepted (again, often unconsciously) negative attitudes or beliefs about themselves and their own group. For example, women can internalize sexist beliefs about themselves and other women, as seen in women blaming women for sexual assault perpetrated by men, judging other women based on their appearance and dress, and criticizing women who are outspoken but not men who act similarly (Cowan, 2000). Internalized oppression is not only bias about our own group, but also about ourselves, such as when a woman blames herself for her own sexual assault or doubts her ability to be a leader because of messages she has received that a leader "should" communicate or act in certain ways.

Interpersonal oppression and privilege relate to discrimination and privilege that are enacted within interpersonal interactions and relationships. This kind of oppression can be active, intentional, and conscious. Examples of active and intentional interpersonal oppression include a heterosexual youth bullying a gay youth by name calling or a White cisgender manager not hiring an applicant because they are transgender or Latine or both. The latter example illustrates how interpersonal oppression may be enacted at a relational level but may have effects beyond the individual or the relationship, in terms of blocking access to resources or opportunities.

However, just as we have internalized oppressive biases that we are not aware of, we often enact those biases in our interpersonal interactions without intention. "Microaggressions" are everyday, seemingly minor (to the agent) instances of interpersonal oppression (Sue, 2010). Examples of experiencing microaggressions include:

- A same-sex attracted person having to hear the term "gay" used as a negative descriptor of something or someone.
- A Black woman professor who is told she is a "credit to her race."
- A U.S.-born Asian American man who is asked regularly where he is from.
- A White woman who is labeled as aggressive when she disagrees with others.
- A nurse from a family who has used welfare benefits has a conversation with a colleague who says "People on welfare just don't want to work."
- Instead of speaking directly to the patient who is physically disabled, a doctor directs all questions to their non-disabled partner who is accompanying the patient.

Often, microaggressions can appear harmless to the agent, or even well intentioned. But they are oppressive to the target because of the way they are socially repeated, connect to systemic hierarchies, and are cumulatively negative. Microaggressions are like a poke. Imagine someone pokes you once. It could seem to the poker that they are being affectionate or friendly, or just getting your attention. You, the pokee, might not like it, but it is just a poke, right? But if you experience 20 pokes in the same place, you will likely have a bruise. And if you experience 200 pokes in the same place, you will likely have a wound. And if you have that wound, then even a single poke will hurt a LOT.

Interpersonal oppression can also be passive. Passive interpersonal oppression is a kind of collusion; if we see oppression and do nothing about it, then aren't we then partly responsible for its continuation? For example, a commonly discussed experience among women in leadership positions is how their ideas in meetings are ignored or glossed over until a man brings up the same idea. Men may recognize this dynamic but choose not to speak up about it or try to change the dynamic. Similarly, standing by when others are speaking in sexist ways about women; making jokes about the dress, accent, or food of those from other countries'; or disparaging as lazy those who are unemployed or financially insecure are forms of passive interpersonal oppression.

Institutional oppression and privilege are related to discrimination and privilege that are embedded in our cultural norms and our social organizations and institutions, such as schools, policies, or the legal system. Some historical examples of oppression in the United States through laws include denying the right to freedom for Black people through slavery, denying access to a process of becoming a citizen for Asian immigrants through the Asian Exclusion Act, denying the right to vote for women or people who were not landowners, denying the right to marry for gay and lesbian couples, denying the right to obtain education for people with disabilities. The laws that supported these direct denials of rights have since been overturned. However, research finds that there continues to be discrimination in our social institutions (Golash-Boza, 2018). Examples include bias within the criminal justice system, gerrymandering in creating voting districts, racial profiling for citizenship checks, and the relative exclusion of the contributions of people of color, women, and other marginalized groups within the teaching of history in schools. Institutional privilege means that people in the privileged groups are able to access resources and rights more easily and without challenge. These are all examples of the ways that oppression and privilege are not only individual and interpersonal, but are also institutional. Despite the fact that in many cases there are no longer laws supporting institutional oppression, the cultures, policies, and procedures within institutions are based on social understandings that reflect the prejudicial and oppressive worldview. In addition, the ways that individuals with power act within institutions maintain the institutional culture, connecting intrapsychic, interpersonal, and institutional oppression. The "-isms" (racism, ethnocentrism, sexism, hetero-sexism, classism, ableism) are the experiences of oppression that are related to specific hierarchies of power and privilege.

In sum, oppression is the experiences one is subject to as a result of belonging to a group that is of lower status within social structures. Oppression is both not having privileges that others have and having negative experiences that others don't have such as marginalization or exclusion, insult, exploitation, or violence. Negative or unfair treatment is not always oppression. Whether such treatment is (structural) oppression is based on the reason for that treatment and the connection to systemic hierarchies of distinction as we discussed above. Furthermore, oppression is not only negative experiences or unfair interpersonal treatment from people who are actively biased or discriminatory. Oppression is also reflected in our internalized views of ourselves and others, our intentional and unintentional behaviors, our acceptance of systemic hierarchies, and the policies and practices of our organizations and social institutions.

Reflection Questions

Consider your own identities in relation to race, ethnicity, gender, social class, or ability:

- Do you belong to groups that are not dominant in any of these hierarchies?
- What kinds of experiences do you have because you belong to groups of lesser social status? Do you understand these experiences as experiences of oppression? Why or why not?
- If you do not belong to any of these subordinate groups, what kinds of experiences do you *not* have—that is, what experiences of oppression have you not had to experience? Not experiencing negative things because of your dominant or relative status is actually a kind of privilege, which highlights how privilege and oppression are interdependent.

Unconscious Bias: Examples of Color-blind Racial Ideology and Unconscious Racism

One of the more difficult aspects of understanding oppression and privilege is recognizing how bias and prejudice can exist outside of your awareness. Even more challenging is realizing that individual and institutional efforts to minimize the impact of oppression or distance oneself from it are sometimes ineffective or can actually cause harm. Color-blind racial attitudes or ideology (also known as color evasiveness) is an example of this.

How Do I Say? Why not use "colorblindness"? Colorblindness is a term that describes individuals with a genetic condition leading them to perceive color differently from the general population. The experience can range from difficulty distinguishing between two colors like red and green to not being able to see any colors. Using the term "color-blindness" to refer to color-blind racial attitudes conflates racial discrimination with a genetic condition linked to ability. As such, we recommend using color-blind racial attitudes or color-blind (racial) ideology, not "colorblindness."

Color-blind racial attitudes are an ideology exemplified in statements such as, "I don't see race" or "I see people as human beings only. Skin color doesn't matter." Those who ascribe to color-blind racial ideology are often intending to focus on the humanity of all people with the aim of being fair and not discriminating. However, color-blind racial attitudes tend to deny the realities experienced by people of color that skin color *does* matter in our society (even if it shouldn't). A growing body of research over the last 20+ years indicates that these seemingly well-intentioned attempts to minimize or de-emphasize racial differences are actually associated with increased racial tension, prejudice, and the denial of racism and its effects, particularly at the institutional level (see Neville et al., 2013).

At this point, you might be wondering *why* the impact of a color-blind racial ideology is so vastly different from the intention, particularly if you ascribe to this ideology. Under the norms of a color-blind racial ideology, even noticing racial differences or inequities may be seen as "racist": one is discriminatory for noticing race, or "using the race card." Simultaneously, ignoring or minimizing race-related topics, not acknowledging the pain of racism, and avoiding discussions of privilege or oppression is considered to be "nice" or normative. But denying that one sees color (race) and espousing that ignoring racial difference is the preferred way to interact across racial diversity denies the social consequences of race, racial power dynamics, and racism. For people of color who experience these social consequences, color-blind racial ideology means that their racialized experiences are not acknowledged or seen as real, and that speaking about their experience of race or racism is censored. Furthermore, the lack of acknowledgment of racial inequities through the color-blind ideology relates to the maintaining of the system of racism because one cannot change and eradicate racism without first acknowledging that there is racism. Being silent about experiences of race and racism or actively ignoring the issue (even if it's arising from positive intentions), therefore means enabling racism to continue. This same analysis can be applied to other categories: ignoring the ways that women's experiences are different than men's, or minimizing the barriers that people with disabilities face, results in erasing very real and salient differences in current experience, especially experiences related to oppression and privilege.

Another reason why color-blind ideology is ineffective as an anti-racist strategy is that prejudicial attitudes are often not in our consciousness. Decades of innovative research indicate that we have **implicit bias**, not only about racial groups but also about other social categories such as gender, social class, sexual orientation, religion, etc. Through numerous studies, Mahzarin Banaji and colleagues have illustrated that human biases are not only explicit and conscious, but also implicit and unconscious, often going against our own perceptions of ourselves (Banaji & Greenwald, 2016). The implicitness of biases is particularly troubling because even when you don't want to hold biases, you can still have them and can act in ways that demonstrate those biases, particularly in spontaneous behaviors or responses (Dovidio et al., 2017; Greenwald et al., 2009). Of note, this research also indicates that target group members (e.g., people of color, when considering race) are vulnerable to unconsciously internalizing negative messages about their own group, although not to the same extent as dominant group members do (see Nosek, Banaji, & Greenwald, 2002).

Research on **aversive racism** finds that implicit attitudes affect behaviors. Through a series of social psychology experiments, Dovidio, Gaertner, and colleagues showed that even well-meaning White people who consciously espouse egalitarian beliefs and deny racial prejudice can still discriminate in ways outside of their awareness—a phenomenon termed *aversive racism* (see overview of multiple studies in Dovidio et al., 2002; Dovidio et al., 2017; Gaertner & Dovidio, 2005). In one such study, White college student participants were asked to evaluate the qualifications of a fictitious Black or White applicant for college admissions and to describe what criteria they used most in their evaluation. The qualifications were manipulated to be consistently strong (strong grades and SAT scores), weak (weak grades and SAT scores), or mixed (weak scores and strong grades, or strong scores and weak grades). Results indicated no discrimination when applicant qualifications clearly identified as strong or weak. However, there was discrimination when the qualifications were ambiguous, with participants rationalizing their racially biased choices based on the ambiguous criteria. For example, when White people had strong scores and weak grades, they were admitted because they had strong scores, but when Black people had strong scores and weak grades, they were rejected because of the weak grades. This study and others indicate that aversive racism is more likely to manifest in less than clear-cut situations where preferences could be attributed to or justified by non-race factors, such as in job interviews where no candidate has the perfect fit, but each person has different strengths.

These researchers have also looked at the relational effects of aversive racism (see overview of multiple studies in Dovidio et al., 2002; Dovidio et al., 2017; Gaertner & Dovidio, 2005). They demonstrated that White people's explicit (conscious) racial attitudes predicted their impressions of how friendly they acted in an interaction with a Black person, but that their implicit racial attitudes better predicted the Black person's evaluation of their friendliness in the same interaction. Thus, Black and White people in the same interaction had different perceptions of how it went: White participants reported a positive experience and Black participants reported unhappiness with the interaction. Both people assumed that the other person shared their impression. In yet another study, these researchers demonstrated that aversive racism and discrepant views on interactions affects productive teamwork. They differentiated White college students on the basis of their implicit and explicit racial attitudes as prejudiced (high in both implicit and explicit discriminatory racial attitudes), non-prejudiced (low in both), and aversive racist (low in explicit discrimination and high in implicit racial bias). Black people paired with these three kinds of White people were less trustful of both prejudiced and aversive racist White people. And the racial attitudes of White people affected the success of the dyad: predictably, the most effective team was the non-prejudiced White person and the Black person. But it was the pair of the well-intentioned but aversively racist White person with the Black person who was least effective. These findings have particular implications for understanding why implicit attitudes are so important. In a work setting that is predominantly White, most White people will have productive pairings with other White people. But most Black people will be paired with White people, and their work productivity and effectiveness will depend on whether the White person has done the work to unlearn implicit bias, work that involves more than good intentions and personal belief that one is not biased (see Chapter 10 for more on what that work looks like).

Relative, Ascribed, Contextual, and Intersectional Privilege and Oppression

Privilege and oppression are not absolute and binary within a given person. A person is rarely completely privileged or completely oppressed. Because of this, it's helpful to think about relative privilege, ascribed privilege, and how privilege can be contextual and intersectional. Within specific hierarchies of privilege, there is a dominant group status at the top (e.g., White people are dominant within the racial hierarchy, and cisgender men are dominant within the gender hierarchy). But many hierarchies have multiple groups that are not dominant, and these groups may have relative and ascribed privilege in relation to each other. **Relative privilege** considers how there may be more than two categories within a hierarchy, and how oppressed groups relate to each other in regards to the power and privilege within that hierarchy. It is different from, but related to intersectional privilege (see below), because it is about multiple categories within the same social hierarchy, rather than the intersection of multiple identities in different social hierarchies. For example, within our hierarchy of gender, cisgender women are not privileged in relation to the dominant group of cisgender men. But cisgender women *are* privileged in relation to trans women. Similarly, relative privilege often relates to ascribed privilege, because it is often the dominant or most privileged group that has the most influence over how the hierarchy is created.

Ascribed privilege is privilege that is controlled by the dominant group and given or "ascribed" to a minority group in order to maintain the power and privilege of the dominant group itself. Ascribed privilege differs from actual privilege because (a) the group that benefits from ascribed privilege does not actually have the most power to create or maintain that privilege, and (b) the ascribed privilege most benefits the dominant group, rather than the relatively elevated minority group. During slavery, for example, wealthy White men developed rules that elevated limited income White men above enslaved Black people as a way to prevent the groups from aligning their social class worker interests.

Ascribed privilege calls attention to the ways that prejudice between oppressed groups within a given social category has a different nature and effect than prejudice directed from the privileged group to an oppressed group. Oppressed groups do not have the power to define the nature or boundaries of statuses within a hierarchy, including their own group. Thus, the White men that were elevated above enslaved Black people could not, themselves, choose how they were defined or the social class privileges they did or did not have access to. This was given to them (ascribed) by the dominant group (the group with the most power). It is often the case that endorsing ascribed privilege simultaneously maintains one's own oppression, as well as undermining possibilities of making connections to resist oppression. This may be particularly relevant when some groups are elevated or offered ascribed privilege *within* a social category. An example would be people who identify as gay or lesbian having prejudice against people who identify as bisexual. Some authors (e.g., David et al., 2019 in relation to race) talk about prejudice among oppressed groups within a social category as "lateral internalized oppression," where someone with an oppressed status within a social structure has internalized negative views about *other* oppressed people within that same social category. Cross-minority prejudices within a given hierarchy are understood as internalized oppression because they work to maintain the privilege of the dominant group (e.g., heterosexual people) within the overall hierarchy, and are therefore detrimental to all who have subordinate status within that social category.

Privilege can also be contextual. When we talk about privilege, we are usually talking about our society in general, but within sub-cultures or specific contexts, some groups can have more relative privilege than others. For example, women within the context of nursing or preschool education or library science have contextual privilege in terms of representation and inclusion in those fields, as compared to men.

Finally, experiences of privilege and oppression are intersectional. Although we can talk about what it means to have limited income as if all people experiencing poverty are similar, we know that experiencing poverty encompasses a huge range of experiences. Some of these experiences are related to other hierarchies of power and privilege. For example, you have likely heard the fact that women make less money than men on average, reflecting ways that women are not privileged in relation to men. When you look at pay at the intersection of race and gender, however, you see that White women make more on average than Black, Latine, and Indigenous American women—evidence of White women's racial privilege and relative privilege within the larger category of women. In fact, White women make more on average than Black, Latine, and Indigenous American men (U.S. Department of Labor, 2020). Another example is how our impressions and stereotypes about Black men experiencing poverty are not necessarily the same as those we have about White women experiencing poverty, or how we might think and interact differently with a person who is experiencing poverty and is disabled, compared with someone who is not disabled. Our access to power (remember, the ability to influence an outcome) is affected by the impressions and stereotypes that others put upon us.

We know we've given you a lot to digest so far and hope you are managing to receive all the information. Understanding that oppression and privilege matter and affect you even when you don't want it to can be challenging to sit with, especially if you didn't think about this before. But it's important knowledge to have before considering the ways that hierarchies of inequity affect the lived experiences of all people, which is the focus of the next sections. So, if you find yourself having a hard time with the material, we invite you to take a little break to reset before diving in again.

Effects of Hierarchies of Oppression and Privilege

This primer focuses principally on understanding concepts, rather than examining the breadth and depth of the effects of these hierarchies. However, it is the effects of oppression and privilege that make these concepts matter so much. In later chapters focused on specific hierarchies, we describe effects on ideology and touch on effects at systemic, interpersonal, and individual levels. But having a basic understanding of the breadth and depth of effects is vital to understanding the meanings of oppression and privilege.

Systemic oppression has had serious and long-standing compounded material costs, and continues to exact material costs today. The racial and gender inequities we see in educational, housing, and/or financial opportunities are rooted in histories of colonization, slavery, and laws that understood people of color and women as less than fully human. Systemic oppression also has serious psychological costs: experiencing oppression relates to depression, anxiety, lower self-esteem, and suicidality. These psychological costs are detrimental in their own right and also contribute to material costs. Systemic material issues such as limited income neighborhoods where healthy food is less available interact with and contribute to health inequities, which also interact with psychological costs. Thus, material, health, and psychological effects are cyclical and interacting. Systemic oppression also has detrimental effects for those who are privileged, including effects on worldviews, relationships, and losses to the society that affect all members (Goodman, 2011).

Exploring Effects of Oppression through the Example of Racism

Let's look at race as an example of the wide-ranging effects of systemic oppression and privilege. Since the Civil Rights Movement of the 1960s, more direct and explicit legal and institutional enactment of racism has decreased. It is no longer typical for laws and institutions to explicitly discriminate on the basis of racial categorization: In fact, there are now laws that prohibit such discrimination. Because of this, some people may think that race and racism no longer matter. But race and racism still have far-reaching impacts on our lives today. The concluding paragraph of the 1998 American Anthropology Association statement on race illustrates this point well:

> The "racial" worldview was invented to assign some groups to perpetual low status, while others were permitted access to privilege, power, and wealth. The tragedy in the United States has been that the policies and practices stemming from this worldview succeeded all too well in constructing unequal populations among Europeans, Native Americans, and peoples of African descent. Given what we know about the capacity of normal humans to achieve and function within any culture, we conclude that present-day inequalities between so-called "racial" groups are not consequences of their biological inheritance but products of historical and contemporary social, economic, educational, and political circumstances.
>
> (American Anthropological Association, 1998)

The "tragedy" they refer to is the successful integration of the historic racial worldview into our ideology, and into our relational, cultural, and institutional practices. This integration is so pervasive that many of us don't often think about these racialized ideas when those ideas aren't connected to the oppression for our own group. But we can clearly see these continued effects if we direct our attention and raise questions about what we see.

Institutional-Level Effects of Race and Racism

We can, for example, easily see that race matters and racism exists when we consider institutional oppression and major structural racial inequities. For example, as we mentioned previously, there is a disproportionately low number of people of color in positions of power in the United States, which means there is a disproportionately high number of White people, particularly wealthy cisgender White men. For example, in 2020, White people made up about 60% of the U.S. population but constituted (Lu, Huang, Seshagiri, Park, & Griggs, 2020):

- 80% of the Supreme Court.
- 81% of the Senate, 74% of the House of Representatives, and 94% of state governors.
- 88% of military chiefs (who are all men).
- 80% of those who direct the major news organizations.
- 76% of those who lead the 25 highest-valued companies (who are all men).
- 96% of those who lead the top 25 universities.

The inequities continue when you look at other areas, such as

- Healthcare—8% of White ("non-Hispanic") people were uninsured in 2019 compared to 19% of "Hispanic" people (U.S. Census Bureau, 2020). African Americans are twice as likely to die of diabetes compared to White people.
- Income—Median household income is approximately $75,000 for White ("non-Hispanic") people compared to approximately $55,000 and $46,000 for Latine and Black people, respectively (U.S. Census Bureau, 2021). Within Asian Americans there is significant variability by ethnicity (e.g. median household income for Vietnamese and Koreans is less than $55,000, but median income for Indians and Filipinx is $75,000 or above [Golash-Boza, 2018]).The average yearly earnings for White men in 2000 was about $50,000, while Native American men earned about $30,000 on average (Golash-Boza, 2018).
- Poverty—It is estimated that 1 in 3 Native Americans live in poverty in the U.S. (Institute for Policy Research, 2020). In Asian Americans, a clear bimodal distribution is noted for those who are economically advantaged in comparison to those who are in poverty (e.g., 25% of Mongolians live in poverty; Budiman & Ruiz, 2021).
- Unemployment—7% for White people in 2020, compared to 11% for Black people and 10% for Latine people, including 12% for Puerto Ricans (Statista, 2021).

In listing the inequities above, we are pointing to ways that racial categorizations and legacies have blocked access for people of color to resources, opportunities, and achievement with significant material costs, meaning costs that directly impact economic advancement. These costs most heavily affect people of color, of course. But racism is costly to *all* people in the United States (and elsewhere). There is a collective loss when everyone in a society is not able to reach their full potential, to develop and contribute their gifts to society. By one measure, for example, the wealth gap between White and Black Americans "is projected to cost the US economy between $1 trillion and $1.5 trillion in lost consumption and investment between 2019 and 2028" (Losavio, 2020).

We often hear about these inequities on the news, or read about them in social media, or hear politicians or protesters talking about them. And if you have been affected by these inequities, it is very personal (and painful). But if you have not been oppressed by racism, then reading about these inequities may sometimes seem abstract or far away, more about concepts and numbers than about people. This is particularly true if you are not familiar with the history of race in the United States (and connections to current experiences), if you haven't considered how race is a worldview and how we are socialized into that worldview, if you haven't had much interaction with people of color or people who are racially different than you, or if you have thought about race and racism as the result of individual "bad apples" and intentional behaviors.

Individual and Interpersonal-Level Effects of Race and Racism for People of Color

In addition to tracking structural inequities and considering material costs, inequities often become more personal when we think about them at the people level. The pervasiveness of racism and its embeddedness into every aspect of life are added burdens that tax people of color physically and psychologically (Carter et al., 2019). Numerous studies have found links between experiencing racism and hypertension, headaches, cardiac problems, chronic stress, and asthma (e.g., Carter et al., 2019; Gee et al., 2007; Pascoe & Smart Richman, 2009). Other studies have linked racism to elevated levels of anxiety, depression, post-traumatic stress symptoms, and suicidal thoughts (e.g., Carter et al., 2019; Carter, et al., 2017; Donovan et al., 2013; Liu & Suyemoto, 2016; Wang, Lin, & Wong, 2021). These effects relate to the effects of not having privilege and the effects of experiencing oppression. We see these effects both individually and intergenerationally for people of color, in relation to access to resources and opportunities, and exposure to risks.

The effects of racism also relate to the drain on intrapsychic resources that comes from the everyday stress of having to navigate these inequitable systems, a process termed racism-related stress (Harrell, 2000). For example, racism-related stress encompasses the emotional and physical cost of constantly having to decide whether to identify and name microaggressions (and macroaggressions) or whether to hide one's authentic responses and emotional experiences to avoid being accused of being too angry, too sensitive, too humorless (Sue, 2010). Both "choices" exact a toll. The former in having to manage the minimization or dismissal of racism experiences by others, oftentimes those in positions of power to address them (e.g., teachers, supervisors, police officers); the latter in having to manage feeling silenced and helpless in the face of insult or harm, or feeling like a fraud or "sell out." And research shows that people of color regularly experience microaggressions (Sue, 2010) and so, regularly face that choice. For example, racial microaggressions were an almost ubiquitous experience among Black women college students in one study (96% reported experiencing them at least a few times a year; Donovan et al., 2013). Similar to studies with other people of color, these experiences were associated with psychological distress.

As these invalidating experiences accumulate, people of color can become justifiably wary or vigilant to possible harm when interacting with White people, which can result in seeking safety and belonging through self-segregation with racially similar peers (see Tatum, 2017). Other consequences of this invalidation include anger, fear, hopelessness, or internalized racism where a person of color might denigrate their own racialized group, view themselves as somehow inferior or damaged because of their race, distance from other people of color, or have prejudicial preferences for White people (see David, Schroeder, & Fernandez, 2019). We go into more detail about internalized racism in Chapter 4 when we talk about racial identity development, but we want to underscore here that racism does real damage to the psyche and body of people of color. And, over the lifespan, research suggests these experiences result in a "weathering" effect that wears the body down and is thought to increase people of color's vulnerability to disease and contribute to premature aging (Geronimus et al., 2006).

Effects of Race and Racism on White People

The system of racism is most harmful to those who lack racial privilege and power (i.e., people of color). However, an important but rarely discussed issue is that racism is also damaging to the racially privileged group. Racism hurts White people in the United States in a number of ways (Goodman, 2011: see Table 3.1): by taking away knowledge of their ethnic heritage and connection to the histories of their families, people around them, and the land on which they reside; by contributing to cognitive dissonance and distortions; by contributing to feelings of anxiety and guilt and fear, including fear that one's status may be impacted if gains among people of color are made; and by causing isolation and segregation from others. These effects influence White people's decisions and behavior: for example, decisions about where to live (e.g., gated communities), where to educate children (e.g., "good" schools that are predominantly White), and where to socialize (e.g., places of worship or organizations that are populated by other White people).

Such self-segregation and social distancing decisions are costly both materially and relationally, in that these "protections" are expensive to secure and result in shallow or non-existent relationships across racial difference. And without meaningful exposure to and discussions with people of color that center their experiences, it is very challenging for White people to unlearn implicit biases or to develop accurate knowledge about others and themselves (Dovidio et al., 2017; Suyemoto & Hochman, 2021). Robin DiAngelo (2018), who identifies as White, brings this point home in her book *White fragility: Why it's so hard for White people to talk about racism*. In it, she asserts that White people struggle with understanding racism because they do not see themselves in racial terms, and racial socialization is not something they are taught to learn and understand. This tendency to not notice or think about race and racism and to project this non-seeing over to others' experiences by indicating that one's race does not matter (i.e., color-blind racial ideology and evasiveness) results in psychological responses like denial, defensiveness, minimization, withdrawal, guilt, and shame around topics of race and racism, all of which shuts down learning and serves to maintain White privilege and advantage.

Table 3.1 Costs of oppression to privileged groups

Psychological Costs: Loss of Mental Health and Authentic Sense of Self

- Socialized into limited roles and patterns of behavior
- Denial of emotions and empathy
- Limited self-knowledge and distorted view of self
- Discrepancy between external perceptions and internal reality
- Pain and fears (of doing and saying wrong thing, of retaliation from oppressed groups, of revealing self for fear of judgment, of different people and experiences)
- Diminished mental health (distorted view of self and reality, denial, projection)

Social Costs: Loss and Diminishment of Relationships

- Isolation from people who are different
- Barriers to deeper, more authentic relationships
- Disconnection, distance, and ostracism within own group if one acts differently

---

Intellectual Costs: Loss of Developing Full Range of Knowledge

- Distorted and limited view of other people's culture and history
- Ignorance of own culture and history

Moral and Spiritual Costs: Loss of Moral and Spiritual Integrity

- Guilt and shame
- Moral ambivalence (doing right thing versus social pressures and realities)
- Spiritual emptiness or pain (disconnection from other human beings, violation of one's spiritual values)

Material and Physical Costs: Loss of Safety, Resources, and Quality of Life

- Violence and unrest (restricted ability to move about freely; increased fear for self and others; limited desirable places to live, work, go to school, recreate)
- Negative health implications (e.g., stress and stress-related illnesses)
- Loss of valuable employees, clients, and customers
- Loss of knowledge to foster societal growth and well-being
- Waste of resources (to deal with effects of inequality)
- Diminished collective action for common concerns

Source: From Goodman, D. (2011), *Promoting diversity and social justice: Educating people from privileged groups* (2nd ed.). Routledge. Used by permission.

Our intention in this section is to increase understanding of how socialization into systems of oppression and privilege hurts us all—not in the same ways, but in ways that create barriers to wholeness, acceptance, authenticity, and interpersonal connection. Similar kinds of effects apply to inequities related to ethnicity, gender, sexuality, ability, and social class. But people often don't attend to these effects, especially if they are in privileged positions. There is a significant body of research in the social sciences that establishes and examines the effects of all of these hierarchies of oppression for individuals, groups, and societies. In future chapters, we touch on some of those effects, and we encourage readers to seek out the research and more intentionally direct your attention to structural inequities, material costs, psychological costs, and effects on relationships and individuals. Doing so clarifies the importance of unraveling our assumptions about oppression and privilege, and how they affect our lives. One of the major points we hope you are understanding from our example of the effects of racism is that we can't choose whether we are affected by racialization and race. This is what it means to be a systemic issue. However, at the individual level, we *can* choose how we engage with the *system* of racism and its effects. This is true for other systemic hierarchies as well.

Beyond Good Intentions

As this chapter shows, understanding hierarchies of privilege and oppression is much more complex than we might first think. It can be hard to consider ways that we might have power that we didn't actually earn and that other people don't or can't have. But not thinking about these hierarchies doesn't make them not exist. Whether we acknowledge these systems or not, we are usually aware of them at some level. Consider your reflections on the questions we asked above about which groups are systemically privileged and which are systemically oppressed in our society, and about what kinds of privileges and oppression people experience. In addition to the examples you came up with at the personal level, what are some examples of systemic evidence that privilege and oppression actually exist and affect people's lives? How is this evidence different from our feelings of how we would like it to be?

Considering how we would like things to be versus how they are can highlight how privilege and oppression are systemic, not just individual. It can also help us see how prejudice and oppression aren't always conscious, deliberate, or active. We can think about discrimination as occurring on various continuums: conscious and deliberate to unconscious and unintentional; active to passive; direct to indirect. Hate crimes are examples of conscious, deliberate, active, and direct discrimination at the interpersonal level. Most microaggressions are examples of unconscious, unintentional, and active discrimination at the interpersonal level.

We are all susceptible to internalizing the messages from our culture. As we mentioned above, research on prejudice and attitudes towards oppressed groups suggests that most people, even those who actively value equity and justice, hold stereotypical and negative attitudes towards non-dominant groups (e.g., people of color, women, transgender people, sexual minorities, people experiencing poverty, or disabled people). As hierarchies of oppression and privilege are part of our culture, we are socialized into beliefs, expectations, assumptions, and behavioral norms that foster or maintain prejudice. An analogy is that we are on a moving walkway that is constantly moving us towards maintaining the system of privilege and oppression. We can't simply stand still. We must either walk in the other direction or work to stop the walkway or change the direction. While discrimination can be enacted through passivity (e.g., not intervening when someone tells a racist joke), anti-discrimination cannot.

In sum, hierarchies of privilege and oppression are not created or maintained by any one person; instead, these hierarchies are part of the social fabric of our lives. Privilege and oppression are social phenomena and not characteristics or choices of individuals. If you are White, for example, you can't choose to not have White privilege—it will still be there even if you don't want it. Think about this in relation to the items from McIntosh's list above, or the examples of positive advantages. You, alone, can't change those things for your own individual experience. Similarly, if you are oppressed, you can't simply decide or choose not to be. You can't completely control the existence of the stereotypes about your group, or control whether someone will shout out a sexist slur. You can't personally root out the implicit ablist attitudes that other people might have, that might affect whether or not you are seen as competitive for the job you want. You can't magically change the physical environment to make it equally accessible for you if you are in a wheelchair. In sum, you can't just decide you won't be privileged or oppressed.

However, you *can* choose to actively contribute to changing the system overall. You can work to spread the positive advantages that all people should receive, but that are currently available only to those who are privileged. You can challenge yourself to confront the negative advantages you have and try to undermine them. You can work to have oppression affect you less, developing positive coping approaches. You can also resist the existence of oppression, contributing to changing the systemic meanings. A person who is in a privileged position can engage in **ally or accomplice** action, which is action or intention that aims to undermine and challenge the system of privilege and oppression that benefits the agent themselves.

> *How Do I Say?* Ally versus accomplice or co-conspirator. Some activists and scholars have suggested a distinction between "ally" and "accomplice," with the latter indicating a person whose social justice beliefs are coupled with action that requires some level of personal risk (e.g., speaking out in public against racism, taking action that might lead to arrest), while the former does not involve such action. Others view "ally" as a verb, not a type of person, that describes the process and action of challenging a system. From this perspective, it is impossible to be an ally all the time or to self-identify as an ally. See Chapter 10 for much more on the meaning of ally and accomplice, and how to take action to resist oppression.

A person who is a target of oppression can engage in action as an **advocate,** aiming to undermine and challenge the system of oppression that oppresses them. We discuss this in much greater depth in Chapter 10, but we wanted to introduce this possibility here, because we find that the idea of contributing to positive change can help us stay open to learning about these difficult ideas.

Resources for Learning More about Power, Privilege, and Oppression

The Humanities Project at Arizona State University has compiled and added to checklists of privilege related to different statuses, similar to Peggy McIntosh's "*Invisible Knapsack.*" Statuses addressed include White, male, cisgender, heterosexual, sexual (versus asexual), able-bodied, middle-upper class, social class: https://projec thumanities.asu.edu/perils-and-perks-of-privilege.

Anderson, S. K., & Middleton, V. A. (Eds.) (2018). *Explorations in diversity: Examining the complexities of privilege, discrimination, and oppression* (3rd edition). Oxford University Press.

Arizona Humanities Council. (n.d.). Perils and perks of privilege: A workshop series. Arizona State University. https://projecthumanities.asu.edu/perils-and-perks-of-p rivilege.

Dovidio, J. F., Hewstone, M., Glick, P., & Esses, V. M. (Eds.) (2010). *The SAGE handbook of prejudice, stereotyping and discrimination* (pp. 3–27). Sage. https://dx.doi.org/10. 4135/9781446200919.

Johnson, A. G. (2018). *Privilege, power, and difference* (3rd edition). McGraw-Hill.

Kimmel, M. S., & Ferber, A. L. (Eds.) (2017). *Privilege: A reader* (4th edition). Routledge.

Plous, S. (2002). Home page. Understanding prejudice. https://secure.understandingp rejudice.org/.

Section Two

Understanding Hierarchies of Oppression and Privilege: Race, Ethnicity, Sex and Gender, Sexuality, Disability, and Social Class

In this section, we examine six social categories of inequity. In each chapter, we start by naming erroneous assumptions about the social category and related statuses, assumptions that are often linked to how these constructs are oversimplified and decontextualized. After providing a simple definition of the category and related system of oppression, we explore the category in a bit more depth, beginning with the social construct, associated meanings, and assumptions about statuses and categorizations within the category. We also explicitly consider identity in relation to each category, briefly exploring ways that individuals negotiate imposed or socially constructed meanings of these categories and seek to create positive self-concepts. Finally, for each category, we explore the associated system of privilege and oppression (the "-ism": e.g., racism, classism, ableism). We do this to help readers understand how the social category might affect people because of where they are in the social hierarchies embedded in our culture. This structure also continues to center privilege and oppression, as we did in Section One, and explore how the concepts we define in these chapters are not only about individual differences but also about access to power, which includes resources, opportunities, and the ability to influence outcomes.

We know that the concepts we discuss in this section are complicated and difficult. Researchers and professors who have been studying these concepts for years don't always agree on their meaning. The variability in meanings is related not only to the complexity of the concepts, but also to the fact that meanings change over time and might vary because of the contexts in which they developed and used. For example, consider these questions: who is White and how is this determined? Who is male and how is this determined? How have these meanings changed over time? Meanings and the language we use to reflect our meanings *do* change, sometimes quite rapidly. For example, when we (the authors) were growing up, the terms "cisgender" and

DOI: 10.4324/9780429059599-6

"transgender" were not readily available. Some people may have identified in these ways or understood these ideas, but they were not a widespread part of our social discourse.

Given the challenges in grappling with diversity concepts that are dynamic, complex, and difficult, you might be wondering why defining them here is necessary at all? As we mentioned at the start of Section One, basic definitions provide shared language to start from, which is important if we are going to talk with others about these issues. Furthermore, we frequently hear many of these social category words in the news, in social interactions, in schools, or elsewhere. But if these concepts are so complex, and the meanings are controversial, then are we even sure we are talking about the same thing? If we have an initial shared meaning, then we are at least starting from the same point. This is particularly important in a classroom or group discussion, where there might be multiple interpretations of the same concept, making a difficult subject even more challenging to discuss and learn about. For example, consider this conversation between Pat and Chris:

PAT: Black people can be just as racist as White people.
CHRIS: No, only White people can be racist.
PAT: That is the most ridiculous thing I've ever heard.
CHRIS: You really don't understand what's going on in the world.

One way to understand this conversation is to decide who is right, Pat or Chris? But another way to think about this interaction is to consider what is behind the assertions, and whether there is a way that Pat and Chris can better understand each other's perspectives. What if Pat and Chris were to step back together and see that Pat's definition of racism focuses on individual acts of prejudice in interpersonal interactions based on race, while Chris's definition links racial bias to the system of privilege that favors White people? By clarifying that they have different starting points, perhaps they can learn from each other's perspectives about who can or can't engage in racism. Understanding their different perspectives can contribute to a deeper conversation about the purposes and implications of different perspectives, including whose needs are served or why one might personally seek to accept or reject different perspectives.

As with Section One, throughout these chapters we invite you to engage in a number of reflection exercises, to consider your own assumptions, experiences, and effects from these constructs. For example, we will be asking you to consider the stereotypes that our society holds about different kinds of people. You might find this uncomfortable, particularly if you think naming stereotypes is linked to others (or you) believing them. But we can't address something we won't acknowledge or talk about. So, we are encouraging you to take the risk to be honest about what thoughts and feelings come up for you about these concepts, what kinds of ideas are in our society, what you may have been taught or socialized to believe, and what kinds of biases you may have internalized from that teaching. We encourage you to remember that these concepts are challenging to dig into, and to discuss your ideas and responses with others. Again, you may ultimately still disagree with the meanings and perspective that we present, but you will know exactly what you mean and why you stand behind it, rather than your meaning consisting of an assumption you have never questioned.

Our hope is that you will come away from these chapters with a broadened understanding of possibilities. And with as many questions as answers. We hope that these explorations of understandings and reflections on your own experience will spark further curiosity about these concepts, about how they work in our society, and why and how we continue to act in ways that contribute to maintaining hierarchies of privilege and oppression. We encourage you to explore further, using the resources offered in each chapter, as well as the wealth of information available through an internet search or your library. Even if, or especially, if you disagree with things we have said in these chapters, or if you think that we have presented a biased view of these issues, learning more about what research says about how these social hierarchies affect our lives can help you shape your own informed understanding and more effectively communicate your viewpoint to others.

Resources for Learning More about Hierarchies

In each chapter within this section, we provide resources for learning more that are specific to the content of that chapter. The anthologies listed below contain readings that apply to multiple hierarchies of oppression and privilege. These anthologies usually contain conceptual and research-based essays as well as personal narratives, examples, stories, and poems.

Adams, M., Blumenfeld, W. J., Chase, D., Catalano, J., Dejong, K., Hackman, H. W., Hopkins, L. E., Love, B., Peters, M. L., Shlasko, D., & Zúñiga, X. (Eds.) (2018). Readings for diversity and social justice: An anthology on racism, antisemitism, sexism, ableism, and classism (4th edition). Routledge.

American Sociological Association. (n.d.). Home page. Contexts: Sociology for the public. http://contexts.org. This website has a variety of articles related to structural inequality, oppression, and privilege.

Andersen, M. L., & Hill Collins, P. (Eds.) (2020). Race, class, and gender: An anthology (10th edition). Cengage Learning.

Anzaldúa, G., & Keating, A. (Eds.) (2002). This bridge we call home: Radical visions for transformation. Routledge.

Grusky, D., & Hill, J. (Eds.) (2018) Inequality in the 21st century: A reader. Routledge.

Rosenblum, K. E., & Travis, T. C. (Eds.) (2016). The meaning of difference: American constructions of race and ethnicity, sex and gender, social class, sexuality, and disability (7th edition). McGraw-Hill.

Rothenberg, P. S., & Accomando, C. H. (Eds.) (2020). Race, class, and gender in the United States: An integrated study (11th edition). Macmillan.

4   Understanding Race and Racism

Erroneous assumptions that many people have about race in the United States today include:

- Race is only or primarily about differences in visible physical appearance.
- Racial categories are biologically based.
- Race is the same as ethnicity.
- Race (and racism) is only relevant to non-White people.

Unraveling these assumptions means exploring the relation of race to hierarchies of privilege and oppression, which involves considering the history of the concept of race, the racial worldview that contributes to the creation of racial categories and hierarchies, and how race is not an inherent characteristic of people but is instead a process of socialization into that racial worldview.

Many people today have learned to think about race primarily or solely in relation to physical characteristics. That is, they learn to think that race is a social category based on physical characteristics such as skin or hair color, the shape of facial features like eyes or noses, or body types. This definition focuses on race as a category of difference rather than distinction (as discussed earlier), making it appear neutral without tangible influence and consequence. However, social science research (and likely your own observations and experiences) makes it clear that race is not neutral. The race you are perceived to be affects how you think about yourself and your identity. It affects how others treat you. It affects the opportunities you have access to, whether directly because of your race, or indirectly because of the ways in which the opportunities you currently have relate to the opportunities that your family and ancestors were able to have. Race matters in our society because of the meanings we associate with the concept and the status categories within the larger social construct.

Defining Race and Racism

Race is a social category to which individuals self-assign or are assigned by others, usually on the basis of physical characteristics, with the purpose of creating or maintaining hierarchies of power and privilege.

DOI: 10.4324/9780429059599-7

Racism is the system of judgments, beliefs, actions, norms, and social/ institutional practices that protect White supremacy, racial privilege, and hierarchy.

Some Possible Responses to the Material in This Chapter

Some people believe that race doesn't matter, that racism doesn't exist, that those who point to the ways racism is woven into the fabric of society are "snowflakes" or the PC police. There is even a push to ban Critical Race Theory, which presents history and research about the existence and wide-spread influence of race and racism (Sawchuk, 2021). Alongside (or because of) these realities are contemporary movements that center race and anti-racism efforts such as the Movement for Black Lives (formerly known as Black Lives Matter) and Stop Asian Hate. With this backdrop, you may be entering this chapter with some (a lot of?) apprehension that can manifest as shame or guilt around previous thoughts/actions, fear about being seen as biased by others in your class, frustration around having to learn something you see as irrelevant or biased, or even boredom that you are required to read about a topic you feel you know already. Contrastingly, you might be excited or open or curious to explore race and racism more.

What bubbles up for you in the reading of this chapter is important information to notice and engage mindfully, without judgment. Naming your emotions helps with this process—"oh, I'm having an experience of guilt again" or "I'm experiencing anger at what they are saying." The more you're able to hang in there with this chapter, including completing the questions and exercises, the more you'll be able to learn and therefore personally choose your meanings around race and racism and what you stand behind. Our goal is not to tell you what to think, but to invite you to consider possibilities that we encourage you to examine further through your own research into history, science, and social science literature.

For example, did you have a response to the definition of race we provide above, which emphasizes that race is not biologically based but socially constructed? As we mentioned in Chapter 2 around social categories and hierarchies, your racial socialization might influence how you respond to these assertions, and others throughout the chapter. If you're familiar with the topic through personal experience and/or previous learning, this chapter might bring up feelings of anger, sadness, or helplessness about how race has been used to oppress you and/or people of color in your community. You may experience feelings of relief or validation that there is language to describe your own experience.

Contrarily, if you're new to the study of race and racism or if your previous learning has emphasized that race is a biological construct, the definitions above, and the chapter as a whole, may cause confusion, disbelief, and feelings of defensiveness. You might be wondering:

- How can something that seems so real be something that people just made up (and continue to make up)?
- Racial groupings have been around a long time, they mean something, don't they? What about physical differences, those are "real," right?
- How can you say it is about privilege and oppression: physical differences are genetic so isn't race biological? Doesn't that make it real?

Such responses and questions are far from unusual. They reflect the misinformation about race that relates to the history of the concept and to the ways that race, as a system of domination, has been created and maintained.

Did you also notice your responses when you read the words "White supremacy" and "privilege"? Maybe they made you uncomfortable for some reason or defensive or angry. One of the reasons you may have these responses relates back to our socialization into a system that names race and racial oppression only in relation to the subordinate group without similarly naming race and racial privilege when it applies to the dominant group. Such invisibilizing of the dominant group and the systemic nature of racism has the byproduct of making the dominant experience so normative and unquestioned that simply calling attention to Whiteness and dominance causes discomfort, as in the naming of White supremacy. Sometimes people feel personally attacked, as if saying that White *supremacy* is bad is saying that White *people* are bad, or even that they, if they are a White person, is bad. Feelings of guilt, denials of being racist, or distancing from group members if you are White are also common when learning about racism from a systemic (versus individual) lens.

We say all this to help you understand the responses that might arise for you. It's our hope that such knowledge will help you meet these responses with compassion and continued openness to the learning.

Exploring Meanings of Race

Race as a distinct category of identification and social positioning is a fairly recent conceptualization, emerging in the 18th century as erroneously purporting that physical, biological characteristics were connected to personality characteristics and abilities and that people belonged to racially distinct groups that differed on these associated characteristics. White Europeans (especially Western Europeans) were placed at the top of the hierarchy of groups and other "racial" groups were seen as inferior. The connection of race to biology supported the idea that these differences were unchangeable and inherent.

Considerable research since the 18th century has debunked the idea that race connects biology with personality traits and abilities, or that race is distinctly categorical. In addition, as hard as it might be to comprehend, biological and genetic evidence undermines the idea of any biological basis to our racial categories, in spite of the fact that physical differences are, indeed, biological (e.g., Pounder et al., 2003; Smedley & Smedley, 2012). Instead, researchers today acknowledge that the creation of race as a social categorization in the 18th century was one way that White gentry and governments in the United States and Europe justified the invasion, enslavement, and genocide of Native Americans and the system of chattel slavery (the lifetime enslavement of people of African descent and their offspring), as well as other acts of domination and discrimination against non-White peoples (e.g., Fredrickson, 2015).

To reflect the current research and understanding, we can consider race as a worldview, a process of socialization into creating categories of hierarchy and assuming meaning based on these categories. Some researchers use the language "racialization" or "racialized groups" to reflect this process— emphasizing the process by which people become socially racial*ized*, rather than considering race as a thing, or as "real" categories. In the United States, the primary racialized categories are White, Black, Asian American, Native or Indigenous American (including native Hawaiian and native Alaskan), and Latine.

How Do I Say? The terms we use here are considered respectful at the time this book was written, although there is always some controversy about terms. Because language is dynamic, some of the terms used historically to identify racialized categories are considered offensive now. Egregious terms to avoid include: colored people, Negros, Oriental, mulatto, and Caucasian. Some individuals will have negative reactions to the terms Hispanic and American Indian, or other terms that you might have been told are appropriate or sensitive (even terms in this book). When referring to an individual, it is generally best to ask what term they feel is most respectful for themselves and their racial group.

Multiracial people are people who have identifiable heritage from multiple racialized groups and are identified by themselves or others in this way. An emerging racialized group in the United States is Middle Eastern North African (MENA, including Arabs) or SWANA (South West Asian and North African). "Emerging" means that the people in this group are increasingly being racially identified and experiencing racial discrimination based on how others racially categorize them.

Race is not the same as ethnicity (see more on this in "Ethnicity" in Chapter 5). Each racialized group includes multiple ethnic groups. For example, White Americans include most people from European ethnic backgrounds including English, Irish, German, and French; and Black Americans include the African American descendants of chattel slavery in the United States as well as most people whose families emigrated from Africa and the Caribbean (who may or may not identify themselves as African American).

We say "most people" from various places because race is not wholly related to national or geographic origin. People within a racial group may be of ethnicities that are not commonly associated with their race, such as a White South African person who ethnically identifies as South African, or Black people who have emigrated to the United States from France or China or Polynesia and may ethnically identify with those cultures or with both specific African heritage and the ethnic heritage from those cultures (e.g., Nigerian and French or Kenyan and Chinese).

Although race is not the same as ethnicity, many racial groups have associated pan-ethnic cultures that can relate to ethnic origins prior to coming to the United States (or, in the case of Indigenous Americans, to similarities in culture prior to colonization), and/or to cultural patterns that have emerged in the United States related to their racialized experiences. For example, research in psychology often explores Asian American values such as collectivism that have been demonstrated to be more highly endorsed in Asian immigrants and in U.S.-born Asian Americans of diverse specific ethnicities (e.g., Indian Americans, Korean Americans, Vietnamese Americans) as compared to White European Americans (Park & Kim, 2008; Oyserman et al., 2002). Many Asian cultures are more collectivistic than American, European, or European American cultures, so a pan-ethnic experience emerges in contrast to the more dominant ethnocultural norms. This pan-ethnic experience is then associated with race. Some pan-ethnic cultural patterns relate to racialization itself. For example, African Americans in the United States developed strategies for surviving within and resisting the dehumanizing effects of slavery and subsequent anti-Black policies and attitudes, this includes the practice of socializing Black girls and women to exhibit strength at all costs (West et al., 2016).

Race as Social Construct

We can understand more about the ways in which race is a social construction related to privilege and oppression when we consider the messages we receive about different racial groups. Racial stereotypes reflect some of the messages that we receive about different racial groups. Thinking about stereotypes can be uncomfortable (triggering), but in our experience, students can all too easily come up with a long list of stereotypes that they have heard or seen about racial minority groups.

Reflection Questions

Take a moment and reflect on the stereotypes you have heard about Black people, Asian Americans, Latine, Native Americans, SWANA, and Multiracial peoples.

Complete the list below, by writing down as many stereotypical descriptors for each as you can (at least five for each group).

To really engage in this activity, write it down, don't just think about it.
White people are …
Black people are …
Asian Americans are …
Latine are …
Native Americans are …
SWANA people are …
Multiracial people are …
Look at the lists you have generated. How do you feel looking at this list? How easy or difficult was it to generate this list? What does engaging in this activity and reflection tell you about your assumptions or socialization about racial minority groups?

It's Complicated: You may have a difficult time with this question because you are afraid that answering it might be racist or stereotyping. The fact that so many people have this concern is an indicator of how emotionally charged issues of race are. We know that the complete answer to our question is, for example, "Black people are all different, just like people of any race." While this is true, it is also true that we have been taught stereotypical ideas about what Black people are like. Here, we are asking you to take an honest look at the ideas that you have been exposed to. We are asking you to step beyond concerns about being "politically correct" to consider what ideas you have been exposed to that are stereotypical. Although many people think we shouldn't consider these group experiences because that would mean "seeing" race which can be seen as racist, we think that avoiding thinking about these stereotypical ideas contributes to creating racial tensions. If we can talk about them, we can change them. Research on color-blind racial attitudes supports this, as we discussed in Chapter 3.

Our experience in doing this kind of thought exercise is that people generally do have many ideas about specific racial groups, and are aware of stereotypes, even if they don't believe them or actively want to reject them. Some of the stereotypes that typically emerge from this exercise include:

- White people are selfish, can't dance, racist.
- Black people are criminal, violent, stupid, "poor," lazy, like watermelon, strong, physical, over-sexed.
- Asian Americans are foreigners, bad leaders, smart and good at math, can't drive, exotic (women), sexless (men), eat dogs, carry disease, own nail salons.
- Latine are "illegal," lazy, religious/Catholic, family oriented, uneducated, sexually available (women), on welfare with too many children, housemaids.

How Do I Say? Terms such as "illegals" and "illegal aliens" are inaccurate and disrespectful. People are not, themselves, illegal or legal and terms such as these are dehumanizing. The term "undocumented immigrants" which more accurately refers to the documentation status, is experienced as more respectful.

- Native Americans are primitive, savage, alcoholics, lazy, spiritual, nature-loving, exotic, dead (extinct).
- SWANA people are terrorists, sexist, abuse women, religious, cab drivers.
- Multiracial people are confused, unwanted, White wannabes.

Students are often surprised at how easily they can generate 10 or 20, or even more stereotypical ideas for the racial minority groups. The ease with which most people come up with answers to these questions for people of color (once they get over the fear of seeming racist) reflects the pervasiveness of the social constructions of race in our society. Students often have more difficulty coming up with stereotypes about White people, and often observe that the stereotypes they do come up with are either not very consequential (e.g., White people can't dance) or are related to being racially privileged. When we ask students or other folks about how it feels to see these lists in writing, we hear words like "angry, sad, hopeless, bitter." Sometimes we also hear words like "relieved" because the elephant in the room has been named. And occasionally we hear "hopeful" with a reflection that becoming aware of the stereotypes we have been exposed is a first step towards debunking them and challenging our unexamined assumptions.

In addition, people often have a relatively narrow idea of racial group meanings, without being fully aware of this. Let's take a minute to complicate the racial assumptions and meanings. For example, consider your answers about the different racial groups in relation to your thoughts about being multiracial: is your understanding of what Black multiracial people are like different than "just" Black people? Are your stereotypes of multiracial White people the same as your stereotypes of White people? Consider also how your answers might shift if we specified other kinds of intersecting identities: stereotypes of race are often strongly gendered. For example, scholarship in the social sciences has explored our social constructions and stereotypes of Asian American men as emasculated and non-sexual and of Asian American women as sexually exoticized (e.g., Han, 2006; Mukkamala & Suyemoto, 2018). Our social constructions of race tend to have intersectional assumptions related to class, sexuality, and ability as well. Would the answers to the following questions be different than what you came up with above: What are rich Black people like? What are disabled Native Americans like? What are gay SWANAs like? What are trans Latine like? What are ethnically Syrian White people like?

How and Why the Social Construct of Race (and Racism) Was Created

But where did the *idea* of race and the associated erroneous assumptions come from? As we mention above, one of the biggest misconceptions about race is that it is genetic or biological, versus a social construct. This myth is important to unravel because it's the foundation of justifying racial hierarchies and therefore racism. If we believe White people are genetically superior because of their race, then it's easier to justify the overrepresentation of White people, particularly cisgender White men, in positions of power across all categories of life in the United States, from the government to business to education to the criminal justice system to the military. Understanding that race is not biological means that what you see with your eyes—like this overrepresentation of White people in power and the underrepresentation of other racialized groups—has other explanations that require more (un)learning to understand. Examining how our ideas about race originated is good place to start.

In ancient cultures, the term race *was* used, but it referred mostly to difference, without the kinds of associations of characteristics, personal qualities, and abilities that racial categories are now associated with. The idea of race as a distinct biological difference between people with implications for inherent characteristics and abilities emerged in the 18th century. This meaning of race, which included a hierarchy of races and the idea of White superiority, is linked to the spread of European colonization, where race was used to justify invasion, colonization, and slavery (Smedley & Smedley, 2005). Through a racial hierarchy lens which put European colonizers at the top while viewing other groups as *inherently* inferior, it became acceptable for European colonizers in the Americas to subjugate non-Whites through, for example, the violent seizure of the land of Indigenous peoples and the intergenerational enslavement of people of African descent.

Although scientists of the time failed to prove the inherent inferiority of people categorized as non-White through such methods as the measurement of bones and skull size, the idea of race and racial hierarchy continued to be propagated by government policies and people with greater power. Over time, in spite of the lack of research support, more ideas about characteristics and traits became associated with different racial groups. These ideas were consistently characterized by assigning more negative characteristics to people who were not White. Many of these ideas are clearly evident in early social science texts arguing against racial mixing. For example, Gobineau states:

> The white race originally possessed the monopoly of beauty, intelligence, and strength. By its union with other varieties, hybrids were created, which were beautiful without strength, strong without intelligence, or, if intelligent, both weak and ugly … all civilizations derive from the white race, that none can exist without its help, and that a society is great and brilliant only so far as it preserves the blood of the noble group that

created it, provided that this group itself belongs to the most illustrious branch of our species.

(Gobineau, 1853, pp. 209–210)

Debunking the Race Is Biology Myth

The idea of race as biological and related to inferior or superior character-istics has been rejected by an overwhelming body of contemporary scientific and anthropological evidence (American Anthropological Association, 1998). For instance, the scientific mapping of the human genome and that of other species clearly shows we are one of the most genetically homogeneous species on the planet, sharing approximately 99.9% of our genetic material with each other (Collins & Mansoura, 2001). In fact, what we now know is that there is more biological and genetic variability within the people in socially con-structed racial categories than between the people who belong to different racial categories (Ford & Kelly, 2005). There is also more variability in phe-notype within a race: an Italian American person could have skin much darker than many African Americans or other people of color and still be classified as "White." Thus, although phenotypical differences are, indeed, biological, these phenotypical differences don't actually define the boundaries of racial groups. Research also shows that many of the phenotypical differ-ences we attribute to race are actually attributable to where our ancestors lived, with, for example, people living closest to the equator with a lot of direct sun possessing darker skin and those living closest to the poles where there is less and weaker sunlight possessing lighter skin (Marks, 1996; Wang & Sue, 2005). So, many of the physical characteristics we use to assign people to racial categories are superficial and linked to ancestry and migration patterns, not to deeper cognitive, emotional, or physical abilities.

In spite of this lack of scientific evidence for the idea of race, the develop-ment of racial ideas of White supremacy in the United States and elsewhere became the basis of laws, institutionalized practices, and social norms and behaviors that denied rights and benefits to people of color (Zinn, 2015) his-torically and currently. For instance, the notion of race and racism has justi-fied genocide of Indigenous Americans; and colonization, land theft (e.g., the Homestead Act of 1862), lynching and murders of Mexican Americans in the 1900s, and abuses through the border control. It has shaped access to free-dom and human rights (e.g., slavery, separation of families at the U.S. bor-ders; hate crimes against Arab Americans and Middle Eastern Americans); education opportunities (e.g., denial of public education for Black people and other people of color; racial segregation in schools); the ability to exercise the right to vote and testify in court (e.g., poll tax, People vs Hall); and immigra-tion and citizenship (e.g., the Asian Exclusion Act; the Johnson-Reed Act that banned immigration from Asia, the Polynesian Islands, and the Middle East; Native American exclusion; recent policies specifically aimed at Mexican and South American undocumented immigrants).

In sum, the science of today and an examination of U.S. history make clear that race is not biological. People in power (primarily White men at that time) constructed the meaning of race in order to protect their racial privilege and deny access of resources and benefits to others (people of color). Moreover, those in power have periodically changed the boundaries of racial categories to maintain the privileges of the dominant group as different challenges to the hierarchy have arisen. These historical events and decisions have reverberations in our present day lives, most central of which is that our society continues to ascribe to a racialized world view that supports and normalizes the privileging of White people and the oppression of people of color. We examine this socialization in more detail in the next section.

Reflection Questions

- What did you learn, if anything, about the origins of race in your early schooling, grades kindergarten through 12th grade? What did you learn about the existence and history of racialized groups and the creation of racial hierarchies?
- Did your learnings reflect the science and history presented in this chapter? What kinds of social norms and values affect what you learned? How did learning or reviewing this material here make you feel?
- What would you like to learn more about or research on your own? What motivates you to do so? How will you approach your research so you encounter different views and evidence? How will you decide what is "true"?

The Changeable Boundaries of Racial Categories

That the boundaries of racial groups have changed over time to serve different functions in relation to privilege also emphasizes how race is a social construct. If race had a clear basis in genetics or biology, then the boundaries of race would be fixed within that genetic basis. But the boundaries of the categories have defined and changed at various times and in relation to various groups of people in order for the group with more power (in this case, White people) to maintain their power and economic status. For example, rules of **hypodescent** assigned lineage of biracial Black and White children of enslaved Black women to the mother, in contrast to European patriarchal lineage traditions and laws for the progeny of White women.

How Do I Say? Hypodescent is the assignment of a mixed status person to the subordinate status. In relation to race, the assignment of a multiracial child to the race of the subordinate parent. Hyperdescent is the assignment of a multiracial person to the more privileged racial category. Although hyperdescent may mean greater access to privilege for an individual, it has historically been used when it would benefit the privileged group, as noted in the examples below regarding Indigenous Americans.

Post-slavery, hypodescent was used to maintain the boundaries of Whiteness and its commensurate privileges designating biracial Black and White people to the socially subordinate racial status.

Although there was no research evidence to support it, the views of early geneticists were used to justify the practice of hypodescent, whereby anyone who had "one drop of Black blood," typically 1/16 heritage but ranging from 1/8 to 1/32, would be considered legally Black, even though their heritage was mostly White (e.g., 15/16 of their "blood heritage" was from White people) and even if they looked White (Omi & Winant, 1994; Tucker, 2004). Through this conceptualization of race, if one's great-great grandparent was Black (and even if the parents, grandparents, and three other great grandparents were White), then one would be considered Black. The major question is: why couldn't this logic work the other way around (i.e., hyperdescent)? What if 1/16 of "White blood" permitted a person to be designated as White?

The emphasis on hypodescent served a purpose: during times of slavery it ensured that descendants of enslaved people were also confined to slavery and post-slavery, and it ensured those descendants were not eligible for rights and privileges reserved for White people (such as voting, serving on a jury or attending schools and colleges). Applying hypodescent to enslaved African people served the purpose of ensuring that Black people were constrained to subordinate status. But hypodescent was not applied to all people of color, which emphasizes how racial categories are created and recreated to serve the function of maintaining the hierarchy of oppression (for people of color) and privilege (for White people). In contrast to the "one-drop rule" is the "blood quantum" system developed by the U.S. federal government to determine who was or was not Native American. Blood quantum required Native Americans to prove they were "sufficiently" Native American in order to be entitled to recognition by the federal government as Native, reflecting the idea of **hyperdescent** (Schmidt, 2011). Recognition was essential to Native Americans' attempts to protect land, resources, and identity, and access health care, the ability to live on the reservation, or other benefits or protections controlled by the Bureau of Indian Affairs subsequent to colonization and displacement of Indigenous people. But it was in the best interest of the colonizers and the U.S. federal government to decrease the number of Indigenous people, which led to the hyperdescent policy, where Native people needed to meet a percentage threshold, like 25%, of native "blood" in their ancestry (Spruhan, 2006). Furthermore, the blood quantum required for recognition could also change when it benefitted non-Indigenous people. For example, when land was parceled to individual tribe members (rather than held by a collective tribe), individuals with less than 25% of blood quantum and little connection to the nation could sometimes receive land (Harmon, 2021).

Individuals have also legally contested the boundaries of various racial categorization rules and their associated lack of privileges. Takao Ozawa's attempt to be classified as White is one such challenge. Ozawa was a businessman who was born in Japan. He emigrated to the United States where he attended high school and college, married, and raised his children. After living in the United States for 20 years, he applied for U.S. citizenship in 1914, when naturalized citizenship was available only to "free White persons" and "aliens [non-citizens] of African nativity and to persons of African descent." Ozawa argued that he held "American" values and that when he stayed indoors, his skin was light, sometimes even lighter than others who were considered "White," such as people of Spanish or Portuguese descent. He did not challenge the restriction of naturalization to only White people and those of African descent, but instead challenged the boundaries of the categories by arguing that he, a person of Japanese heritage, should be categorized as "White." The Supreme Court denied his application, stating: "the federal and state courts, in an almost unbroken line, have held that the words 'white person' were meant to indicate only a person of what is popularly known as the Caucasian race … we see no reason to differ" (Sutherland & Supreme Court of the United States, 1922a). However, a year later, in 1923, the Supreme Court ruled on the naturalization case of Bhagat Singh Thind, who was originally from Punjab, India. Coming after the Ozawa case, Thind argued that he *was* a member of the Caucasian race according to anthropological science. The court decision noted that Thind may have met criteria of having Aryan blood but he was not Caucasian "as that word is popularly understood" (Sutherland & Supreme Court of the United States, 1922b). The boundary of "Whiteness" was defined as Caucasian in one case, but when Thind sought to be within that boundary *because* he was Caucasian, the boundary was redefined.

Rules of hypo- and hyperdescent, and legal history such as that of Ozawa and Thind illustrate that racially minoritized individuals don't have the power to define their own race, an example of the cultural imperialism aspect of oppression described by Young (1990; see Chapter 3). Said another way, it is the racially privileged group that has the power to determine racial boundaries. This is important because we often think about race, racial categories, and the effects of race as related to racial identity, the way an individual *personally* thinks about their own race and chooses to label themselves. However, race is a social and systemic category, which means that your socially ascribed racial categorization will have effects regardless of whether race is important to you, whether you identify with the race that others categorize you as, or whether you want those effects (more on this later).

Racial Identity

Colloquially, racial identity can be as simple as identifying as Native American because your family has always done so. But racial identity can also be understood as much more complex than choosing a name or label for one's racial background. This is because an individual's racial identity develops in interaction with the social meanings of race and the groups that are formed within the associated hierarchy. Here, **racial identity** relates to how people negotiate the social meanings of race, that is, how they create their own meanings of what being categorized as a particular race means to them, for their own lives and self-understandings *in the face of the social meanings*. If you're a person of color, this usually means a developmental process of exploring meanings and experiences related to feelings of belonging and connection to a racial group, as well as meanings and experiences related to racial oppression and working to find ways to create a positive sense of identity even as social messages might be conveying stereotypes and oppressive ideas about who you are because of your race. If you're a White person, racial identity relates to whether and how you perceive race and your own categorization as White, your awareness of race as a system of privilege and oppression that benefits you and other White people, and your willingness to address the systemic inequities related to race.

Reflection Questions

- What racial category do you endorse when people ask you what race you are, or when you have to fill out a form that asks you about your race? What contributes to your identifying in this way?
- What kinds of experiences do you *personally* associate with being of this racial category?
- How do these experiences relate to or challenge the stereotypical ideas about this racial group that you generated?
- How much have you thought about your experiences as related to your racial category?

After reflecting on and exploring your own racialization and racial identity, take a few moments to reflect on how your experience would be different if you were of a different racial background, or if people perceived you that way.

Racial identity development theories provide a lens to understand how individuals psychologically make sense of being racialized—or seen as a person with a race. Psychology researchers have created various models of racial identity for both people of color and for White people (see Table 4.1).

Table 4.1 Overview of racial identity development

Conformity

People in this status generally accept and/or lack awareness of racial inequity and White supremacy. Race may be seen as personally or generally unimportant (low racial salience). Instead, there is an emphasis on individual experience and common humanity. People may actively endorse color-blind racial attitudes. People in this status accept White privilege and White European American culture as dominant and normal, and (unconsciously) emulate or assimilate. Although it may be more comfortable to avoid confronting the realities of racism, conformity attitudes and beliefs are challenged by lived experiences, observations, and facts, contributing to cognitive dissonance.

People of Color in Conformity are more affected by internalization of negative attitudes about their own group and/or themselves, although they may not have awareness of these attitudes or their effects.	White people are more likely than (U.S. born) People of Color to hold Conformity racial attitudes, especially if they have less exposure to racial diversity.

Awakening/Dissonance

Movement into the Awakening/Dissonance status may be catalyzed by personal or observed experiences of racial discrimination. One begins to notice that racial categorization has effects on lived experiences. One may experience confusion about beliefs previously held about oneself and others of similar or different racial categorization. There is an emerging recognition that privileges, benefits, and access to resources that are available to White people are not as readily available to people of color. Both people of color and White people often feel distressed, confused, and/or disillusioned, especially if they began with a stronger belief in meritocracy.

People of Color in Awakening/Dissonance may experience conflict in the way they feel about themselves and their own racial group. They begin to more actively see their own oppression and more consciously attribute negative experiences to racial bias. They may seek to minimize the personal effects of race and racism to protect a just world view and a sense of personal agency and control.	White people in Awakening/Dissonance may see the impacts of racism on people of color but continue to be less aware of the privileges experienced by White people, or the systemic nature of White privilege. They may be more likely to see racial issues as individual and interpersonal rather than institutional and societal. White people in this stage may respond to the difficulty of perceiving inequity and associated feelings of guilt, shame or anger with attempts to minimize the importance of racism, especially current (rather than historical) effects. They may hold on to color-blind racial attitudes, asserting that not seeing race is a way of being non-racist. White people may move from here into *reintegration* (Helms) or into Exploration and Immersion (below). *Reintegration* is a regression to Conformity attitudes accompanied by a stronger allegiance to White dominance and blaming of people of color for their experiences of inequity.

Exploration and Immersion

People in this status begin to more fully and intentionally explore the effects of race and racism for their own and others' experiences. Having recognized the effects and injustice, they are seeking to reject the racialized ideas, their own (internalized) prejudice, and the acceptability of racial oppression. They perceive the world through a racialized lens, seeing racial discrimination everywhere, including perceiving microaggressions and unintentional racism. This experience is emotionally intense and painful, and individuals often feel unable to maintain a sense of personal well being, build perceptual distance, or develop emotional buffers (armor).

People of Color in *Exploration and Immersion* immerse themselves in exploring the history, meaning, and experiences of being of their racial group. People of color with immersion attitudes may distance themselves from relationships with White people and seek out relationships with people from their own group or people of color generally. They may develop or express anti-White attitudes that focus not only on White supremacy but also on White people as a group. They may also develop or ascribe to group-endorsed prescriptions or meanings of what it means to be or act "authentically" of the group. This stage can be problematic for multiracial individuals if they do not experience acceptance from the group with which they identify.

People of color in this stage are seeking to develop a counter-narrative to dominant negative messages and attitudes about their group and to embrace the strengths, resiliencies, and joys of the group. They seek to more actively understand and perceive racism within the dominant U.S. culture as a means to reject and resist this experience. They often become more outspoken about race and racism and feel angry and a sense of urgency for change. They may be perceived by others as generally angry (or even irrationally angry).

White people in *Exploration and Immersion* are beginning to understand the experiences and effects of race and racism not only as abstractions, but also as concepts that shape their own personal experiences. They are generally seeking to better understand both the experiences of people of color and the experiences and meaning of being White, including White privilege. White people who are deeply immersed often feel guilty about having privilege and being White, anxious and fearful about being perceived as racist, and angry about not having previously learned more about race, oppression, and privilege. They struggle with developing a positive sense of themselves as White people.

Some White people may precede this stage with an experience of *pseudo-independence*, which involves an abstract but depersonalized understanding of racism and (over) identification with people of color, including seeking connections with people of color and rejecting connections with other White people. This may contribute to a paternalistic approach or to looking to people of color for answers to resolve the issues of racism. In *pseudo-independence*, White individuals have not yet engaged the development of what it personally means to be White, and have not yet recognized their personal responsibility to resist or address racism.

Introspection, Emergence, and Redefinition

People in this status are emerging from the intense and often rigid and reactive attitudes associated with Exploration and Immersion. They are seeking to develop an understanding of themselves and the social system of race and racism that is more complex, nuanced, and (hopefully) intersectional while retaining the insights they have gained into racialization, privilege, and oppression. They are engaging a process of (re)defining themselves with greater mindfulness, active choice about who and how they want to be, and increased self-compassion, rather than being reactive to meanings of race that have been imposed on them. They are also better able to recognize how racism is institutional and systemic, not only intrapsychic and interpersonal. Both people of color and White people have greater understanding and skills for developing authentic intimacy across racial differences.

People of Color in _Introspection, Emergence, and Redefinition_ have come to a place where they recognize how race shapes experience generally and personally, and how this constrains development, opportunity, and well-being for people of their group. They recognize that racism has serious effects and locate problems due to discrimination within the system rather than within themselves, which provides protection against internalization and greater clarity about coping and self-care in the face of racism. In this stage, they are recognizing that one kind of constraint relates to a narrow focus on race and racism. They recognize that a reactive stance of intense and angry immersion can be rigid, confining, and exhausting and are seeking to develop a more personalized and holistic understanding of themselves both in relation to and independent from their racial group. They are more able to recognize how their anger is justifiable, but does not have to be personally consuming. They are also developing a greater awareness of how other people of color experience racism and how other systems of oppression interact with racism.

White people in _Introspection, Emergence, and Redefinition_ are developing a greater understanding of what it means to be White that is less driven by feelings of anxiety, guilt, fear of judgment, and defensiveness. They are working to develop a sense of themselves as White people who benefit from racial privilege without self-blame, recognizing that they too are caught in a system of racism. They are better able to differentiate blame from responsibility. They may feel a sense of loss that is less about loss of comfort or privilege and related more to an awareness of the ways that racism creates distance in relationships and worldview, contributing to a sense of isolation and sadness. Simultaneously, they develop recognition that working to resist and undermine racism is a means towards bridging the imposed distance.

Integrative Awareness and Commitment

In this status, both People of Color and White people have developed both personal and systemic understanding of how race and racism shape worldviews, relationships, experiences, and opportunities. They understand the connections of race to power, privilege, oppression, and hierarchy. They have personalized this understanding by considering how they have, themselves, been shaped by race and racism and how they understand themselves as a racialized person. From these foundational understandings, individuals in *Integrative Awareness and Commitment* can develop a strong sense of how they can and will make choices about negotiating issues and effects of race and racism. Individuals in this status appreciate racial and cultural diversity and are committed to advancing equity. They often have greater insight and awareness of their own developmental process of identity and conscientization, and the ways that cycles of new experiences of dissonance and exploration may be necessary for continual growth.

People of Color. The deep understanding of the dynamics of race and racism characteristic of *Integrative Awareness and Commitment* contributes to an understanding of the importance of solidarity among oppressed racialized groups, and oppressed peoples more generally. This understanding contributes to a commitment to support and advance equity not only for one's own group, but for others as well.	*White people.* For White people, ally/accomplice development is an integral part of *Integrative Awareness and Commitment.* Although a well-intentioned "nonracist" identity may be developed without commitment to action to address racism, a deep recognition and personalized understanding of White privilege and the power basis of race is generally accompanied by recognition of responsibility for advancing equity.

Note: Integrated from models presented in Cross (1995); Helms (1995); Sue, Sue, Neville, & Smith (2019); Sue et al. (2019): Suyemoto & Hochman (2021); Thomann & Suyemoto (2018).

These models describe the personal experiences and attitudes that individuals may have as they make sense of their own racialized experiences. Separate models exist because the racial context for people of color and for White people is drastically different due to all of the issues we have discussed here. But the models also have shared elements because the pervasiveness of race and racialization in the U.S. context is socialized into all of us. As illustrated in the Racial Identity Development Table, most of these models for people of color and for White people consider five attitudes or stage/status possibilities: Conformity; Awakening/dissonance; Exploration and immersion; Introspection, emergence, and redefinition; and Integrative awareness and commitment.

We note that racial identity is more complex than these simple categorical types of attitudes. And the multiple models of racial identity development for people of color in general or for specific groups of racial minorities, as well as the models of White racial identity, White racial consciousness, or White ally development are also much more complex than this brief overview. But these models are often helpful foundations for people to understand their own negotiation of race and racism and to consider how their personal attitudes and development of awareness and understanding might affect their learning, their emotional reactions to learning about oppression, and their interactions with others who may have different attitudes or be in a different stage in their journey of awareness and understanding.

Exploring Racism

Racism is the system of judgments, beliefs, actions, norms, and social/institutional practices that protect White supremacy, racial privilege, and hierarchy.

When people think about racism, they usually think about direct, intentional, and obvious interpersonal discrimination against people of color. But **racial oppression** is more multi-faceted than stereotyping, name calling, or interpersonal violence. As we discussed in more depth in Chapter 3, racism can be indirect, unintentional, or subtle. As we mentioned there, most people hold racially biased attitudes, even if they actively believe in racial equality and equity. In fact, research indicates that holding color-blind racial attitudes is related to increased racism of other kinds, because the denial of racial distinctions relates to maintaining racial prejudice (Neville et al., 2000). Indirect, unintentional, subtle, and even unwanted racial attitudes affect interpersonal interactions and judgments in ways that are often outside of our awareness, but still have negative material costs for those who are the targets (e.g., blocking access to resources or achievement, Dovidio et al., 2017) and psychological costs (e.g., costs to self-esteem and well-being, increased body dissatisfaction, anxiety, and depression) for people of color (e.g., see reviews in David et al., 2019 and Sue, 2010).

Historically, we can see extreme examples of racism in legal and institutional practices. In the United States, the attempted genocide of Indigenous People and chattel slavery of African people are two obvious examples. Most people are also aware of Jim Crow laws, and the long legacy of policies, laws, and social practices that exclude and oppress African Americans even to this day. There are many, many other legal institutional examples such as exclusion from citizenship naturalization for immigrants from non-European countries, unconstitutional imprisonment of Japanese American citizens during World War II, denying access to education for non-White people, anti-miscegenation laws that denied the right to marry for inter-racial couples where one partner was White, and so forth (see pastkey.org for timelines of racism).

The Civil Rights Movement that began in the 1960s led to laws that formally forbade discrimination based on race. But racism still exists at individual ideological, interpersonal, and institutional levels, in spite of these laws. Ideological and interpersonal racism is visible when White doctors prescribe less pain medication for Black compared to White patients even when reported pain levels are similar (Morden et al., 2021), when police officers profile Black and Latine motorists as criminal (Harris, 2020), and when students presume women of color professors are receptionists or janitors (Niemann et al., 2020). Two examples of cultural and institutional racism are mainstream media and education. White people, who experience racial privilege in our hierarchical system, have many examples of their experiences, stories, histories, and role models in mainstream media. Can you think of five White movie stars? Can you think of five Black, Asian, Latine, Indigenous American, or SWANA movie stars? Similarly, our educational curriculum includes the history, experiences, and perspectives of mostly White European Americans. For example, when we ask our college student classes what they have learned about Latine people in the United States, there is often very little that students can think of having learned. Within our discipline of psychology, there is a large amount of research on Latine cultural identities, families, acculturation, experiences in therapy, psychological effects of discrimination, and much more. But most psychology majors know almost nothing about Latine experiences.

The experience and effects of racial oppression are often intergenerational. A prime example of this, that intersects with social class, is the history of economic exploitation and racial oppression that began with chattel slavery. Even after slavery was outlawed, laws and social practices such as red-lining, segregated schools, and discrimination in hiring blocked the economic advancements and achievements of Black people in the United States. In case you haven't heard of red-lining, it's the practice of denying access to financial services (e.g., mortgages) in ways that disproportionately affect communities of color. Because of this practice, White Americans were able to take advantage of federally backed mortgages in the 1930s and use the equity from the homes they were then able to afford to finance other investments, such as down payments on future homes or college education for their kids. Black Americans were largely denied these federally backed mortgages, which meant their children and grandchildren did not have access to the opportunities that such investments provided. The results: today White home ownership is 30% higher than that of African Americans, contributing to the significant wealth-gap between the groups (U.S. Department of Housing and Urban Development, 2021).

As we talked about in Chapter 3, the flipside of oppression is privilege. **Racial privilege** is the unearned privilege that a person receives because they are categorized "higher" on the racial hierarchy. We offered some examples of White privilege from Peggy McIntosh in Chapter 3. Many of these examples are about individual or interpersonal experiences. But racial privilege also affects our experiences with cultural and legal institutions. Consider the examples of media and education above: if you are White, you have had the privilege of seeing people like you in the media and learning about the experiences and accomplishments of people like you in your educational curriculum. These institutional experiences contribute to the privilege of seeing oneself as centered in positive ways (which is part of Young's "cultural imperialism" as discussed in Chapter 3). This is the opposite of marginalization and erasure, which are part of oppression. Similarly, if you are White, your ancestors had access to education, home ownership, and preference in hiring that contributed to intergenerational achievement and success for many White people in the United States.

There are hundreds of examples, articles, books, and other resources that detail the history and current practices of ideological, interpersonal, and institutional racism. And that describe the complexities that challenge what is often denial of racism, and the tendency to place the detrimental effects of racism on the targets of racism (people of color), rather than acknowledge there is a systemic issue. Delving into these examples and complexities is beyond the scope of this primer. What we would like you take away from this section is some thoughtful consideration of what racial oppression and racial privilege might look like today; and how it affects all people in detrimental ways, but is particularly harmful to people of color.

Reflection Questions

Reflecting on shared experiences:

- What are some examples of oppression that people of color experience? Are there experiences of oppression that are common across racial minority groups?
- How do experiences of oppression vary among groups? What are examples of oppression for specific different racial minority groups? How do these experiences of oppression relate to the ways that each group is understood within the social construct of racial categorizations?
- What are some examples of privilege that White people experience?
- What are some of the relative or ascribed privileges that some racial minority groups are given as compared to other racial minority groups within our racialized system? Claire Jean Kim (1999), for example, talks about the "triangulation" of Asian Americans and African Americans where Asian Americans are relatively privileged in relation to ascribed intelligence or merit and African Americans are relatively privileged in relation to ascribed nativity and belonging as an American (for more on relative and ascribed privilege, see Chapter 3). Another example is the basic recognition as a racialized group: for example, there is no racial category for SWANA people in the U.S. census.
- In Chapter 3, we talked about the ways that oppression and privilege operate at individual (worldview and internal ideas), interpersonal, and institutional levels. Do your examples reflect these different levels? Are there examples that you could include to reflect different levels?

Reflecting on personal experiences:

- What are your *personal* experiences of oppression or privilege in relation to race?
- If you are White, what are some of the privileges that you experience because you are White? These may be things that you don't experience (e.g., not being called names, being assumed

that you were accepted into your college or hired into your job because you were qualified, not being stopped by police for little or no reason) or things that you do experience (e.g., respect, acceptance, seeing people like you in positions of authority). Think about the individual level (e.g., ways that White people think about themselves, others, the world), the interpersonal level (e.g., ways that White people are treated by others), and the institutional level (e.g., systemic inequities, both currently and historical inequities that continue to have effects now).

- If you are a person of color, what are some of your experiences of oppression? Include things that are denied to you. Consider the individual level (how you have been taught to think about yourself and your group), the interpersonal level (how you have been treated by others), and the institutional level (e.g., systemic inequities, both currently and historical inequities that continue to have effects now).

- How have your experiences of oppression or of privilege affected how you think and feel about yourself? How do they affect how you approach developing relationships with others?

Remember, our purpose here is not to create guilt or anxiety because of the privileges we might have, but to be open to understanding privilege and becoming aware of how the racialized system of privilege and oppression affects us all. We might not want to have these privileges and have others denied them, but that doesn't mean that we don't benefit from privilege if we have it. Generating examples of specific experiences of oppression and privilege helps us see what is so often ignored and better understand how the abstract constructs actually affect people's lives. This is the first step in being able to challenge the system of inequity, if this is what you seek to do.

There is increasing recognition of the need to address the continuing systemic racism in the United States and across the globe. Individuals and organizations have been working to resist racial oppression since racial ideology was first created, and we have certainly made progress in multiple ways. However, racial oppression continues. Currently, for example, the Movement for Black Lives (M4BL: previously named Black Lives Matter) is at the center of both activism and controversy. Some White people and people of color believe the term "Black Lives Matter" asserts that Black people are somehow exceptional, that Black lives matter *more*. This leads to responses of "All lives matter." But the slogan "Black Lives Matter" is addressing the fact that historical and current racism has dehumanized Black people and created a social norm that Black lives *don't* matter. Until Black lives do matter, it is impossible for all lives to matter. The Movement for Black Lives invites us all to consider how participating in anti-Black oppression creates harm for all of us, to understand how our own humanity is undermined by systemic racism and anti-Blackness. If you can see the validity in this perspective, what might you do to contribute to a solution? If you cannot, then how do you make sense of the continued social construction of people of color as less than White people, and of the continued disparities between White people and people of color, not as individuals, but on the larger scale of groups and categorized people?

Resources for Learning More about Race, Racism, and Racial Identity

Race and Racism

DiAngelo, R. (2018). *White fragility: Why it's so hard for White people to talk about racism.* Beacon Press.

Golash-Boza, T. M. (2018). *Race and racisms: A critical approach* (Brief 2nd edition). Oxford University Press.

Goodman, A. H., Moses, Y. T., & Jones, J. L. (2020). *Race: Are we so different?* (2nd edition). John Wiley and American Anthropological Association.

McDermott, M. (2006). *Working-class White: The making and unmaking of race.* University of California Press.

Miller, J. M., & Garran, A. M. (2017). *Racism in the United States: Implications for the helping professions* (2nd edition). Springer.

Mukhopadhyay, C. C., & Henze, R. (2014). *How real is race?: A sourcebook on race, culture, and biology* (2nd edition). Rowman & Littlefield.

New York Times. (2019). The 1619 project. https://www.nytimes.com/interactive/2019/08/14/magazine/1619-america-slavery.html.

Smedley, A., & Smedley, B. (2018). *Race in North America: Origin and evolution of a worldview* (4th edition). Routledge.

Racial Identity

Helms, J. E. (2019). *A race is a nice thing to have: A guide to being a White person or understanding White persons in your life* (3rd edition). Cognella.

Tatum, B. (2017). *Why are all the black kids sitting together in the cafeteria? And other conversations about race* (3rd edition). Basic Books.

Also see the list of anthologies and readers in the Section Two introduction. These anthologies contain conceptual essays as well as personal narratives, examples, stories, and poems.

5 Understanding Ethnicity and Ethnocentrism

As we discussed in Chapter 2, culture consists of many experiences (see Figure 2.1). The dialect we speak, food we eat, ways we communicate, and ideas we have about what is normal or positive behavior are all part of ethnic culture. The stereotypes we hold and the structures of inequity that we create or maintain are also part of our ethnic culture, as they are part of the norms and values and worldview that we develop. People often confuse ethnicity with race, as we noted in Chapter 4. Other erroneous assumptions are that ethnicity is only or primarily about a label or self-chosen identity; that people who identify a particular way ethnically always act in such-and-such a way (e.g., all Mexican Americans speak Spanish); and that the United States is an ethnically diverse melting pot where all ethnicities are equally valued and there is no dominant ethnic culture. Unraveling these assumptions entails understanding how the term "ethnicity" is used in ways that combine ethnic cultural background, ethnic identity, and ethnocultural affiliation; and examining how ethnicity is not only cultural difference but also a distinction related to hierarchies of privilege and oppression.

Defining Ethnicity and Ethnocentrism

Ethnic culture: An ethnic culture is a kind of culture based in a shared history and ancestral heritage usually related to a geographical location or a history of ancestry from a geographical region.

Ethnicity: Ethnicity is social categorization related to one's ethnic heritage.

Ethnocultural affiliation: Ethnocultural affiliation relates to how much a person is actually affected by or connected to a given culture, whether the culture of their ethnic heritage, the dominant culture of the region one has emigrated to, or any other culture. It relates to the ways that one's thinking, feeling, and behavior are actually oriented towards or influenced by a specific ethnic culture.

DOI: 10.4324/9780429059599-8

Ethnocentrism: The idea that the culture of one's own ethnic group is centered, both in one's own experience and one's own judgment of what is normal, acceptable, good, or valuable.

Ethnocentric monoculturalism: Ethnocentrism that is backed by the power of the dominant culture. Ethnocentric monoculturalism relates to cultural imperialism as an aspect of oppression, so that the dominant culture involves the system of judgments, beliefs, actions, norms, and social/institutional practices that protect and privilege the dominant group and marginalize or oppress values and practices of different ethnicities.

> *It's Complicated:* Ethnic groups are characterized primarily by shared culture, and shared culture develops through proximity, which is why ethnicity is often connected to a geographical location. Sometimes we think about ethnicity as synonymous with nationality, but the extent to which people within a given nation share similar culture can vary, and people who are not of the same nationality can share an ethnic culture. For example, some ethnic groups are related by a geography that encompasses multiple nation states, such as the Hmong in Asia and Kurds in the Middle East, while other ethnic groups are a minority group residing mostly within one nation state such as the Rohingya in Myanmar and the Tutsis in Rwanda. For many of these groups, their ethnic minority status and distinct ethnic cultures have resulted in persecution and displacement by the dominant ethnic cultures.

Some Possible Responses to the Material in This Chapter

Before we go on, let's pause here to address possible responses to the material. You might have noticed we do this in every chapter. It's our invitation for you to check-in with yourself to notice, name, and normalize what is happening internally as you read. In recognizing your responses, you increase the likelihood those responses won't derail you from the learning.

Your responses to this chapter may be similar to your responses to the previous chapter on race and racism, although maybe not as intense. So, you might experience confusion, disbelief, or feelings of defensiveness when we point out that that your values, assumptions, and worldview are perspectives influenced by your ethnic culture and not ones that are objectively right or ubiquitous. That we're pointing to the ways ethnic differences are related to hierarchies of privilege and oppression might also bring up anger or frustration, particularly if you believe that you (and others) appreciate and embrace all cultures, have an idea that all cultures are treated equally, or think that our cultural differences don't matter beyond individual preferences and experiences. Alternatively, you might experience excitement around learning how worldviews arise or even have an *"aha"* moment related to why past interactions with individuals who didn't share your ethnic culture might have gone badly.

If you're like some of our students, learning about ethnic culture may cause you to wonder whether having ethnic pride is a bad thing. One of the questions we get often is, "Is it ethnocentric to love my culture?" We want to put your mind at ease by telling you up front: it doesn't have to be. You can love your culture while *also* respecting and appreciating other cultures. Problems arise when love of one's culture equates to denigration and subjugation of other cultures. Read on to learn more about this.

Exploring Meanings of Ethnicity

Ethnic culture is particularly influential for an individual because it is so pervasive and because socialization begins so early: our parents and family pass on their ethnic culture from the moment we are born (or even before!). Language is a good example: language is part of ethnic culture, and as infants we hear our specific ethnic language from our family beginning with their first interactions with us. The sounds and meanings in a specific language vary, and this shapes many aspects of who we are and how we develop, not only in our thinking and social relationships but even in our sensory capabilities and brain development. For example, young infants (around 6 months of age) can distinguish between all sounds in human spoken languages. But infants soon start to get more specialized in their native language(s): they get better at distinguishing between sounds in the languages they are exposed to and worse at distinguishing between sounds that don't exist in the languages they are exposed to. Thus, a typical monolingual English speaking adult cannot easily hear the subtleties required in the "uo" vowel in Vietnamese (e.g., in the name Phuong) and a typical monolingual Japanese speaking adult cannot hear the distinctions between and English /l/ and /r/. This contributes to accents that people have when speaking, which we may use socially as an indicator of ethnic background (and ethnic belonging).

Ethnicity is not the same as race. Ethnicity relates to cultural worldviews and behaviors (see below), while race is about categorization historically created to maintain hierarchies that are related to phenotype (see more about race in Chapter 4). As we mentioned in Chapter 4, each racialized group (Asian, Black, White, Latine, Native American, SWANA) includes many ethnicities or ethnocultural affiliations. For example, a person may be racialized as White and be ethnically affiliated as Italian or Italian American, Irish, French, Swedish, and so forth, or a person may be racialized as Black and be ethnically affiliated as Afro-Caribbean, or African American, or Bajan (Barbadian), or Nigerian, or Sudanese American.

How Do I Say? Ethnicity and race are often confounded, but this can erase important experiences that are central to people's experiences and self-concepts. We encourage you to consider what kind of language you can use to be clear about when you are talking about ethnicity versus race. For example, not all White people are European American and not all people who are ethnically European are White. If you are talking about ethno-cultural experiences, then "European American" is the right language for the group of people, but if you are talking about racial privilege, then "White" is the right language for the group. If you are talking about both, then you can put them together: "White European American."

The distinction is often clearest when we are talking about specific ethnicities and racial categories that are not simultaneously pan-ethnic categories (e.g., the difference between White and Danish or Black and Haitian). But while some of the language used for racial groups is clearly referencing something different than ethnic culture experiences (e.g., White, Black), the language used for other racial categories (e.g., Asian American, Latine, Indigenous American, Middle Eastern North African) is the same language that is used to describe a pan-ethnic experience. Sometimes, you can avoid this issue by being specific about the ethnic reference, such as naming the specific native nation or specific ethnic background, rather than using a pan-ethnic label.

Mostly, we are encouraging you to consider the differences between racial and ethnic categorization and identities and to avoid confounding race and ethnicity in language.

Sometimes our expectations of how race and ethnicity "should" go together are not at all accurate: a person who "looks" Black or brown or White could be ethnically affiliated as Mexican, as South African, or as Tongan. We can't tell their ethnicity from their physical appearance or racial categorization.

Although we often confound race and ethnicity, it is important to conceptually differentiate these concepts because they have different kinds of effects on people's lives. Markus (2008) defines race and ethnicity similarly to how we do. She goes on to describe how ethnicity and race are different in relation to claiming, imposition, and hierarchy implications:

> Ethnic differences refer to differences in frameworks of meaning, value, and ways of living (practices) that derive through association with a particular ethnic group and are noted, claimed, or appreciated by those associated with the group ... Racial differences, by contrast, refer to differences in societal worth that people outside the group impose and that people associated with the group do not claim and, in fact, often resist. These status differences determine a hierarchy among groups.
>
> (Markus, 2008, pp. 661–662)

Although we can differentiate race and ethnicity, these concepts and experiences are also related. One way ethnocultural experiences and race can be connected is when cultural practices emerge from our shared experiences as part of a racialized group. For example, racial socialization in African American families and communities are cultural practices that prepare young people to cope with and resist anti-Black racism; teach about heritage, history, and culture; and develop pride in being Black, and in the resiliency and strengths that Black people have even in the face of racism (Hughes et al., 2006). For African Americans, ethnocultural ways of living and frameworks of meaning have been strongly shaped by the shared historical experience of slavery (which is, of course, directly related to racism), partly because of the overwhelming nature of this experience and partly because the practice of chattel slavery also involved ethnocultural stripping or suppression, where languages and cultural practices from African home countries were prohibited. Simultaneously, we can see how this is still different from racial meanings of being Black, because some Black people in the United States, such as Nigerian immigrants, don't share this history and ethnocultural experience. Their ethnocultural referent is the culture of Nigeria, in interaction with the new cultural experiences they are encountering in the United States.

> *It's Complicated:* Black immigrants who come to the United States with ethnocultural affiliations that don't reflect the shared history of chattel slavery may nonetheless acculturate to some aspects of African American ethnicity because of the ways that legacies of chattel slavery continue to exist in our worldview, interpersonal practices, and institutions. Thus, the children or grandchildren of immigrants may have less association with the ethnoculture of their immigrant heritage and develop stronger ethnocultural affiliation with the pan-ethnic cultures that have developed in the U.S. that are more strongly affected by connections with racialization (e.g., African American, Asian American, pan-Latine).

Another way that race and ethnicity are related is when ethnocultural experiences become associated within our racialized worldview with a racialized category. This happens when we assume that people of a particular race will have specific ethnocultural practices, even if that practice is not part of the specific ethnic culture within the race. For example, non-Asian people in the United States often assume that all people who "look" (East) Asian use chopsticks as their primary utensils. But this isn't necessarily true. Thai culture, for example, *primarily* uses forks and spoons. (There are exceptions to this within Thai culture, especially because Chinese culture and the use of chopsticks spread in Thailand through immigration.) The assumption that all people who look a particular way have particular cultural practices is an instance of racializing ethnocultural practices and is also an example of stereotyping.

It's Complicated: The term "Asian American" encompasses over 4.6 million people with dozens of different ethnicities. People in the United States from Asian heritages or people who are racialized as Asian are often grouped into pan-ethnic subgroups related to specific geographical region, such as South Asians, Southeast Asians, or East Asians, to emphasize shared experiences and histories. The racial construct of "Asians" tends to focus on East Asians (e.g., Chinese, Japanese, Korean) and marginalize other subgroups such as Southeast Asians, Filipinx and South Asians. For example, while Filipinx and South Asians are also classified as racially "Asian," they are phenotypically different from what many people in the U.S. envision when they think about an "Asian" person. And the stereotype of the "model minority" usually does not consider the refugee history of Southeast Asians.

Ethnicity is *one* kind of culture but it is important to remember that culture is a much broader variable. Many of the other diversity issues we are talking about have cultures related to the group. As examples:

- Part of the creation and differentiation of social classes are the associated cultural aspects, such as cultural values and practices associated with working-class, middle class, or upper class (e.g., Stephens et al., 2014).
- Many deaf people differentiate between deaf (with a little "d") and "Deaf" (with a capital "D"), where the former simply means not hearing while the latter reflects a cultural understanding, affiliation, language, and identity (National Association of the Deaf, 2021).
- Research has examined many aspects of gay culture (and its distinction from the dominant culture which is heterosexual; Gerstner, 2006).

In addition, there can be **ethno-religious cultures**, which focus on the secular cultural aspects of a religiously identified group, separate from the belief or doctrine or spirituality or relation to deity/deities. An ethno-religious culture combines the historical geographic history and heritage with religious history and heritage that creates a more specific kind of cultural experience. Jewish culture is an example, where many people identify ethnically as Jewish regardless of their actual religious practice and doctrinal beliefs; others may identify as Jewish both ethnically and religiously. Although we can discuss the differentiation of the bases of these experiences, they are rarely disentangled in discussing identity, at least on the surface level. But these differences are important (again) because exploring these nuances can help us understand how we might be talking about different things and therefore misunderstanding. Engaging the nuances also helps us understand not only *that* we might be talking about different things, but *how* we might be doing so.

Ethnicity and Ethnoculture as Social Constructs

Ethnic culture is created by people and changes over time. Like all culture, as discussed in Chapter 2, some parts of ethnic culture are more visible: such as food, music, holidays, and related customs. Often people think of these aspects as how to understand ethnic culture. But other parts of ethnic culture that are harder to see have a major influence on our thinking, feeling, and behavior, even if we are not aware of this influence. Values, assumptions, and social norms affect how we see ourselves and the world, and the default ways that we interact with others. The values and social norms we have been socialized into determine what we think of as "normal" and acceptable, and what we think of as different or unusual, or even weird or pathological.

Reflection Questions

- What is American culture? What are Americans like? If you like, start with easier things like, food, music, or holidays. But also think about the values that are central to American culture, the ways that we expect others to act, or ways that American culture might fall on the example variables we discussed above, or those in the iceberg figure in Chapter 2.
- Now, think about a different ethnocultural group, in the United States or elsewhere. What is Lakota culture like? Or Swedish culture? Or Peruvian culture? What is Mexican American culture like? Or African American culture? Or Iranian American culture?

The culture of the United States ("American" culture) is an example of an ethnic culture, in that people within the United States share cultural norms, values, and practices. If you were brought up within the United States without much exposure to other ethnocultural practices, you may have a harder time answering the question about the values or norms of American culture because you are so embedded within the U.S. ethnic culture yourself. Often, our students find that it is easier to see the less obvious aspects of their own ethnocultural affiliations if we get more specific about the kinds of norms, values, and practices that are part of culture. Table 5.1 offers some examples of norms and values that people from different ethnocultural backgrounds might vary within.

It is beyond the scope of this primer to discuss all of the cultural variables that vary among ethnic groups in the United States and globally, or to present the findings from research about how the ethnocultures of specific ethnic minority groups reflect these variables or others. What we most want you to take away from this discussion is the idea that ethnic culture is far more than food, dress, music, or holidays and that we are frequently unaware of how much our ethnic culture has shaped our thoughts, feelings, and behaviors.

Table 5.1 Examples of ethnocultural variables, stances, and applications

Ethnocultural value or norm	Possible stances and related attitudes	Examples of application
The relation of people to nature		
	People are meant to master the natural environment and use it for the good of human beings. People are meant to protect and care for the environment for the good of all living things and the earth.	Differences in views about drilling or fracking for oil, attitudes about climate change, approach to environmental protection such as expanding or reducing national parks or protected waters versus human use (e.g., for agriculture, ranching, fishing, etc.) or choices about vegetarianism.
Time orientation		
	Oriented towards past, present, future. Value that is put on the importance of history, timeliness, future planning, spontaneity, or mindful attention to what is happening in the present moment.	Differences in judgments about people who are early or late, meanings of "productive" time such as judgments about people who "waste time" or people who don't "savor the moment," expectations of pace when interacting with service workers such as servers in restaurants, bank tellers, or store cashiers, response to urgency at work.
Meanings of family		
	Who is included in "family": • Default meaning of "family" is nuclear family (parents and children). • Default meaning of "family" is blood extended family (including grandparents, aunts, uncles, cousins). • Default meaning of "family" includes "fictive kin" or "chosen family" who are members of a klan or community. Expectations of family roles, rights, and responsibilities of different family members.	Norms of caretaking for children and elders, family rights for visitation or adoption of children, immigration policy related to "family unification" and who is included amongst those who can be sponsored in for citizenship. The extent to which family or specific family members should be involved in each member's decision making (e.g. career choice for adult children, decisions about moving or immigration).
Communication process		
	Includes multiple variables such as: • Kinesics: communication through the body, including facial expression, eye contact and gaze, or gestures • Paralanguage: aspects of language beyond the words, including tone, inflection, loudness, pauses, silence. • Directness: points are made in a direct, abstract and linear fashion, or more indirectly, personally, or metaphorically through stories, allusions, analogies, examples, etc.	Views of people as too loud, too effusive, too emotional or evasive, judgments about appropriate level of eye contact, judgments of people as "inscrutable" (difficult to read from expression), too quiet, difficult to follow, ineffective in communicating viewpoints. These views then relate to things such as social censure in public spaces (too loud on the bus, too loud in the cafeteria) or issues with more material consequences such as whether someone is seen as having leadership ability related to career advancement.

Ethnocultural value or norm	Possible stances and related attitudes	Examples of application
Individualistic or collectivistic orientation and self construal		
	Individualistic orientation emphasizes independence, individual agency and decision making, individuality (uniqueness), and advocacy for one's own rights, advancement, and self-actualization. Individuals raised in an individualistically oriented culture are more likely to have an independent self-construal emphasizes internal traits or characteristics with an emphasis on independent identity (who I am). Collectivistic orientation emphasizes relational interdependence, decision making informed by multiple perspectives, and group harmony and well-being. Individuals raised in a collectivistically oriented culture are more likely to have an interdependent self-construal that emphasizes how one's understanding of one's self is based on connections to others, with one's character changing with context as connected to interpersonal roles and others' view of oneself.	Views of people as overly dependent or as selfish. Ideas about mental health and independence or dependence relate to this value. For example, should people make their own decisions about college major, career, or romantic relationships or should major and career decisions be collaboratively decided with the family or made primarily in relation to family needs? Norms about expression of views and assertiveness also relate here: is it important and valued for people to express their personal views and opinions regardless of whether that might create conflict or harm others, or is it better sometimes to prioritize harmony and the group's well being? Norms about motivation and achievement also relate here: is there a greater emphasis on collaboration, cooperation (including a desire to follow or emulate others), and advancing the goals of the group, or is individual achievement and personal excellence more important with a related emphasis on competition?
High or low context communication		
	• Low context communication is where the meaning of the communication is in the words themselves and is usually more direct. Associated with individualistic ethnocultures. • High context communication is where the meaning is not only in the words, but also in the context, including the relationships between the people communicating, the situational context, the specific choice of words, and what is not said versus what is said. High context communication is more likely to be indirect and requires a greater understanding of the cultural context and unspoken rules. Associated with collectivistic ethnocultures.	Views of people using high context communication as inarticulate or evasive because it seems that they are not making their meaning clear; that is, they are not making every aspect of their meaning explicit in a way that is perceptible to those who are used to low context communication. Views of people using low context communication as lacking subtlety, being disrespectful, or rude. They may be seen as disrespectful because they are unaware of relational rules that govern effective or expected communication (e.g. who should speak first or say more, given relational roles and positions). A high context communication approach also expects meaning to be conveyed in what is not said, as well as what is said, which may lead to misunderstandings about communications or intent. For example, low context critique or feedback may be experienced as stronger or more judgmental than is meant, or as aggressive or rude.

Note: Informed by Condon & Yousef (1974); Markus & Kitayama (1991); Kluckhohn & Strodtbeck (1961); Sue et al. (2019).

As we talked about in Chapter 2, if almost everyone around us shares our culture, we may not even perceive that our experiences are cultured. Even if we are aware that our culture is only one of many, we may have difficulty understanding when ethnocultural differences arise. Our own ethnocultural values become much more obvious when we are in an ethnocultural context that is different from our own, or when we are interacting with people who are from a different ethnic culture. However, even when that is the case, we may not immediately be aware that there is a cultural difference or dis- connection. For example, I (KLS) have some friends who have been married now for quite some time. When they first got together, they liked to take walks in the park on the paths. Somehow, though, they had a difficult time actually staying on the path, so their walks would look like the picture in Figure 5.1. They would consistently end up off the path and have to readjust to get back on the path. What made this happen?

Eventually they realized that they had an ethnocultural difference related to their most comfortable or ideal physical distance (called proxemics). One of them felt more comfortable being closer and so moved to close the distance, but the other one moved away to maintain a less close distance that was more what they were used to. So, as a couple, they ended up off the path.

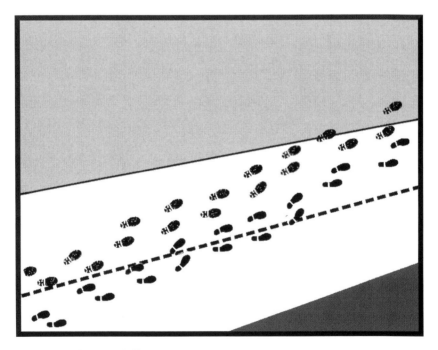

Figure 5.1 Differences in Proxemics
Source: Developed by Thanh Nguyen and Karen L. Suyemoto. This work is licensed under a Creative Commons Attribution-NonCommercial-ShareAlike 4.0 International License. Used by permission.

Neither is right or wrong, it's not like closer distance is good and farther distance is bad. What is challenging and takes us off the path is when one of us thinks we're doing one thing and the other one thinks we're doing another thing. We are not necessarily aware that we are starting out with different places and that we need to negotiate that difference.

Ethnic Identity and Ethnocultural Affiliation

Ethnic identity relates to how people personalize the social meanings of ethnicity, that is, how they create their own understanding of what their ethnicity means to them, for their own lives and self-understandings. People often assume that "ethnicity," or one's ethnic *heritage*, inherently relates to one's current ethnic *identity* and to ethnocultural *affiliation*, particularly for people of color, Indigenous people, and immigrants in the United States. People think that a person with heritage from a specific location or background will identify that way and will think and act in ways that relate to that ethnic culture. However, this is not always the case. For example, a Latine person whose grandparents emigrated from Chile might have much greater familiarity with American language, holidays, cultural practices, relational norms, and values, than with Chilean culture. This person might identify as American, as Chilean, as Chilean American, or as Latine (a pan-ethnic identity that may also be related to racialized grouping).

Ethnocultural affiliation is about how much our experience relates to a specific ethnic culture—how much we ascribe to the values and norms, engage in the behaviors, and so forth. That is, how much we engage in the modal practices and beliefs. The difference between ethnicity or ethnic identity and ethnocultural affiliation is often glossed over, and this can cause confusion. For example, if someone asked me (GSK) my ethnicity, I might say Korean or Korean American, because my parents and family came from Korea to the United States. But by saying that I am ethnically Korean or even Korean American, others might assume that this means that I am strongly affiliated with this culture. This may or may not be true—I might have values and behaviors that are characteristics of Korean ethnoculture, such as liking kimbop, being interdependent in my relationships, and having a tendency to conform for the sake of maintaining social harmony. *Or* (like the grandchild of Chilean immigrants above), I might be very acculturated to the U.S. ethnoculture, and instead like to eat hamburgers and dislike kimbop, have a very independent approach to decisions and achievement, and be a strong non-conformist with a high tolerance of interpersonal conflict. Some people identify their ethnicity in a certain way without participating much in the practices, values, or norms of the ethnic culture. Gans (1979) calls this "symbolic ethnicity." While it serves to create symbolic connections to our heritage and to others who share that heritage, it does not have much meaning in terms of understanding an individual's worldview and associated behavior. Rather than simply assigning a label to our identity based on our heritage, we can more fully explore the influence of our ethnic cultures on our worldview and relationships if we consider ethnocultural affiliation, or what it might mean in our lives to be associated with an ethnic culture, to believe and act in ways that are consistent with that culture, and to be influenced by the social norms and expectations of that culture.

Understanding ethnocultural affiliation relates to considering the difference between modal practices and individual manifestations of culture. **Modal practices** are those aspects of the ethnic culture (or any culture) that are characteristic of what "most" people do within a culture. Modal practices come to define the culture. For example, in relation to some of the ethnocultural values and norms in Table 5.1, the **dominant European American culture** in the United States is oriented towards mastery over nature and future time.

How Do I Say? Why do we describe the dominant culture in the United States as European American? Although some people believe that the United States is a melting pot of cultures, U.S. culture has been strongly shaped by the norms and values of the Europeans who colonized North America and initiated the United States as a nation, and codified laws and practices into U.S. institutions. Culturally, "American" is most similar to European American values, norms, and ethnic practices with lesser influence from other ethnicities or pan-ethnic regions. Considering analogies for culture might be helpful here. Some people see the United States as a melting pot of cultures, where all cultures melt together, while others see it as a salad, where different ethnic cultures retain their flavor and character while contributing to a more delicious whole. We see U.S. culture as a stew, where there is a dominant flavor. In a beef stew, for example, the carrots in a stew do affect the overall taste, but the carrots taste more of beef than the beef tastes of carrots.

In contrast, **individual manifestation** considers how a particular individual engages with or reflects a culture. Just because someone is a part of the identifiable cultural group doesn't mean that they will agree with or embrace *all* of the values or practices that characterize the cultural group. A particular European American might be future oriented but might feel strongly about living in harmony with nature. Furthermore, how one ethnically identifies and the extent to which one actually participates in or embraces the ethnic culture are not the same thing: one could identify as American and be oriented towards harmony with nature and current and past time, as well having family meanings, communication processes, and self-construal that are different from the modal American practice. However, it is likely that this person would feel a lesser fit and sense of belonging to the dominant European American ethnic culture with which they identify, and with the people who share that ethnic identity. Having said all of this, it is also important to remember that cultures change. For example, given the current climate change activism and increasing awareness, the dominant culture in the United States might have a much greater emphasis on harmony and caretaking of nature in five or ten or twenty years.

One's ethnocultural affiliation influences the congruence between the modal practices and individual manifestation. Other concepts that relate to this are enculturation and acculturation, which relate to the ways that individuals are affected by the interaction of cultures These terms are often used when discussing immigrant experiences, where an ethnic heritage culture (e.g., Syrian culture) interacts with the culture of the new, or destination, country (e.g., the United States). **Enculturation** addresses the process and experience of socialization and affiliation to an ethnic heritage culture: for example, how much the child of Syrian immigrants has been socialized into Syrian cultural norms, values, beliefs, and practices. **Acculturation** addresses the process and experience of socialization and affiliation to the new host culture: for example, how much this same child of Syrian immigrants has been socialized into American cultural norms, values, beliefs, and practices.

Reflection Questions

- What is the ethnic background(s) of your family?
- What is your ethnic identity (that is, how would you answer the question: what is your ethnicity or ethnicities)?
- What are some of the modal values, beliefs, and behaviors associated with these ethnicities (see Figure 2.1)? When you think about the values, beliefs, or behaviors related to your ethnicity, which of these do you embrace or reject?
- How are you similar to or different from others in your ethnicity?
- Are processes of acculturation and enculturation a part of your experience and do they influence what you embrace or reject? What else might influence your personal experience in relation to the shared ethnoculture or the group?
- How much do you know about the ethnic cultures of groups other than your own?
- How did you learn about these cultures?
- What kind of things influence us to learn about (or not learn about) ethnic cultures other than our own?
- How does your ethnicity and your race interact? Imagine you are from same ethnocultural background, but of a different race (e.g., if you are Dutch and White, imagine being Dutch and Black). Or imagine you are of the same race but of a different ethnicity (e.g., if you are White and ethnically identify as European American, imagine being White and having a strong Brazilian ethnocultural affiliation, or being Amish; or if you are Black and

African American, imagine being a Black immigrant from Kenya). How would your experience be different? How does this reflection affect your understanding of the interaction of race and ethnicity?

- How does your ethnicity interact with other statuses of privilege and oppression related to different social categories? In a personal way? In relationships with others who are like or unlike you in relation to ethnicity, race, or other statuses?
- How would you and your life be different if you were from a different ethnocultural background?

Exploring Ethnocentrism

Ethnocentrism is the idea that the culture of one's own ethnic group is centered, both in one's own experience and one's own judgment of what is normal, acceptable, good, or valuable.

Ethnocentric monoculturalism refers to ethnocentrism that is backed by the power of the dominant culture (Sue, 2004). Ethnocentric mono-culturalism relates to cultural imperialism as an aspect of oppression, so that the dominant culture involves the system of judgments, beliefs, actions, norms, and social/institutional practices that protect and privilege the dominant group and marginalize or oppress values and practices of different ethnicities.

There are hundreds of ethnicities with dozens of variables within each that are related to ethnic culture. This multiplicity challenges the ways that ethnicity can be used as a meaningful categorization system that could guide our expectations of other people given the huge range of how individuals, even within an identified group, might think, feel, and act. Thus, many people have fewer ideas (stereotyped or otherwise) about what some *specific* ethnic groups or people might be like. Many people in the United States, for example, have little idea about the experiences (or even existence) of ethnic groups such as Hmong, Beninese, or Guyanese. It is more common to have ideas about what a pan-ethnic group is like (e.g., Asian Americans), but these ideas are often influenced by the interaction of racialization and ethnicity, as we described above.

We also have ideas that our own ethnicity is best. **Ethnocentrism** is where we center the culture of our own group, both in terms of the experiences we have and in terms of evaluating what is normal, acceptable, good, or valuable. Many people are ethnocentric to some extent—believing how we and our families think and act is a good way to be. Ethnocentrism becomes problematic, however, when we believe that how we think and act is inherently better than others, rather than simply different. When we have limited experience with other ethnocultural experiences and when our own ethnicity is socially dominant, we may be less knowledgeable about others and more likely to consider our own experience as *inherently* normative and positive. We are more likely to develop ethnic stereotypes, which sometimes, but not always, overlap with racial stereotypes.

Although the United States is a country with many immigrants from various places and related ethnocultural backgrounds, there is a dominant culture which is largely related to European American ethnoculture (rather than, for example, Asian American, Latine American, Native American, African American, or Middle Eastern American), as we discussed previously. Can you identify how the dominant European American culture in the United States stands on the example variables in Table 5.1?

The dominant European American culture in the United States:

- Values mastery over the environment, seeing natural resources as something that can (or should) be used for the comfort and advancement of human beings.
- Emphasizes the nuclear family.
- Emphasizes eye contact when listening.
- Values empirical and statistical information.
- Promotes a linear dispassionate presentation.
- Is individualistically oriented, with associated emphasis on independent self-construal, individual achievement and competition, and relatively low context and direct communication.

The dominance of the European American culture in the United States is enforced through **ethnocentric monoculturalism**. Ethnocentric monoculturalism reflects the ethnocentrism of the dominant group married to the power of that group to determine norms of acceptability, health, and behavior more generally. The idea that immigrants from diverse ethnocultural backgrounds *should* assimilate into the dominant European American ethnoculture, and stop believing, valuing, or behaving in ways that differ from that dominant European American culture reflects an ideology of ethnocentric monoculturalism. The issue of difference versus distinction is relevant here: can we imagine a society where diverse ethnocultural experiences co-exist, and contribute together to something that benefits from that diversity?

Currently, many practices that reflect diverse ethnocultural backgrounds are judged negatively, and the people with these practices experience **ethnocultural oppression.** Conversely, **ethnocultural privilege** is the privilege that one experiences from living within a context where the dominant ethnic culture matches one's own. In Table 5.1, we discuss differences in views and judgments that might be made of people who have other views. These judgments are examples of ethnocentrism. But when ethnocentrism connects with dominance, these can also be examples of ethnocentric monoculturalism, ethnocultural oppression, and related ethnocultural privilege.

A very concrete example is judgments about dress. Some ethnic and ethnoreligious cultures value modesty or simplicity more than the dominant norm in the United States. Some ideas or practices among these (many) cultures include that women should not expose their arms or legs, that long sleeved shirts are expected for men, that men and women should cover their heads, that belts and ties are prohibited, that colors should be plain, that jewelry is forbidden, and many other variations. People who dress in these ways may be judged as strange, stared at, or even assaulted. Dress is an important example of the ways in which cultural norms can be imposed because how a person dresses usually has so little effect on their actions or capabilities or interactions. And yet, there are strong judgments nonetheless.

A less concrete example at the individual and interpersonal level is to attribute judgments such as "lazy" or "inconsiderate" to people from other cultures (e.g., Afro-Caribbean culture) who transgress U.S. dominant norms of punctuality because they have greater present time orientation. In Table 5.1, we also discuss the consequences of not aligning with the dominant cultural norms related to communication process, including judgments about being too loud or unclear in communication. These judgments are made without consideration of the diversity of ethnoculture. Another example is related to individualism and collectivism: East Asian Americans who are more ethnoculturally affiliated with heritage country collective cultures that value harmony are often judged as overly conforming and dependent, which relates to stereotypes of Asian Americans as good workers but poor leaders because they lack independent creativity or initiative.

At an institutional level, there are many examples of ways that the dominant European American culture has been oppressively imposed. One example is "English only" attitudes and laws. Another example is rationalizing the exclusion of non-European immigrants based on fears that these immigrants would undermine the "American way of life." A more specific example related to family norms is the many cases of removing Indigenous American children from the community when their immediate parents are not available to them due to illness or death, and placing them for adoption with European American nuclear families. This oppressive practice reflects an understanding that these children would be "better off" with a nuclear family of two parents than being raised by extended family related by blood or Indigenous community intimacy. Ethnocentric monoculturalism is also reflected in our educational system. For example, children in kindergarten are often taught about how to read and express emotions, based in European American cultural norms. Children in schools are also taught that each child must "do their own work" and learning games often emphasize competition between children or groups. These approaches privilege ethnocultural values of individualism and competition. Children whose families already embrace these values have an easier time and experience less negative judgment from teachers and peers, reflecting their ethnocultural (and usually out-of-awareness) privilege.

Reflection Questions

- What kinds of social messages have you received about your ethnicity and your ethnic background? Where have you gotten these messages from? How have these messages made you feel about yourself?
- Think about your ethnocultural values, norms, and experiences. Are the ways that you think and act similar to or different from others around you? Are they similar to or different from what you have been taught in school or what you see in the media and culture around you?
- Have you observed or experienced exclusion, negative judgment, or oppression related to your ethnocultural practices, values, norms, and experiences (e.g., language, dress, ways of interacting, time orientation, etc.)? What do you think is the basis of these negative judgments or oppressive actions? How do these observations or experiences make you feel?
- If you have not had many of these experiences, how do you understand your privilege in relation to culture and ethnicity? Have you generally taken for granted that your cultural values and practices are "right"? Have you thought about how your values and practices *are* a part of culture?

In Chapter 2, we talked about the ways that oppression and privilege operate at individual (worldview and internal ideas), interpersonal, and institutional levels. How do your examples reflect these different levels?

As we have said before, cultures and ethnocultures change. In our lifetimes, we have seen major changes related to ethnocentric monoculturalism in the United States. Some concrete examples include the kinds of food that are available in our supermarkets and restaurants, the range of music that people listen to, the translation of signs and important legal documents (e.g., voting ballots) into different languages, or even the attention to the existence of cultural diversity that is now discussed in teacher education (for people seeking to be teachers) or psychologist training (for people becoming psychologists). As a nation, we have a greater understanding that culture, and ethnoculture, matters. And we are talking much more about it. These changes have been facilitated by organized movements (e.g., for bilingual education or requirements for document translation) and by cultural shifts related to greater travel and to the much greater availability of information and cultural products (e.g., music and art) enabled by the internet. But there has also been backlash to these changes, and there are widely discrepant views about opening or closing doors for immigration and whether American culture is enriched or threatened by embracing multiculturalism. How has your experience been enriched by exposure to diverse ethnocultural perspectives and practices?

Resources for Learning More about Ethnicity and Ethnocentrism

Bayor, R. H. (Ed.) (2016). *The Oxford handbook of American immigration and ethnicity*. Oxford University Press.

Bizumic, B. (2019). *Ethnocentrism: Integrated perspectives*. Routledge.

Matsumoto, D., & Juang, L. (2011). *Culture and psychology* (6th edition). Cengage Learning.

Also see the list of anthologies and readers in the Section Two Introduction. *These anthologies contain conceptual essays as well as personal narratives*, examples, stories, and poems.

6 Understanding Sex, Gender, and Sexism

Some of the assumptions that we are erroneously taught in the United States about sex and gender include the beliefs that:

- Both sex and gender are completely and absolutely defined or dictated by "real" biological differences.
- These biological differences create an essential and absolute binary (male versus female).
- Sex and gender are inherently related to each other.
- Personality characteristics and abilities are inherently associated with the binary categories of male and female.

Unraveling these erroneous assumptions means considering more deeply how sex and gender are social constructs. This includes considering how biological differences are not as clear cut, as consistent, or as absolute as we might assume. And considering how even existing biological differences are not what creates meanings and influences social interactions in relation to sex and gender.

Defining Sex, Gender, and Sexism

Sex is a socially constructed medical categorization, conceptualized as distinctions related to specific physical or biological characteristics, including chromosomes, gonads (i.e., internal sexual organs: ovaries, testes), hormones, genitalia (i.e., external sexual organs: vagina, vulva, clitoris, penis, scrotum), and secondary physical sex characteristics (e.g., breasts, width of hips, amount of body fat, pitch of voice, facial and body hair, size of Adam's apple).

Gender is a socially constructed categorization related to intersections of identity, expression, and social expectations and roles. Connected to gender categorization are the socially developed expectations about how people "should" act and the personality characteristics and behaviors they are expected to have given how others perceive their sex.

Sexism is the system of judgments, beliefs, actions, norms, and social/institutional practices that protect and privilege the gender binary (man or

DOI: 10.4324/9780429059599-9

woman) and place cis men in the dominant, privileged position within the assumed binary. **Cissexism** is a kind of sexism that maintains the assumption of the binary, by privileging those who "fit" the constructed binary and targeting trans people.

Some Possible Responses to the Material in This Chapter

Learning about sex diversity, gender fluidity, and ways of complicating our assumptions of sex and gender binaries might be revelatory for you if you're new to the topic or are questioning your sex and/or gender categorization. Such knowledge could bring up a variety of emotions like relief, hope, fear, nervousness, or confusion. Whatever comes up, we invite you to see this as a beginning in your unlearning process and movement toward greater understanding of how sex and gender are socially constructed.

On the other hand, learning that sex and gender are actually not biological or binary may make you feel deeply uncomfortable. Assumptions of binaries are often taken for granted. Many of us feel very strongly about our own experience as a man or a woman and rely on our personal felt experience that our gender is *real*, meaning—to us—it is completely hardwired and biological. The mere suggestion that gender (and therefore the gender binary) is socially constructed can result in a resistance tailspin. This resistance can manifest emotionally as dismissal, denial, minimization, disbelief, or outright anger; and can manifest behaviorally as aggressive questioning or outright avoidance of the reading. But note that we are not saying that your felt experience of gender is not real or important. We are asking you to consider that the gender *categories* of man and woman might not be as universal to everyone as we often assume.

We invite you to be on the lookout for these responses in yourself and others. As we have indicated previously, noticing, naming, and normalizing your responses might give you a bit of distance from your reactions so that you can take in different perspectives more fully. It also helps to remember that exploring the ways that sex and gender are more complex than a biological binary doesn't mean that your own experiences as a man or as a woman (if you have those experiences) isn't real or valid or important to you.

Exploring Meanings of Sex and Gender

Most people have an expectation that sex and gender will "align" in particular ways (that are, themselves, socially created), but this isn't always the case. We will discuss this more below, but to understand the complexity of these concepts and experiences, we need to begin with unraveling the assumption that sex determines gender or vice versa. That is, we need to unravel the assumption that if your body seems to fit the male categorization, for example, then your gender will (or should) be as a boy or a man. We also need to unravel the related assumption that if you identify your gender as a boy or a man, then your body should fit the male categorization and if it doesn't, you should make physical changes so that it does. Although sex and gender are not the same thing, they are often seen as interactively determining meaning and experience; sex influences gender meaning, development, and identity because the ways that people are categorized by others based on others' perception of their sex influences the gendered social expectations and roles that are ascribed or imposed upon them. Said another way, if you are "read" or "coded" (seen by others) as male, then you are expected to dress and act in stereotypically masculine ways and engage in "manly" pursuits.

Sex and Gender as Social Constructs

Sex is a socially constructed medical categorization, conceptualized as distinctions related to biological differences in chromosomes, hormones, internal and external reproductive organs, and secondary sexual characteristics. One's designated sex assigned at birth is often *assumed* based on external genitalia, which may or may not align with all of the physical or biological characteristics listed here (more on this below). Thus, it may be more accurate to discuss "sex assigned at birth" rather than simply "sex." In our current U.S. culture, we often think about sex as binary, meaning we have two sexes: male and female. People often support this binary view by pointing to genetics, stating that the pairing of XY sex chromosomes makes a person a man and the pairing of XX sex chromosomes makes a person a woman. But these are not the only possible make-ups. Some people have XXY (called Klinefelter Syndrome) and some have XO, meaning only one complete X sex chromosome (called Turner Syndrome). Thus, even at the basic chromosomal level there is more variation than we might assume.

In addition to chromosomes, our sex is related to hormone levels (e.g., estrogen and testosterone), internal and external reproductive organs (e.g., ovaries and testes, vagina and penis), and secondary sexual characteristics (e.g., facial hair, muscle mass, wider hips, larger Adam's apple). Our usual expectation is that biological aspects connected with sex categorization such as chromosomes, hormones, internal and external reproductive organs, and secondary sexual characteristics will all line up together to be congruent with *either* a male or female binary category. Although this is the case for most people, nature is actually more variable than we think, with considerable **sexual diversity**. There are people whose chromosomes are XY (considered male), but who have less testosterone and more estrogen which contributes to a physical appearance and secondary sexual characteristics (e.g., lack of facial hair) that others categorize as female. There are also people who have chromosomes that are XX (considered female) and internal or external organs that others categorize as male. And, as we discuss below, there are people whose internal or external sexual anatomy doesn't fit neatly within the binary categorization approach at all.

How Do I Say? Some people use the term "intersex" when referring to people who don't fit the binary categorization of sex. Such labeling is complicated, however, because it creates a new category, rather than reflecting how we might conceptualize sex as more of a continuum, not strict categories. Terms like "sex diverse" or "sexual diversity" acknowledge this continuum.

The continuum and range within biological sex characteristics have always existed. But within the U.S. culture, we have created the idea of *only* two categories—male and female—that all people "should" fit within neatly and completely. We have this idea even though there is considerable evidence of biological sex variability beyond a binary construction. The two-category idea is so strong in the current U.S. understanding that we "push" people into this sex binary, socially and biologically (Fausto-Sterling, 2020). For example, it has been common practice to perform medically unnecessary surgery on babies who are born with variation (e.g., a larger clitoris or a urethral opening located on the penis shaft; InterACT and Human Rights Watch, 2017). These surgeries place infants at risk not only from possible negative consequences of surgery generally, but also from the possibility of negative side effects such as loss of nerve sensation. Additionally, in cases where children are born with variation among chromosomes, hormones, internal and external reproductive organs, and secondary sexual characteristics, doctors may intervene to create greater "alignment" into either male or female. For example, doctors may assign a sex based on the appearance (natural or surgically created) of the external genitals and instruct the parents to raise the child within that gender (see gender, below). The rationale presented is that the children would be so negatively affected by being different and so traumatized by others' negative reactions (e.g., bullying) that it is better to make them fit into the male or female category.

There are many problems with this rationale, such as the physical risk and damage as well as the psychological and relational impact on those children who end up not experiencing themselves (their gender) as the sex assigned (InterACT and Human Rights Watch, 2017). Given this, the question we ask you to consider is whether it is the infants' bodies that are the problem or whether the problem is our rigid binary system? Take a moment to ask yourself how you would feel if your physical body didn't fit neatly and "absolutely" into prescribed male or female biological or physical characteristics? Would you want others to think you were "abnormal" or "weird"? Do you think you would deserve ridicule or bullying? How would you feel about your body? *Why* would you feel this way? Would you want to undergo multiple surgical operations and/or other medical procedures that are often painful and dangerous? If so, why would you want to do that? Would you want others to make this decision for you? In these questions, we are asking you to consider the social basis of our judgments and expectations about sex and bodies.

Our experience is that people in the United States often find it challenging to consider that the idea of binary sex categories is socially constructed, rather than something that is biologically inherent, "natural," and therefore "real" in a way that should not (or cannot) be questioned. As we mentioned in Chapter 2, we can often see how our ideas and meanings are socially constructed rather than absolute if we look at how meanings vary within different cultures or have changed over time. Within the United States, for example, the category or identity of "intersex" dates to the early 1900s and only recently has become a more frequent part of our discourse about gender. Similarly, surgical intervention is also relatively new. Thus, while the assumption that most people are male or female is not new, the idea that physical bodies *must* be absolutely male or female and they should be manipulated to ensure they fit into this binary is relatively recent in the United States.

Furthermore, other cultures, both historically and currently, have recognized the existence and experience of what we in the United States now call "intersex" people: Hebrew texts describe social roles of intersex people, some Hindu deities are intersex, and *guevedoces* in the Dominican Republic are all related to what we now call "intersex." Often, these conceptions include ideas about gender, or gender roles, as well as sex. Many Indigenous nations, for example, recognize and often revere two-spirit people.

How Do I Say? Two-spirit is a relatively recent intertribal term that centers traditional Indigenous conceptualizations of sex, sexuality, and gender that reflect, for example, fluid gender presentation, fluid gender roles, same-gender love, and/or gender identity that is different from sex assigned at birth. Among some Indigenous scholars, two-spirit is a reclamation of a cultural and spiritual way of being that historical European colonization sought to erase through violence, intimidation, and "re-education," and that prior western-derived terms of lesbian, gay, bisexual, or transgender do not fully capture.

For example, Margaret Robinson (2020, p. 7), an Indigenous two-spirit scholar, states: "Two-spirit identity enables Indigenous people 'to negotiate boundaries between bisexual, gay, lesbian, queer or trans communities and our own nations (Brotman et al., 2002). In gender and sexual minority Settler communities, two-spirit identity makes Indigeneity visible and serves as a buffer against assimilation.'"

Although cultural conceptions of those not fitting into binary sex categorizations may include additional gender categories or more fluid understandings of gender, one may be "intersex" and have a definitive identity within gender binary categories as male or female. It is not the case that the existence of sex characteristics determines gender binary categories, as we discuss below. It is also not the case that the sex characteristics that an individual has, or the sex category one is assigned (or identifies with), inherently determines gender.

Gender as a social construct, is a categorization that connects our ideas about physical sex and related binary assumptions to our *assumptions* about people's identity, personal characteristics, and abilities. Gender is therefore about how we, as a cultured society, create expectations about people (including ourselves) given how we *perceive* their bodies. These expectations include how people with different gender statuses "should" act, the personality characteristics we expect them to have, how they will/should interact with us, and how we should interact with them. In these ways, gender serves as an invisible filter that both describes the categories we expect people to fit neatly into and prescribes the rules we expect people to follow depending on their category. This gender filter can also influence how we act and respond to others without us even knowing it. You can recognize the impact of your filter, though, if there are moments when you feel unsure and uncomfortable about how to interact with someone because their gender category isn't immediately apparent to you. Although gender as a social construct relates to categorical expectations, gender experience or identity may be more self-determined by creative expression and exploration of personal or social gender meanings (see more below).

Like sex, we have created an idea that gender is binary, that people are either boys/men or girls/women. We also assume that a person's gender identity is *determined* by the sex category they are assigned to. So, people often think that what boys and girls are like is "hardwired" into our biology, our genes, and our associated appearance. So, if someone "looks" like a male (boy) then they "should" like trucks and sports and be less emotional and relational. These ideas and assumptions do not reflect the complexity of human experience: like other structural categories explored in Section Two, gender is a socially constructed categorical system that reflects a system of privilege and oppression that we need to explore further.

Some aspects of biology related to sex categories do affect our behaviors and characteristics, such as the ways in which testosterone affects activity or aggressive behavior. But even if levels of testosterone are related to male genes, hormones, or organs, that doesn't necessarily mean that being active or aggressive is inherently male, or that those who identify as male must be active or aggressive to be healthy or "normal." Our assumption or expectation that this will be so comes from how we are socialized to think about men and women (or boys and girls), and the ways that we associate perceived biological differences with rigid ideas about behavior, thinking, and feeling.

Reflection Questions

What comes first to mind when you consider the questions below?

- What are boys/men like?

Within this, try to think broadly about how boys/men think, feel, and behave. For example, think about personal characteristics (e.g., emotional, active, relational, etc.), but also think about things like how boys/men act (e.g., how they talk or move) and how boys/men think or feel. Think about what you have learned or seen about things that boys/men like to do, and the things they don't like to do. And about how boys/men dress or don't dress, how they do their hair, how they decorate their rooms.

- What are girls/women like?

Within this, try to think broadly about how girls/women think, feel, and behave. For example, think about personal characteristics (e.g., emotional, active, relational, etc.), but also think about things like how girls/women act (e.g., how they talk or move) and how girls/women think or feel. Think about what you have learned or seen about things that girls/women like to do, and the things they don't like to do. And about how girls/women dress or don't dress, how they do their hair, how they decorate their rooms.

If you are like most people in the United States, you can come up with a pretty long list reflecting what boys/men "are like" and what girls/women "are like," and those lists will include many ideas that are binary and opposites. For example, boys/men are active, loud, logical, and oriented towards things rather than people, while girls are passive/quiet, emotional, and oriented towards people rather than things. Even if you don't actually think that boys/men are like X and girls/women are like Y, you are aware that these are the meanings that are associated with the social categories. These meanings are taught to you in so many ways through socialization by family and other people, as well as through formal education. For example, in the books we read and the movies we see, boys and men are portrayed to act in particular ways and girls and women act in other ways.

But, is this *inevitable?* There are boys who like pink and are really emotional and not very logical, and girls who love the color blue, competitive sports, and logic puzzles. Characteristics and behaviors exist on continuums, with a lot of variation. However, we have stereotypical assumptions about gender categories, assumptions that are so strong that we censor people who don't meet those assumptions. For example, if women are "too assertive," they are seen as "bitchy" and boys are often teased if they cry or show fear or vulnerability, rather than being emotional in acceptably "masculine" ways such as being angry or aggressive.

As with all the social structures we discuss in this book, we invite you to question why we are so strongly drawn to categorizing people as man or woman. And why we create these categories in ways that are quite narrow, rather than being able to encompass the breadth of our experiences as humans. What would boys/men be like if raised in a society that expected and taught them to be quiet and emotional? Or encouraged them to express how they felt at different moments and contexts, quiet or loud, vulnerable or aggressive? It is really hard to consider what boys/men or girls/women might be like if they were socialized differently, because we have ourselves been socialized in ways that have shaped us to believe in these associations, and even to internalize them within our own identities and our feelings about how we "should" be or who we are.

One way we can see more clearly how gender is a social construct is by looking at how ideas about what a man or a woman is (or should be) have changed over time and context. For example, cis women in the United States and Europe were once seen as incapable of logical and rational thought, and therefore unable to succeed in higher education and untrustworthy to vote (at this time, people didn't even name or consider trans women). Furthermore, our expectations about women vary in relation to other identities and statuses, such as race or social class. A century ago in the United States, the dominant (heteronormative) expectations of middle-class cis White women were that they would marry a cis White man and have little to no influence or activities in careers or politics. The man was the person in charge: he made the major life decisions for himself, his wife, and his children (especially female children). The woman was not expected or even allowed to work outside the home, and when she did, her wages belonged to her husband. Her role was to care for her husband, the children she was expected to have, and her home. However, Black women (whether cis or trans) under slavery were forced to work, not permitted to marry, and forced to have children who were then considered the property of the White plantation owners (see discussion of sexism below).

Gender Identity

Thus far, we have been discussing the social construct of gender: the prescription of a strict binary categorization and the ideas about how women/girls and men/boys should be within that binary. We become aware of how we have been socialized into these ideas by considering our associations with the meaning of gender generally and the meanings of gender categorization or statuses. But gender is not only an abstract idea, it is also a central part of our self-understandings or identity. **Gender identity** is the personal negotiation of social ideas related to gender as a category, and the ways that an individual sees themselves and acts in relation to those ideas. Here, we invite you to consider that an individual's gender may be more related to the ways in which they *experience* themselves in the world than it is related to what other people think they "are" or "should be" based on their body or on ideas imposed on them by others. For many of us, the way we experience ourselves may fit into the binary idea of gender and also fit into the ways that we or others characterize us based on our bodies. But many people experience their personal gender as more complex and not as either/or man/woman. For these and others, the box that others might put them in as a man or a woman is less of a comfortable "fit" compared to their own sense of themselves.

Again, we make assumptions that what we perceive is what should be: if we see somebody who "looks" like a boy, we assume they have a penis and have been assigned the sex of male at birth, and we think that person *should* identify as a boy and think and feel and act "like a boy." Oftentimes, this is the case: most people are **cisgender** (or simply **cis**), meaning their experience of their own gender, their gender identity, matches the social expectations based on their assigned sex and the perceptions of others. But what if they feel more like a girl, or like what we, in our cultured society, define as a girl? What if they like to wear dresses and make-up or play with dolls? What if they don't like sports at all and do like talking about feelings and watching romantic comedies? What if they experience themself as more like what people expect a "girl" to be? This person may identify as a girl/woman, reflecting their own experience of gender, rather than the categorization that our hierarchical system might impose. Or they may identify as a feminine man. Or they may identify as **transgender** or trans or non-binary or (gender)queer.

How Do I Say? Transgender is the term used when a person's gender identity is inconsistent with their sex ascribed at birth. As noted here, some people may have a personal identity, or identify as and with transgender, but one could have the experience of transitioning gender or having one's gender not match assigned sex without having a personal transgender identity. Also, as noted in Chapter 3, cisgender or transgender is written without hyphenation and should definitely not have an "ed" at the end (e.g., the terms should not be "cisgendered" or "trangendered") because it is an identity and status, not something that "happened" to someone.

The following helpful site presents a long list of terminology related to gender and sexuality: http://www.juliaserano.com/terminology.html.

Some trans people may identify as men or as women and may strongly align with the gender binary and with social expectations prescribed for men and women. Alternatively, some people may identify as non-binary or fluid, which usually means that the person rejects the binary categorization schema, including the idea that they are crossing genders.

It's Complicated: Using the pronouns that actually match people's identity and experience is important. Misgendering through the use of inaccurate pronouns is harmful and oppressive (Gunn, 2020). Using accurate pronouns increases gender equity and inclusion. Many people seek to normalize the process of identifying the pronouns that reflect their identity, particularly if you are cisgender, through stating these on nametags, or in email signatures. In groups, it has become relatively common for individuals to state their pronouns when they introduce or name themselves.

However, not everyone feels safe or comfortable sharing their gender identity publicly, not everyone will fit in to what seem like accepted pronouns (he, she, they), and not everyone is sure of their gender. As such, pronoun "go-rounds" that require people to identify their gender pronouns can be problematic. We might also reflect on the ways that the use of "they" may be creating a third category, rather than challenging the idea of categorization overall or being gender neutral. Some people currently use neo-pronouns—such as xe/xir, ze/zir, fae/faer, ne, ve—either because they experience themselves as gender fluid or because they are seeking a pronoun that is gender neutral (or for other reasons you can unearth if you look into this more).

Reflection Questions

- What is your gender identity? What contributes to your identifying in this way?
- What kinds of experiences do you personally associate with being of your gender?
- How do your personal experiences of gender and your gender identity relate to or challenge the binary construction of men/women or the expected ways of being and stereotypes of men or women?
- How has your gender affected your social experience in the world (e.g., how others treat you or your interactions with others)?
- How does your gender interact with your race and ethnicity? With other statuses of privilege and oppression? In a personal way? In relationships with others who are like or unlike you in relation to social class, race, ethnicity, other statuses?
- After reflecting on and exploring on your own gender and gender identity, take a few moments to reflect on how your experience would be different if you were a different gender.

Exploring Sexism

Many of our ideas about gender are not inherent in male or female bodies (external or internal reproductive organs) or genes or hormones. Gender has more to do with what we *think* boys and girls (or men and women) should be like. It has to do with the *prescriptions* we create for ourselves and others about the meaning of being male or female that create rigid expectations, or stereotypes. We then use these prescriptions to justify differential access to power and privilege. For example, the historical expectations for cis middle-class White women described above that limited their rights to education, voting, and work were justified by stereotypical prescriptions of personality characteristics and skills imposed on our idea of women: these women were seen as inherently characterologically (and biologically) emotional, irrational, nurturing, illogical, and dependent. In the last century, many of the legal constraints on women in the United States have changed, and some of the social expectations and assumptions about personality characteristics and possible skills have also changed. But we still have socially constructed meanings of gender that create gender expectations, prescriptions, and proscriptions for men and women, and these social ideas continue to contribute to **gender oppression** of women (both cis and trans) and of trans people, generally, who experience gendered expectations and cissexism related to not "fitting" within the binary.

Traditionally, **sexism** was a term that reflected the gender binary, focusing on the ways that women were placed in a subordinate position within the gender hierarchy. Although trans people existed, there wasn't any mainstream recognition (or even language), so "sexism" has historically assumed that "women" were cis women. Nowadays, we recognize that sexism against women includes sexism against cis women and against trans women—against people who identify or are perceived by others as women and therefore experience imposed assumptions as women. When we talk about sexism, most people think about **misogyny** or hatred, dislike, or prejudice against women. Misogyny reflects attitudes and actions of **hostile sexism**, related to negative ideas about women's abilities or characteristics and to explicit ways that women are controlled, demeaned, discounted, marginalized, or exploited. Examples might include views that women are intellectually inferior; believing that women are "born" to serve men generally or sexually, or more subtle things like expectations that women should be deferential to men in conversations. Institutional examples include denial of the right to vote historically, current wage discrimination where women make about 85% of what men make (Barroso & Brown, 2021), or the portrayal of women in television and movies as less capable and constantly needing to be rescued, or the lack of portrayals of women as leaders.

While we usually think first of more explicit aspects of hostile sexism or misogyny, Glick and Fiske (2001) have researched how sexism is more complicated than that. They discuss **benevolent sexism**, as another aspect of sexism that is less frequently considered. Benevolent sexism includes ideas that women are pure and should be idealized. Benevolent sexism is reflected in the idea of "chivalry," which is often thought about as ways that men should be courteous or polite to women (e.g., opening doors, picking up the dinner check at a restaurant). Benevolent sexism may seem positive, but these ideas support stereotypes that women are weaker or less capable than men and require the care and protection of men. For example, such stereotypes prioritize and essentialize women's relational and domestic contributions making it challenging for them to be seen as effective leaders or high-achieving professionals, particularly in male dominated fields (Eagly & Karau, 2002). Moreover, ideas supportive of benevolent sexism are often used to justify disempowering or oppressing women and limit women's opportunities. Research suggests that at the national level (within countries), hostile and benevolent sexism are highly correlated, and both are connected to measures of oppression against women that include economic, political, educational, and life expectancy inequities.

Although benevolent sexism and hostile sexism work together to maintain inequity, people (especially women) tend to have a hard time with the concept of benevolent sexism, because it seems to be based in caring for others. Studies also suggest that women internalize benevolent sexism, often at similar rates as men, unlike hostile sexism (Glick & Fiske, 2001). So, if you are feeling a bit upset or angry at the idea that chivalry is bad, you are not alone. Benevolent sexism is so ingrained in our society and is one of the places women are made to feel "special" in an unequal society, and it can seem to offer some benefit to balance other experiences of more direct (hostile) oppression. A question to consider is why some behaviors are only considered courteous or appropriate if done by a man for a woman, and not by a man for a man, or a woman for a woman, or a woman for a man? What does reflecting on that question tell us about our ideas and expectations about gender?

More recently, researchers and theorists have been expanding the traditional view of sexism in light of critiques of the binary categorization. **Cissexism** focuses on the ways that cisgender people are privileged and trans or non-binary people are oppressed. This aspect of sexism focuses on the attitudes, interpersonal, and institutional discrimination aimed at people who do not reflect the prescription that all people should be *either* men or women, should identify their gender according to the sex assigned at birth, and should fit the stereotypes and prescriptions associated with men or women. Fluid, or non-binary folks experience cissexism for not aligning themselves to the gender binary expectations. But trans men and trans women also experience cissexism, even if they align themselves according to the gender binary expectations. While the term "cissexism" may seem new, the discrimination isn't. Girls and boys who don't fit the expectations for femininity or masculinity have been teased or ridiculed as "tomboys" or "sissies" for decades. However, the experiences of oppression directed at those who don't fit sex and gender prescriptions are just beginning to be explored as our changing ideas about gender recognize the range of lived experience and make space for more fluid gender identities and enactments.

It's Complicated: The categories "tomboy" and "sissy" are not treated the same. Because of sexism, girls perceived as tomboys are tolerated more than boys perceived as sissies. It is more socially acceptable for a girl to act "like a boy," than for a boy to act "like a girl." This reflects the fact that U.S. culture (and people socialized into that culture) values what is seen as masculine more than what is seen as feminine. A classic example is the study demonstrating that people equated male characteristics with those of a healthy person, but female characteristics were seen as unhealthy or pathological if not specifically attributed to a woman (Broverman et al., 1970). "Transmisogyny" is the term that captures the intersectional discrimination experienced by trans women.

Sexuality, age, degree and continuation of nonconformity also influence tolerance (e.g., Carr, 2007; Miller, 2011). For example, an athletic teen girl who wears makeup and dates men will likely face less discrimination than an athletic teen girl who doesn't do either, all else being equal. And gender non-conformity (particularly for girls or women) is often more tolerated in children or older women.

In Chapter 3 we talked about the ways that oppression and privilege are two sides of the same coin. **Gender privilege** is the privilege that cisgender men experience given the U.S. patriarchal binary gender hierarchy. The examples of sexism in the paragraphs above all have parallels in privilege. For example, cisgender men have always had access to education, voting, and work based on their gender, although they may have been excluded from these opportunities because of other statuses (e.g., race, immigration, social class, ability, sexuality, or others). Cisgender men also have privileges that are about not experiencing oppression, such as not having to experience sexual harassment or fear rape; although men do have these experiences, they are much less common.

Like other statuses with multiple groups, the privileges that non-dominant groups experience are more difficult to definitively rank. Within gender subordinate groups (e.g., cis women, trans men or women, or non-binary people), there are relative, ascribed, or contextual privileges. For example, Chris is a trans person who was assigned male sex at birth and identifies as non-binary. Growing up, Chris experienced some of the privileges that are afforded to boys by sexism in our society: for example, Chris was often called on in school and wasn't expected to cook or babysit like their sister. But Chris also experienced a lot of teasing for being "girly" and "weak." As a young adult, Chris is perceived as male by many others and so may experience some cis male privileges, such as relative safety in walking alone at night. Simultaneously, Chris does not experience the very basic privilege of being perceived and treated in a way that matches their own identity and sense of self. If others assume that they are a cis male, they will often be treated in ways that inadvertently or actively (even aggressively) refuse to respect their gender identity, contributing to minority stress, anxiety, and depression. But let's complicate the idea of Chris's privilege even more: Chris may be safe at night only if they walk and dress and present as masculine. While this might be how Chris generally presents, if it is not, then they may be particularly targeted for assault or rape because they are perceived as a too feminine man or as trans (i.e., transmisogyny). Some people might think that Chris should just "act" more male, but what does this mean for Chris? First, think about how much effort it would take to change the way you walk, hold your arms, carry things, or other aspects that might be associated with gender. This would take a lot of constant thought and effort. And second, this expectation is basically saying that Chris is not okay as Chris: that they can only be safe walking at night if they act differently than who they are, which brings us back to expectations and prescriptions. Safety from assault or rape is a positive advantage (see Chapter 3)—it is a privilege that should be shared with all people, regardless of their gender.

Reflection Questions

Reflecting on group experiences:

- What are some examples of oppression that women experience? What are the related experiences of privilege that cis men experience?
- What are some examples of privilege that cis people (men or women) experience? The flip side of this question is: what are some examples of oppression that trans people experience?

In Chapter 3, we talked about the ways that oppression and privilege operate at individual (worldview and internal ideas), interpersonal, and institutional levels. How do your examples reflect these different levels?

Reflecting on personal experiences:

- What are your personal experiences of oppression or privilege in relation to gender?
- Have you had to deal with interpersonal or institutional discrimination related to your gender? If so, what has that been like for you? If not, what has that been like for you (and have you thought about this and about other privileges you have)? Have you had to take time and energy to develop strategies to cope with or resist these experiences of oppression and their negative effects?
- How have these experiences of oppression or of privilege affected how you think and feel about yourself? How do they affect how you approach developing relationships with others?

Although we still have a long way to go to dismantle gender oppression, we have made major progress towards greater equity. One example that we mentioned is the increasing recognition of trans experiences, reflected in our language and social practices (such as recognizing that pronouns signal something and should respect a person's identity) and related grassroots and legal resistance to trans marginalization and oppression (such as advocacy for access to bathrooms and sports participation).

Another area where we have made significant process is sexual assault and rape. In the early years of the United States, rape was seen as a property crime—a crime against the (assumedly cis) man to whom the (assumedly cis) woman "belonged." As women were recognized as people (and not property), these laws changed, but continued to allow rape within marriage, reflecting the idea that married women were justifiably under the control or domination of their husbands, who could abuse them as they wished. This began to change most dramatically in the 1970s, when the feminist movement advocated for changes in laws, for services and support for survivors, for changes in medical procedures for rape survivors, and for changes in the social discourse about gender and sexual assault. This continuing advocacy resulted in the passing of the federal Violence Against Women Act (1994), and the related creation of the federal Rape Prevention and Education program. Rates of rape have decreased more than 50% since the early 1990s.

More recently, the #MeToo movement has aimed to empower sexual assault survivors and break the silence that maintains cultural acceptance of rape. What began as a single social media post on Myspace by Tarana Burke has become an international movement promoting changes in social ideologies as well as laws and public policy. Many of the support, advocacy, and resistance initiatives have involved or been led by survivors of sexual assault, reflecting personal resistance and resilience. Although there is much work that remains, we are seeing the positive effects of greater education about sexual assault and changing social discourse about rape culture that aims to address the gendered expectations and socialization we discuss here. Reduction in sexual assault is one example of positive changes in gender ideologies, norms for interpersonal interactions and relationships, and institutional polices, practices, and laws. What are some others that you can think of? How does personal understanding of oppression and privilege contribute to such social changes? What else is needed?

Resources for Learning More about Sex, Gender, and Sexism

Fausto-Sterling, A. (2020). *Sexing the body: Gender politics and the construction of sexuality* (Revised edition). Basic Books.

Kirk, G., & Okazawa-Rey, M. (2020). *Gendered lives: Intersectional perspectives* (7th edition). Oxford University Press.

Serano, J. (2016). *Whipping girl: A transsexual woman on sexism and the scapegoating of femininity*. Seal Press.

The Everyday Sexism Project. (n.d.). The everyday sexism project. https://everyda ysexism.com/.

See also:

Bates, L. (2016). *Everyday sexism: The project that inspired a worldwide movement.* Macmillan.

Evans, M., Lorber, J., & Davis, K. (Eds.) (2012). *Handbook of gender and women's studies.* Sage.

Levitt, H. M. (2019). A psychosocial genealogy of LGBTQ+ gender: An empirically based theory of gender and gender identity cultures. *Psychology of Women Quarterly,* 43 (3), 275–297. https://doi.org/10.1177/0361684319834641.

Shultz, J. W. (2015). *Trans/portraits: Voices from transgender communities.* Dartmouth College Press.

Also see the list of anthologies and readers in the Section Two Introduction. *These anthologies contain conceptual essays as well as personal narratives,* examples, stories, and poems.

7 Understanding Sexuality and Heterosexism

Many people think that sexuality is only about sexual orientation and believe that sexual orientation is defined by the gender of your sex partner in relation to your own gender. But sexual orientation is only one part of sexuality and sexual orientation is not just about who you have sex with. Some other common erroneous assumptions that we hold about sexuality and sexual orientation are:

- Sexuality and gender are the same thing or somehow inherently connected—for example, if you are a gay man, you are effeminate and if you are an effeminate man, you must be gay.
- Sexual orientation is binary—that you are either straight or lesbian/gay.
- Sexuality is consistent: how you feel, act, and identify line up with the label you use for your sexual orientation.
- Sexual orientation is a preference that can be changed *or* sexual orientation identity is static and never changes.

Unraveling these assumptions means considering the multiple aspects of sexuality, more complex relations between gender and sexuality (especially once we complicate gender as we did in Chapter 6), and how our personal experience of sexuality is shaped by the very fact that sexuality is a hierarchical system of power and privilege.

Defining Sexuality and Heterosexism

Sexuality includes sexual feelings, interests, needs, desires, values, and fantasies; sexual experiences, acts, and expressions; and sexual orientation.

Sexual orientation is a social construct historically based on one's own gender in relation to the gender of one's partners in romantic, sexual, or affectional intimate relationships. At its foundation, sexual orientation is understood to be a deeply rooted orientation of one's erotic feelings towards particular people. However, the current labels or identities that people are using to describe their sexual orientation are evolving to embrace a more fluid idea of gender. They recognize sexual attitudes, emotions, or

DOI: 10.4324/9780429059599-10

experiences that are not specifically about the gender of another person in relation to one's own gender. This evolution of understanding sexuality is challenging the historical idea that sexual orientation and sexuality more generally are defined by one's own binary gender in relation to another person's binary gender.

Heterosexism: the system of judgments, beliefs, actions, norms, and social/institutional practices that protect and privilege heterosexuality and heterosexual relationships, related to assuming or maintaining binary constructions of both gender and sexuality.

Some Possible Responses to the Material in This Chapter

Many people have strong beliefs about heterosexuality being the only "normal" and acceptable identity and behavior. These beliefs may be connected to or justified by religion, and often associated religious doctrine that the purpose of sexuality is procreation. There have been hundreds of books, videos, articles, and blogs that promote and refute these arguments, and a deep dive into the perspectives of various religions in relation to sexuality is beyond our scope here. But suffice it to say there really isn't any definitive social agreement, even within religions: people from various religions have used religious texts to argue for both "sides" (that only heterosexuality is acceptable, normal, or healthy/moral *and* that diverse sexualities are acceptable, normal, or healthy/moral). And there are Catholics and Protestants and Muslims and Jews who are sexual minorities, priests and ministers and imams and rabbis who are sexual minorities, and church and synagogues and mosque communities that are affirming of queer people. Here, we are presenting an exploration of sexuality that positions it within social science and scientific research and considerations of systemic power, privilege, and oppression. All that said, some of what we discuss below might be disquieting if it contradicts your religious beliefs.

This chapter might also be especially challenging if it connects with painful experiences you or someone you love has had to endure as a sexual minority person. At the same time, you might feel a deeper sense of understanding and acceptance of yourself and/or others based on the content. As we've mentioned before, your socialization influences how you'll respond to the material. So, please be mindful of your internal experiences if you suspect the material might be upsetting, and take a break when needed.

Exploring Meanings of Sexuality

Sexuality as Social Construct

Many people think about sexuality as only about sexual orientation label or identity. For example, I *am* straight, or I *am* gay. But **sexuality** includes a number of factors:

- Sexual attraction: Who do we feel physically attracted to? Who gives us that tingly feeling? Who do we lust after? Do we feel sexual attraction at all?
- Experiences and behavior: Who do we have sexual relations with? Who have we had sexual relations with in the past? What kinds of ways do we express our sexual desires?
- Sexual identity: How do we personally identify based on important and central aspects of sexuality. Which groups do we connect to or feel most like we belong to? Which cultures or subcultures do we participate in and seek out as part of that group belonging?
- Sexual orientation label: How do we label ourselves or connect to socially constructed categories related to sexuality (e.g., straight, gay, lesbian, bisexual, pansexual, asexual)?
- The multiple ways that sexual feelings can be internally experienced or externally expressed: What kinds of things evoke sexual arousal? In what kinds of actions and interactions do we want to express our arousal?
- Emotional attraction and affection: Who do we feel emotionally attracted to? With whom do we like to spend time, feel comfortable, share our secrets, open our doubts and fears? This relates to emotional intimacy, rather than physical sexuality (e.g., lust), although these aspects of intimacy are often related.

For most people, these different aspects align, in relation to the kind or category of people: that is, most people would answer the various questions similarly and with consistency. For example, a man might say he is sexually and emotionally attracted to men, has sexual relations with men, identifies as gay, and feels romantic affection and love for men. However, some people might have answers to the various questions that don't seem, from the outside, to "match." For example, research indicates that many men and women who identify as heterosexual or straight have stated they feel attraction to people of their own gender, and/or that they have had sexual experiences with people of their own gender (Savin-Williams, 2011). As another example, one of the coauthors once met a man in a gay bar who expressed sexual attraction for other men and had never had sex with anyone other than a man, but he identified as straight: his view was that he had simply not met the right woman yet.

These examples bring up the issue of possible internalized oppression: are these folks who identify as straight/heterosexual denying feelings or possible relationships because they are fearful of the stigma associated with being anything other than heterosexual? On the one hand, at the individual level, people should be able to identify in whatever way they feel best connects to their experience, so perhaps we ask ourselves "what does it matter if they are denying, they should be able to decide their own identity." But when we recognize that there is systemic hierarchy and oppression, our perceptions become more complicated, particularly because research has demonstrated that internalized heterosexism has negative psychological consequences (e.g., depression, anxiety) for those of us who are **sexual minorities** (Newcomb & Mustanski, 2010).

How Do I Say? Current umbrella terminology related to sexuality and sexual orientation aims to be inclusive, to move away from specifying categories that relate to specific genders of the people involved, to encompass a broader range of experiences that are not only about identity, to recognize sexual attitudes and emotions that are not specifically about the gender of another person, and to embrace a more fluid idea of gender.

Many people use "sexual minority" as an umbrella term, which the American Psychological Association (2021) defines as follows: "Sexual minority constitutes a group of individuals whose sexual and affectual orientation, romantic attraction, or sexual characteristics differ from that of heterosexuals." Minority here refers more to the minority experience in relation to power (Wirth, 1945), rather than a numerical minority. Also, some people prefer "person first" approaches that use these terms as descriptors rather than types of people (i.e., they would prefer "sexual minority people" rather than "sexual minorities." In this chapter, we also use the word "queer," which APA defines as "a formerly pejorative term for LGBT individuals. It has now been reclaimed and operates as an umbrella term for any non-heterosexual identity." Our experience is that younger folks often use "queer" and we use this word because we especially appreciate the ways that reclaiming words is part of empowerment and resisting oppression.

At an individual level, it is best to ask people about the language they use to describe their sexuality and what terms they experience as positive or okay. However, most queer folks experience "homosexual" as offensive, particularly as a noun. "Sexual preference" as a synonym or substitute for "sexual orientation" is also experienced as offensive or invalidating, as it implies a personal preference that could or should be changed, rather than an orientation or identity. These terms should be avoided if one is seeking to be respectful.

With this understanding, we might ask different kinds of questions, such as: how might these people experience sexuality or identify if there were no *social stigma* associated with being gay, lesbian, bisexual, or pansexual? Are people really able to decide their own identity if they are socialized within a society that oppresses people who are not heterosexual? Can we imagine a society where it really doesn't matter? What would such a society look like? What would need to change?

Considering these questions helps us see how we have a social construct of sexuality that is not just about identity, but is also about power, privilege, and oppression. Once again, let's try and examine what that looks like, and how it relates to stereotyping and other kinds of oppression.

Reflection Questions

- What are gay men like? When you think about the group "gay men," what do you envision? How do gay men act, think, or feel? How do they dress, or talk, or move? How are gay men similar to or different than straight men? Do you have an image of gay culture, or groups? What models or examples of gay men do you have (and where do these come from)? What are the stereotypes of gay men (remember, we are asking you to consider the stereotypes that you know about, regardless of whether or not you believe these stereotypes)?
- What are lesbian women like? When you think about the group "lesbians," what do you envision? How do lesbian women act, think, or feel? How do they dress, or talk, or move? How are lesbian women similar to or different than straight women? Do you have an image of lesbian culture, or groups? What models or examples of lesbian women do you have (and where do these come from)? What are the stereotypes of lesbian women (remember, we are asking you to consider the stereotypes that you know about, not that you believe these stereotypes)?
- What are straight men like? Straight women? When you think about these groups what do you envision? How do people in these groups act, think, or feel? How do they dress, or talk, or move? How are straight men or women similar to or different than gay men or lesbians? Do you have an image of heterosexual culture, or groups? What models or examples of straight people do you have (and where do these come from)?
- Consider the questions above in relation to other sexuality identities, such as bisexual or pansexual or asexual.
- Do you think that most gay men and lesbian women are like the ideas or models that came to mind?
- Do you think that most bisexual or pansexual people are like those models?
- Do you think that most straight people are like those models?

As with the other social constructs we have explored, we do have socially constructed ideas about people within sexuality categories (Cox et al., 2016; Rice et al., 2021; Zivony & Lobel, 2014). These ideas are shaped by our socialization both directly—such as things we are told about how gay people are, or images of lesbian women we see in books, television, movies—and indirectly—such as the kinds of images we *don't* see of gay or lesbian or bisexual people, or in social interactions such as when a woman is asked whether she is married and when she says "yes," it is assumed that her spouse is a male. Our social constructions of sexual minority people are usually much narrower than our ideas about the dominant group of heterosexual people. For example, in television and movies, we see dozens and dozens of heterosexual people, of all races and genders, of multiple occupations and types of families, of various ages and in various places. So our internal idea or model of straight people is more like the actual experiences of straight people: varied and heterogeneous and intersectional.

One aspect of this narrowness relates to the connection of gender and sexuality. You might notice that the questions above about sexuality categories are placed in intersection with gender (e.g, gay men and lesbian women separately). One reason for this is because these categories, sexuality and gender, are strongly intersectional: being queer means something different for men than for women and there are ways that the stereotypes about gay men, for example, relate to gendered stereotypes and constructs in different ways than for lesbian women (Worthen, 2013). These socially constructed meanings relate to the gender binary that we talked about in Chapter 6, and to the idea of binary sexual orientation that we talk about later in this chapter. The strong intersectional assumption of gender and sexuality also relates to the ways in which we often think about sexuality specifically in terms of sexual orientation which is traditionally defined in relation to the genders of people in romantic, sexual, or affectional intimate relationships. We say that it relates to the genders of people in relationship because it relates not only to the gender that you are attracted to but also to your own gender (we will talk more about this below).

Although highly interacting, sometimes people erroneously perceive sexuality and gender as the same thing. However, sexuality relates to gender only because traditional categories of sexual orientation reference the genders of the people who are participating in a relationship. So, for example, if a cis man and a cis woman are in a relationship, it is assumed that they are both straight in sexual orientation; when a man and a man are in a relationship, it is assumed that they both identify as gay; and when a woman and woman are in a relationship, it is assumed that they both identify as lesbian. This seems pretty straightforward, but it only enables us to talk about sexuality relative to specific relationships between two people. And only if each of the two people in the relationship consistently identifies within the binary categories as a man or a woman. But people may identify differently than their current relationship (as in our example above of the man who is having sexual relations with another man but identifies as heterosexual). People may also identify their sexuality in ways that don't ascribe to binary gender. Over time, we have developed language to describe these more complex identities or patterns of relationships or attraction: for example, if someone is attracted to both men and women, they might identify as bisexual. If someone is attracted to people regardless of gender (e.g., they are attracted to men, women, trans, queer, non-binary, etc.), then they might identify as pansexual. If someone experiences little sexual attraction, then they may identify as asexual (note that this is about feelings of sexual attraction, and not about emotional attraction or desire for intimate romantic relationships).

How Do I Say? Bisexual, pansexual, and asexual are only three of the many terms that people currently use to describe their sexual identities or sexual orientation. There are increasing number of established and emerging terms developing as people describe their lived experiences more fully outside an assumption of binary gender and sexuality (e.g., demisexual, graysexual, or plurisexual). Here are a couple of resources that address different terminology (but note that terminology is also changing and that people may differ in their feelings about what is respectful or accurate): https://www.juliaserano.com/terminology.html# sexuality; https://www.healthline.com/health/different-types-of-sexua lity#d-l.

Sexuality is separate from gender, although our stereotypes often confuse and connect the two (American Psychological Association, 2021).Consider the associations you reflected on before. Did you identify assumptions that conflated sexuality with gender? An example of this conflation is the assumption that a gay man will be effeminate or that a lesbian woman will be masculine or "butch." But not all gay men are effeminate and not all effeminate men are gay. A cis woman in a lesbian relationship can be very effeminate or very masculine or may vary or combine masculine or feminine in myriad different ways at different times. They could also be transgender. Let's explore how that might work. Jessie is a transgender woman whose sex was assigned male at birth and who identified as a boy until their late teens although he was not comfortable as a boy. In his late teens, Jessie began to explore and accept his feelings about his gender and started identifying as trans. A few years later, Jessie affirmed her identity as a woman. Jessie was in a relationship with Mary starting in high school. While Jessie identified as male, people thought of Jessie and Mary as in a heterosexual relationship. Once Jessie affirmed their identity as a woman, people thought of Jessie and Mary as in a lesbian relationship. One thing to notice is how the confusion that arises about Jessie and Mary really comes from our need to categorize them in terms of their gender and the genders within their relationship. Jessie's internal experience may be that they were always attracted to women, so that their sexual orientation towards women never changed. Jessie and Mary, for example, might reject all of this binary and both identify themselves as pansexual, or queer, or they may reject the terminology completely.

It's Complicated: Why is trans included in LGBT if gender and sexuality are different things? Although sexuality and gender identity are distinct, sexism, patriarchy, and rigid gender roles/expectations work intersectionally in the oppression of all queer people. LGB and trans oppression and resistance also have overlapping histories. At the same time, there is tension about the inclusion of trans folks within LGB people and movements. This is yet another reason to move away from listing identities in an umbrella term, and shifting the focus to meanings of sexuality which relate to but are not synonymous with gender.

Sexual Identity

Sexual identity relates to how people make meaning of central and important aspects of their sexuality. Sexual orientation identity, or sexual orientation labeling, is often part of the development of sexual identity and relates to how individuals place themselves in relation to the social construct and categories that are available to them (Savin-Williams, 2011). Sexual identity is a good example of how social constructs and categories change over time and are intersectional. For example, the language of "pansexual," or "asexual" was not readily available until the current millennium. But our understanding of gender and gender identities changed and challenged binary constructions and the traditional categories of sexual orientation, so our language and ideas about sexual identity also started to shift—for example, to consider sexual relationships with trans or non-binary people. Furthermore, as our understanding of sexuality becomes more complicated, our understanding of sexual identity is also becoming more complicated, with consideration of how sexual identity might be an ongoing exploration of the various aspects of sexuality, not only a process of positioning ourselves in relation to traditional sexual orientation categories (Savin-Williams, 2011). As we noted, new identity language and categories have emerged and have been shared within the culture of sexual minority people and, eventually, in more mainstream conversations and discussions.

Like other identities related to structures of social inequity, people who are in the dominant category of sexual orientation are often less aware of the experiences that shape their self-concept and worldview compared to those who are not. Many heterosexual people, for example, simply take their sexuality for granted and don't feel a need to figure out what it means to be heterosexual, try to develop or maintain a positive self-concept around their sexuality, or worry about what others will think of them if or when they reveal their sexual identity. Sexual minority individuals, on the other hand, must constantly grapple with these issues. This is why many models of sexual minority identity development include a focus on the process of self-acceptance and social coming out (e.g., see overview in Dillon et al., 2011).

The emphasis on coming out relates to the ways that negotiating a sexual minority identity often differs from negotiating other minority identities because, unlike race or gender or some disabilities, sexuality is not visible (D'Augelli, 1994). And unlike ethnicity or social class, sexual minority individuals often don't grow up with others who share their identity. So their identities are not necessarily affirmed within their families, and they are usually not enculturated into sexual minority communities through their early family relationships.

Because non-heterosexual sexuality is still stigmatized and oppressed, identity models address working through feelings and experiences of internalized, interpersonal, and institutional heterosexism (Dillon et al., 2011). Sexual identity models also consider how individuals develop supportive relationships and communities and become enculturated and affiliated with sexual minority culture(s). Like other kinds of cultures, sexual minority cultures have their own norms, values, behaviors, rituals, and even language (Gerstner, 2006).

Sexual identity often changes over time, particularly in terms of sexual orientation identity or self-classification. This change can be the case with people who experience themselves as straight, but seems to be particularly true for sexual minorities. This change also emphasizes the differentiation of sexual orientation as "a deeply rooted predisposition toward erotic or sexual fantasies, thoughts, affiliations, affection, or bonding with members of one's sex, the other sex, both sexes, or, perhaps, neither sex (asexuality)" (Savin-Williams, 2011), and sexual orientation as label or identity in relation to the socially constructed categories. Further, it encourages us to consider how our sexual identity may be related to our current developmental, social, and relationship contexts.

Reflection Questions

- How do you understand or experience your sexuality? How would/ do you identify in relation to sexuality? What contributes to your identifying in this way?
- How much have you thought about your sexual and romantic experiences, thoughts and feelings, behaviors, or relationships? Thinking about it now, what kinds of experiences do you associate with being of your sexuality, personally? Do you "fit" into the traditional sexual orientation labels?
- How do your personal experiences and meanings of sexuality and your sexual identity relate to or challenge the social constructions and stereotypes associated with the category you identify with?
- How has your sexuality affected your overall view of yourself? How has your sexuality affected your social experience in the world (e.g., how others treat you or your interactions with others)?
- How does your sexuality interact with your race, and ethnicity? With your statuses in other social hierarchies of privilege and oppression? In a personal way? In relationships with others who are

like or unlike you in relation to status in social class, race, ethnicity, other social hierarchies?
- After reflecting on and exploring your own sexuality and sexual identity, take a few moments to reflect on how your experience would be different if you were a different sexual orientation.

Exploring Heterosexism

Heterosexism is the system of judgments, beliefs, actions, norms, and social/institutional practices that protect and privilege heterosexuality and heterosexual relationships. Heterosexism results in oppression for sexual minority people at the individual, interpersonal, and institutional levels. Some examples include assumptions that sexual minorities are inherently psychologically disturbed, experiences of bullying or name calling, discrimination in housing and employment, intimidation and threats of violence, and high rates of assault and sexual assault (American Psychological Association, 2021). These experiences result in physical harm and death, blocked opportunities, and psychological damage including depression, anxiety, and suicidality. The Nazis' persecution of sexual minority people during the 1930s and 1940s is one of the most extreme examples of oppression against sexual minority people. However sexual minority people have continued to experience violent and extreme oppression in more recent years, such as the murders of 49 people at the Pulse nightclub in Orlando, FL in 2016. Another example is the murder of Matthew Shepherd in 1998, which, with the racially motivated murder of James Byrd, Jr., resulted in changes in federal hate crime legislation (Matthew Shepard and James Byrd, Jr., Hate Crimes Prevention Act of 2009). Despite such changes in legislation, data from 2019 indicate that hate crimes against sexual minority people increased, rather than decreased, as compared to prior years (Hauck, 2019).

How Do I Say? You might be thinking "isn't discrimination against sexual minorities called homophobia?" Homophobia technically means "fear of" or aversion to people who are "homosexual." Homophobia is a term that developed when our discourse about sexuality was binary, where homosexual referred to people who were exclusively attracted to people of their own gender; the meaning of homophobia expanded to address negative attitudes towards sexual minority people more generally, that is, any person who was not heterosexual (also known as queerphobia). Although the word "homophobia" centers on fear, the enactment of homophobia relates to the more active aversion to people who are not heterosexual, and the more active oppression enacted against or experienced by queer people. However, systemic oppression against sexual minorities is not only about fear or active aversion. It is also about the ways that heterosexuality is privileged and normalized and related ways that negative attitudes toward sexual minority people are internalized and enacted, even if that is unintentional (e.g., through implicit attitudes). Heterosexism is a term that captures that greater complexity.

Heterosexism is not only about explicit oppression against sexual minorities, but also encompasses the ways that heterosexuality and heterosexual relationships are taken as the norm while queer sexuality or relationships are marginalized or oppressed. Many people reject traditional homophobia while still participating in heterosexism. For example, Jason is a cis man who identifies as heterosexual. He has many friends that are gay or lesbian, believes in equal rights for marriage, and generally sees himself as gay-positive. However, when Jason met Thanh, who also identifies as a man, Jason asked Thanh whether he had a girlfriend, assuming that Thanh identified as heterosexual. Jason was also deeply uncomfortable when Thanh asked Jason whether he wanted to hook up, while Jason felt complimented when his friend Jennifer (who identifies as a cis woman) asked him the same thing, although he was not attracted to Jennifer, either. Jason's responses suggest that he is uncomfortable with even the *idea* that Thanh might be attracted to him. Why might that be so?

Heterosexism addresses not only the oppression related to sexuality that is experienced by sexual minority people, but also the privileges that are experienced by people who are heterosexual. **Heterosexual privilege** is the unearned benefits that straight, cisgender men and women experience from identifying as heterosexual and being in heterosexual relationships. Some examples include things like easily being able to buy Valentine's Day cards that reflect your relationship (and having lots of choices!), being able to kiss your partner in public without fear, being able to bring your partner to a work event without consideration of other's responses or expectations, or being able to easily and universally marry within your faith.

Reflection Questions

- What are some examples of oppression related to sexuality you have experienced or observed?
- What are some examples of heterosexual privilege you have experienced or observed?

Think here about things that happen as well as things that don't happen (e.g., not seeing many examples of relationships like yours in television and movies). Think also about ways of thinking and feeling. Consider how your examples reflect the ways that oppression and privilege operate at individual (worldview and internal ideas), interpersonal, and institutional levels (see Chapter 2).

- What kinds of social messages have you received about your own sexuality?
- Where have you gotten these messages from?
- Have these messages conveyed that your sexual identity is normal, healthy, and positive, or have they conveyed that your sexual identity is not positive?
- How have these messages made you feel about yourself?
- Have you had to deal with interpersonal or institutional discrimination about your sexuality?
- If so, what has that been like for you? Have you had to spend time and energy to develop strategies to deal with these experiences of oppression?
- If not, what has that been like for you (and have you thought about this and about other privileges you have)?
- How have these experiences of oppression or privilege affected how you think and feel about yourself? How do they affect how you approach developing relationships with others?

As with gender, social attitudes toward sexual minority people have changed substantially since the early 1970s when "homosexuality" was considered a psychiatric disorder by the American Psychiatric Association. These changes did not happen spontaneously, but were largely influenced by the advocacy and activism of sexual minority people and their allies and accomplices. Such advocacy dates back much farther than we might think: the first formal and documented gay rights organization in the United States was founded in 1924 by Henry Gerber, and the Stonewall Uprising in 1969 was a major catalyst for the gay rights movement, which continued to create changes in both social and legal attitudes in subsequent decades.

A significant area of change has been in attitudes and laws related to same sex marriage. Until 2015, marriage between two people of the same sex was not legally recognized in all states in the United States. For gay and lesbian couples this created legal barriers to a large number of institutionalized benefits that heterosexual couples took for granted, including financial benefits of filing taxes as a married couple, employment benefits of spousal coverage for health care, end of life, or health crisis benefits of being able to visit one's partner in the hospital or make health care decisions for one's partner, and parenting benefits of being recognized as the parent of one's child with related social implications.

From 2004 to 2019, attitudes towards same sex marriage essentially reversed: in 2004, 60% of people in the United States opposed same sex marriage while in 2019, 61% of people in the United States supported it

(Pew Research Center, 2019). In 2015, the U.S. Supreme Court ruled that same sex marriage must be legally recognized in all states. Similar to advocacy and activism against oppression in other social categories and statuses, sexual minority people themselves have led most of the resistance initiatives. However, also similar to other structures of social inequity, allies and accomplices supported the efforts resisting oppression at individual, interpersonal, and organizational levels (e.g., the organization PFLAG). The intersections of individual, interpersonal, and legal oppression or privilege are illustrated by one study which found that legalization of same sex marriage resulted in a significant decrease in adolescent suicide attempts, especially for sexual minority adolescents (Raifman et al., 2017). What are other changes you can think of? How have these changes affected you?

Resources for Learning More about Sexuality and Heterosexism

Baumann, J., & the New York Public Library (Eds.) (2019). *The Stonewall reader*. Penguin Books.

Fischer, Nancy L., & Seidman, S. (Eds.) (2016). *Introducing the new sexuality studies* (3rd edition). Routledge.

Hall, D. E., & Jagosie, A. (Eds.) (2013). *The Routledge queer studies reader*. Routledge.

Tolman, D. L., Diamond, L. M., Bauermeister, J. A., George, W. H., Pfaus, J. G., & Ward, L. M. (Eds.) (2014). *APA handbook of sexuality and psychology*. Vol. 1: *Person-based approaches*. American Psychological Association. https://doi.org/10.1037/14193-000.

Tolman, D. L., Diamond, L. M., Bauermeister, J. A., George, W. H., Pfaus, J. G., & Ward, L. M. (Eds.) (2014). *APA handbook of sexuality and psychology*. Vol. 2: *Contextual approaches*. American Psychological Association. https://doi.org/10.1037/14194-000.

Yarber, W., & Sayad, B. (2019). *Human sexuality: Diversity in contemporary society* (11th edition). McGraw-Hill.

Also see the list of anthologies and readers in the Section Two Introduction. *These anthologies contain conceptual essays as well as personal narratives*, examples, stories, and poems.

8   Understanding Disability and Ableism

For many people, what comes to mind from the word "disability" is an image of a person in a wheelchair or someone who is blind or deaf. That is, people tend to think about disability as physical and visible. Another common erroneous assumption about disability is that people with disabilities have limitations on what they can do that extend beyond their specific disability. For example, there are erroneous assumptions that people who are disabled are unable to work, are not (or should not be) sexual, or are inherently unhappy. Many of our assumptions about disability come from an idea that people with disabilities are inherently deficient, that is, they are "less than" what is "normal" or socially acceptable. Unraveling these flawed notions means broadening our understanding of the range and kinds of ability and disability and, most importantly, questioning our idea of "normality." This means considering whether the major challenges for disabled people lie in their own abilities, or in the ways in which we, as a society, view different abilities and the diverse ways that individuals may contribute to their own and others' growth.

Defining Disability and Ableism

Disability: Disability refers to difficulties in functioning experienced by an individual with a health condition in interaction with personal and environmental contextual factors. Areas of functioning may include impairments, activity limitations, and/or participation restrictions. Difficulties in functioning are therefore not inherently related to impairment, but may be contextual or environmental and involve limitations in one or more major life activities. Disability may be present from birth or acquired and may be visible or invisible.

Ableism: the system of judgments, beliefs, actions, norms, and social/institutional practices that protect and privilege nondisabled people and create barriers and oppression for disabled people.

It's Complicated: There is some variability (and debate) in the definitions of disability. Some of these differences relate to the purpose of the entity defining disability (e.g., research, health, legal policy purposes). For

DOI: 10.4324/9780429059599-11

example, the International Classification of Functioning, Disability and Health (ICF) definition, adopted by the World Health Organization (2011), defines disability in relation to health, emphasizing interactions of impairments, activity limitations, and participation restrictions, as we detail in this chapter. The United Nations (UN) and the Americans with Disabilities Act (ADA) focus on identifying the parameters of people with disabilities, so they can then address rights and protections. Across these organizations and definitions, disability is clearly recognized as an interaction between person and environment related to function and effect. We focused on capturing those emphases in the definition we provided above. There continues to be active discussion and refinement of the understanding of the meaning of disability, particularly as scholars and activists call attention to the ways that disability is more of a social construct, rather than a bodily experience. We encourage you to check out the meanings and descriptions of disability in various sources, such as:

- The World Health Organization and ICF: https://www.who.int/publications/i/item/9789241564182
- The Americans with Disabilities Act: https://www.ada.gov/ada_intro.htm
- The United Nations Convention on the Rights of Persons with Disabilities: https://www.un.org/development/desa/disabilities/convention-on-the-rights-of-persons-with-disabilities.html#Fulltext

Some Possible Responses to the Material in This Chapter

As with all the topics we have covered thus far, you likely have established ideas about what it means to be disabled and can point to, if prompted, the feelings or thoughts you typically have when you encounter people with disabilities that are visible to you, like a person in a wheelchair (we'll actually ask you to do just that in a bit). Your notions of and responses to disability might have been informed by previous classes you've taken or through personal exploration motivated by your own situational context (e.g., having loved ones with a disability or experiencing a disability yourself). Having previous knowledge about disability and ableism may make this chapter boring or redundant for you. Alternatively, you might feel seen or supported by the fact that disability is a part of this book, given its typical lack of inclusion in other social justice texts. Disability scholars with whom we've shared early drafts of this chapter have expressed similar feelings, with feedback such as, "I'm glad you're including disability, because it is so rarely discussed or included." But it really should be included more consistently, so that it is not remarkable when it is.

Our experience as teachers reflects the comment above in that students typically learn little about disability and ableism in the classroom. Moreover, those who see themselves as nondisabled are unlikely to have explored the subject on their own. And even those who experience disability or have been formally diagnosed or categorized as disabled may know little about the social construct of disability. We often interact with students in our classrooms who have experienced disability or have formal accommodations who have not been invited to consider what it means to have a disability, or who have internalized stigma about having a disability. So, if you have not learned or thought a lot about disability, you are not alone: we don't say this as an indictment if you're in this position, but to establish a starting point that can influence your possible responses to the material.

Specifically, those unfamiliar with the subject can experience surprise or discomfort at the idea that disability is on a continuum(s), especially if that leads to considering one's own location on these continuums in new ways (e.g., reevaluating how you might fit on the psychological disability continuum if you have been diagnosed with major depression or on the cognitive and learning disability continuum if you have been diagnosed with ADHD). Disbelief that some people with disabilities may not want to be "cured" and fear or anxiety that disability can be a transitory state may also come up as you read. Alongside these difficult emotions can be other emotions like relief or excitement at seeing disability discussed as interactions with the environment, versus as a "deficit" and/or an individual or personal shortcoming that must be overcome.

We invite you to meet whatever comes up for you as you engage this chapter with compassion and curiosity. We know you might be sick of us saying that, but it's so important to your learning that it is worth repeating over and over. Remember: unacknowledged responses have the power to derail your learning, to shut you down from the possibility of gaining a different point of view or of an *aha* moment that contributes to your growth and better alignment between your values and your actions. And we certainly don't want that for you.

Exploring Meanings of Disability

Disability as Social Construct

Reflection Questions

- When you hear the word "disability," what comes to mind? Before reading this book, how would you have defined "disability"?
- What is your image of a person with a disability? In your image, what kinds of things do you see them doing? Just as importantly, what kinds of things do you *not* see them doing?
- Think about media that you have been exposed to (films, television, pictures). Are there disabled people in these media? If so, what is the image that you see? What kinds of disabilities are portrayed? How is the disabled person portrayed?

Let's start with considering the many different kinds of abilities and disabilities. For example:

- **Cognitive and learning abilities** relate to how we think, learn, and process information, such as our abilities in reading, writing, attention, doing math, speaking, understanding what people are saying, and memory. Disabilities in this area include dyslexia, attention deficit, traumatic brain injury, and dementia.
- **Psychological and emotional abilities** relate to how we experience and manage emotions and thoughts, how we perceive the world including other people and ourselves, and how we act in relation to our thinking, feelings, and perceptions. Disabilities in this area include depression, anxiety, and schizophrenia.
- **Physical and sensory abilities** relate to what our bodies can do and how they function. This includes physical senses such as hearing, seeing, and tasting, as well as physical capacities such as sitting, standing, walking, running, or jumping. Disabilities in this area include being blind or deaf, chronic pain, sleep disorders, paralysis, epilepsy, or multiple sclerosis.

Many people expect disabilities to be visible. But clearly, many of the types and experiences in the list above are not visible. Note also that these areas are not clearly distinct or distinguishable. All three of these areas affect and interact with the others. And many diagnoses associated with disabilities (e.g., Down syndrome or autism or depression) affect experiences in multiple areas. These areas are also much more complex than the short sentences above reflect. For example, physical abilities include things we often don't think about such as sleeping or picking up a coin or bodily processing of different kinds of foods. Our purpose in naming these three areas is not to create additional restricting categories, but instead to encourage you to think broadly about the strengths and challenges people have in a wide range of areas.

What defines a **disability** within a range of abilities, strengths, and challenges is the effect it has on activities and lived experience, not the existence of a health condition, impairment, or related experience (Leonardi et al., 2006). Many people experience anxiety, for example, but not everyone who experiences anxiety would consider themself (or be considered by others) to be disabled. Another example is eyesight: many people have a vision impairment, but at what point is the vision impairment considered a disability? Two people may have the same level of ability, but one may experience a significant effect on life activities, while the other does not. This example highlights the ways in which the definition of disability we provide above emphasizes that what is functional depends on the context in which one lives, which is why meanings of disability emphasize interactions of health conditions, impairment, activity limitations, and participation restrictions. The environment in which you live has the biggest effects on the latter two.

Health conditions and related disability can be present from birth or be acquired. They can be related to genetic or biological factors (e.g., diabetes or depression) or to other kinds of developmental or life experiences (e.g., accidents, physical abuse, lead exposure, or vitamin deficiency). The ICF and the WHO distinguish between health conditions (e.g., diseases, disorders, or injuries) and disability, which helps us to understand how disability is related to context, functioning, and effect on living (World Health Organization, 2011). The ICF understands disability as interactions between health conditions and personal and environmental context, resulting in difficulties experienced in any of the following three areas of human functioning:

- **Impairments** relate to difficulty or alterations in the functioning or structure of the body (including the mind), and related experiences—for example, paralysis; sensory limitations or exacerbations (hyperesthesia) in hearing, sight, taste, or touch; anxiety; or facial disfigurement. We often think about impairments as inherently disabling, but this is not the case because often the disability *effect* or limitation comes from activity and participation limitations. For example, someone with facial disfigurement is not inherently limited in activities. Impairments can sometimes be addressed by medical intervention. Even when this is possible, if the effect on life activities comes more from activity or participation restrictions, then this may or may not be the best or chosen kind of intervention. For example, if the effect on life activities is due to a lack of universal access, then the best intervention is related to addressing the activity or participation restrictions caused by lack of access, especially if medical intervention has associated risks or drawbacks (such as loss of social connection or community).
- **Activity limitations** relate to difficulties in executing activities—for example, grasping objects, reading a text, or being in particular social settings (e.g., large crowds) or high places (e.g., working in a high rise). These limitations can often be addressed through assistive devices or personal assistance and/or through accommodations when they interact with participation restrictions.
- **Participation restrictions** are challenges to involvement in any area of life. These are not about impairments in the body or limitations in activity or ability but more about the ways that our social interactions, norms, and physical and social structures are designed. For example, stigma attached to disabilities, buildings without ramps, and webinars without captioning cause restrictions in social and employment participation. These limitations can be addressed through changing our social attitudes and through universal design (more on this below).

Disability relates to interactions among these three areas and not inherently to having a health condition.

Not everyone agrees on what is classified as a disability, because people experience different contexts which create different experiences of impairment, activity limitations, and participation restrictions and, therefore, different effects on life activities. People may also disagree about how much impairment, limitation, or restriction constitutes a disability, and we often make erroneous assumptions about people. If a person works hard and creatively to lessen or manage the impact of impairment, limitations, or restrictions, is that still a disability? What if that effort takes up a lot of time and energy (which itself has an impact on one's life)? People may also disagree about whether a disability can be relatively short-term and transient such as a broken leg or short-term memory impairment from a concussion. Some might see this as a disability, while others may not. Many people also experience disabilities related to aging—should we therefore see being **nondisabled** as a temporary status, especially as life expectancies increase? These questions relate to how we understand the categories "nondisabled" and "disabled" and whether we think about these categories as absolute and, if so, what is the basis of the absolute distinction. Perhaps being disabled or nondisabled is a more permeable or changeable experience than we would like to think. By considering these variations, we are encouraged to more deeply question our assumptions.

How Do I Say? Nondisabled" is the current respectful term. The term "able bodied" is sometimes used in an attempt to be inclusive and acknowledge the impact of ableism. This language, however, is problematic because it implies that disabilities are physical or visible in the body. Disabled people may be able bodied but have impairments such as learning disabilities, traumatic brain injury, or depression. Others find the "abled" aspect of the term objectionable because it suggests that people with disabilities are not able to use their bodies well. People with bodily impairment may or may not experience disability, and even if they experience disability, they may experience their body as having multiple abilities.

As we have noted elsewhere, preferred language changes and what was once seen as respectful (e.g., "differently abled") may now be experienced by some people as disrespectful, because it can be experienced as ignoring the actual existence or experience of disability. There may also be generational, regional, or personal differences.

What makes ability a social construct related to power and privilege, rather than just a kind of difference or even a kind of deficit? The answer to this question, and the complexity of understanding disability, becomes clearer when we question both the meaning of impairment and the reasons why differences in ability become an impairment. Conceptual models of disability include older models of disability as moral or medical problems of deficit that should be rehabilitated, the social model of disability as an issue of social barriers, and the minority model which understands disability as an aspect of diversity related to culture, privilege, and oppression (Dunn & Andrews, 2015).

One way to think about disability is that it is an unfortunate personal deficit. The **deficit approach** views a person experiencing disability as lacking something (mobility, vision, a particular kind of emotional stability) that one "should" be able to do, that "everyone" would "naturally" want to be able to do, or that is needed for functioning successfully.

How Do I Say? There are different views on whether language should center (or not) the experience and identity of disability. That is, should we be "people first" and say "People/person with disability" or "identity first" and say "disabled person." On one side, centering the experience can "reduce" a person to a single aspect of their personhood. On the other side, centering the experience recognizes and affirms that the experience shapes identity as well as access and life outcomes due to structural inequities. The latter perspective is akin to other identities (i.e., Black people or sexual minority people).

The little research that addresses preferred language shows mixed results (see review in Dunn & Andrews, 2015). For example, one study with blind and visually impaired people indicated that most of those who expressed a preference, preferred identity-first language—blind person, rather than person with blindness. The National Federation of the Blind has endorsed this identity-first language. Other studies, however, have found preferences for "person with disability." Results may differ depending on type of disability, age, personal and political identity development, and, of course, by personal preference, although many people do prefer identity-first.

It is always best to ask individuals what they prefer. We also invite you to consider: why are you using one kind of language over another? Is the specific language you are using reductionistic in context?

In this chapter, we use both, and also use "experiencing disability" to emphasize how disability is not necessarily a static or absolute experience.

The disability is seen as something an individual needs to overcome and cope with in order to adapt and succeed; for example, by developing strategies to focus attention to address ADHD or by learning explicit cues to perceive other's emotions to address autism spectrum disorders. It is assumed that any intervention that would "fix" the disability would be welcomed, such as surgery to address deafness or medication to address anxiety. If we hold this deficit view of disability, we might feel sorry for the person with a disability, assume they are suffering and unhappy because they have a disability, and/or evaluate this person in relation to how hard they have tried to over-come the disability or to change the basis of their ability through intervention. This perspective views the disability or the person with the disability as a "problem" to be overcome, with the goal being for people with disabilities to assimilate into the dominant society. These ways of thinking reflect the moral, biomedical, and rehabilitation models of disability, which were dominant and relatively unquestioned until the 1970s. Today they are criticized for stigma-tizing disability, blaming people with disabilities, and maintaining a very narrow view of what is "normal," acceptable, or functional.

In contrast, the **social and diversity models of disability** emphasize the social and environmental context, as well as the issues of power, privilege, and oppression that are the focus of this book. This view starts with the idea that all people have differences in their experiences and "abilities." Most of us can't jump as high as Michael Jordan or think the way that Stephen Hawking could. But we don't usually see our own lack of ability in these areas as "deficits" or "disabilities." So, at what point is a *comparative* "deficit" or lesser ability a *dis*ability rather than simply differences on a continuum of ability? And what makes it so? Furthermore, what makes us value jumping high or thinking in particular ways over other experiences with jumping, thinking, or maybe other experiences period? We might be quite happy with how high we jump, or we might not care about jumping at all and prefer to focus on painting or cooking or simply being.

This social and diversity perspective about disability questions what we mean by "ability" and why we value certain experiences and abilities within our society. It asks *why* and *how* are differences creating functional impair-ment, limitations, or restrictions? The social model of disability emphasizes the match, or fit, between the individual and the social and environmental context. In this model, the functional difficulties that people with disabilities experience are seen as primarily due to the fact that the physical and social environment in which people live is structured to privilege some people on the ability continuums and to disadvantage others. Thus, the primary pro-blem for people with disabilities is the ways our society is structured to sup-port and value only a narrow range of experiences within continuums of experience. For example, consider how sidewalks made of cobblestones or buildings that require stairs privilege people who can walk; how reading material in classes is still often not easily available in forms that are accessible for those with vision impairments; how workplaces are unwilling to accom-modate a flexible schedule that could enable someone with depression to contribute their skills; or how people with a cognitive disability leading to the use of notes for a presentation might be judged as unprofessional, less knowledgeable, or "amateur." The social and diversity models of disability also focus on the ways that social attitudes about abilities create and maintain stigma and negative stereotypes so that functional difficulties are also related to the oppression that people with disabilities experience. This view of dis-ability challenges us (all members of our society) to change our attitudes and environment so that we stop excluding and oppressing people who don't fit within that narrow range.

Rejecting the deficiency model and embracing a social and diversity model of disability doesn't necessarily mean rejecting interventions to address the effects or the existence of the impairment. Although some people advocate for personal and societal acceptance of disability and rejection of interventions (e.g., some Deaf communities' rejection of cochlear implants), others strongly advocate for rejecting the deficiency model and its associated marginalization and oppression (including internalized oppression) while also respecting an individual's choices about how they want to address the health condition, impairment, limitations, or restrictions that relate to disability. Individuals may also experience some disabilities, such as major depression, as inherently distressing regardless of the environmental limitations or restrictions. In these cases, the individuals may welcome interventions to address the issue. But even in these cases, the extent of the disability and related distress is usually greatly exacerbated by social and environmental norms and structures. In the case of depression, for example, stigma and judgmental attitudes about depression as related to a lack of motivation or will power, social expectations about how people should present or relate to others, and rigid workplace and school policies around attendance, combine with a basic lack of knowledge and understanding to not only increase the limitations and restrictions for people experiencing depression, but also exacerbate the depression and increase the actual impairment (Fox et al., 2016).

Disability Identity

Disability identity can relate to personal and social identity processes or to the development of a political identity (Dirth & Branscombe, 2018). Not everyone who experiences impairment will identify as disabled. Some people may not want to accept they have a disability or see themselves as experiencing impairment, limitations, or restrictions, even if these significantly affect their daily living. Others may accept they have a disability but may see this as an experience or an aspect of their lives, rather than an identity: they may feel the disability is not central to their own self-concept. Others may have a personal identity as disabled, but may not see this as a social identity that connects them to a group experience or a shared cultural experience. Still others may have a strong social identity as disabled, including a sense of a shared experience with others who experience similar or different disabilities and/or a sense that the disability offers important and defining experiential opportunities. They may seek out or create communities with shared cultural values, norms, and behaviors including ways of interacting, in-group humor and jokes, and community building events and celebratory days (e.g., International Wheelchair Day or events celebrating the anniversary of the ADA).

Models of developing disability identity share many aspects with identity models for other social hierarchies such as phases or stages of self-acceptance, developing community, identifying and rooting out internalized oppressive attitudes towards disabled people, and developing empowerment, pride, and strategies for addressing discrimination (Forber-Pratt et al., 2017). Developing disability identity in these models relates to rejecting the imposition of meaning from a biomedical model of disability and self-determination of the meaning and personal experience of disability (Dirth & Branscombe, 2018; Forber-Pratt et al., 2017). On a social level, the disability community fosters empowerment, advocating that the meaning of disability should be shaped and informed *by* people with disabilities, rather than *for* people with disabilities.

Experiences of disability and disability identity are intersectional. The image that most people have of a person who is disabled is usually of a White person, but disabilities affect people of all races and ethnicities. An example is police shootings. While recent (2020) reports make it clear that Black people are at greater risk of being shot and killed by police, the fact that 25% of people killed by police are individuals who experience psychological or psychiatric conditions is less well known (Fuller et al., 2015; Schwartz & Jahn, 2020). The intersection of being Black and experiencing psychological disability creates an increased risk that changes this experience of disability and how one copes with or negotiates the activity limitations and restrictions. The impacts of disability and related oppression are particularly affected by social class and resource access, particularly in societies such as the United States where health care is not universal and access to personal assistance and technology relates to being able to personally pay for needed support and having the resources to negotiate complex systems of public care.

Reflection Questions

- Consider your own abilities in various domains. And consider possible health conditions you might have experienced in the past or currently. What can you do easily and what is more difficult for you? Do you experience yourself as disabled or nondisabled in various areas?
- How has this affected your daily life, your relationships, and your activities?
- What kinds of experiences do you associate with being disabled or nondisabled in various domains, personally?
- How does your status as disabled or nondisabled interact with your race and ethnicity? With other statuses of privilege and oppression? In a personal way? In relationships with others who are like or unlike you in relation to social class, race, ethnicity, other statuses?

Exploring Ableism

Ableism: the system of judgments, beliefs, actions, norms, and social/institutional practices that protect and privilege nondisabled people and create barriers and oppression for disabled people.

Ableism creates and maintains the marginalization and oppression of people with disabilities through environmental and institutional practices, as well as through social attitudes. Direct and explicit institutional discrimination has been greatly reduced by the passage of the Americans with Disabilities Act (ADA), which prohibits discrimination based on disability. Importantly, the ADA requires employers to offer reasonable accommodations to enable individuals with disabilities to participate in work, and requires public spaces to be accessible; both of these requirements have significantly decreased participation restrictions. Reasonable accommodations are changes in the work environment or structure that would enable a person with a disability to perform the job, such as providing reserved parking, allowing more frequent rest periods or a flexible work schedule, providing information in formats that are most accessible to the worker (e.g., instructions that are in Braille and instructions that are written rather than verbal). Accessibility requirements include things such as wheelchair accessible transportation and bathrooms, and allowing service animals. Accommodations and accessibility requirements are particularly important because they emphasize how "equal" is not necessarily "equitable."

Historically, people with disabilities have experienced extreme oppression, including widespread and government sanctioned involuntary institutionalization (imprisonment without cause), forced sterilization, and murder by poison by the Nazi regime. Although there are now legal protections for people with disabilities, including the ADA, both involuntary institutionalization and forced sterilization of people with disabilities continue in individual cases (American Baby and Child Law Centers, 2018). Furthermore, although these extremes of violence and dehumanization are no longer socially sanctioned, people with disabilities continue to experience a wide range of **disability oppression**. We discussed above some of the stereotypes imposed on people with disabilities, which highlight how the difficulties encountered by people with disabilities are related not only to what people with disabilities can and can't do (limitations in activities) but perhaps even more so to what those of us without disabilities *think* or assume people with disabilities can and can't do. This assumption contributes to marginalization, powerlessness, and the imposition of cultural imperialism. Furthermore, compared to people without disabilities, those with disabilities experience more direct hostile oppression in the form of physical and psychological violence, including assault, slurs, bullying, avoidance, infantilization, segregation and confinement, and expressions of disgust.

In addition to the examples of stereotyping and more hostile discrimination and prejudice described above, ableism can be intended as benevolent

(Nario-Redmond, Kemerling, & Silverman, 2019). People with disabilities describe experiences of others seeing them as pitiful, incapable, and in need of constant help, or idealizing their struggles, seeing them as heroic for engaging in daily living activities, and praising them as one would a young child. Similar to benevolent sexism, these views are rooted in a view of people with disabilities as less capable, focusing on deficiencies and limitations. Furthermore, having assumptions made about your experiences, your emotions, your motivations, or your abilities takes away your own agency and choice.

Probably the biggest aspect of **ability privilege** experienced by those without disabilities is the assumption and experience of normality. Can we imagine a society where being in a wheelchair doesn't create a major barrier to getting around? What kinds of changes would be needed? As a thought exercise to understand privilege, imagine a building that actively *privileges* people in wheelchairs: a first thought might be that it wouldn't have steps, doorways would be wider, doors would automatically open, and so forth. These are the changes that would address the barriers that currently exist. But did you consider what a building that didn't *also* privilege people who stand and walk might look like? For example, it might also have much lower ceilings: why waste all that living space by having such high ceilings? People who stand would be at a disadvantage because they would always have to scrunch down. We are not advocating for creating inequity for those who are able to stand or who have other abilities, but we do think it is important to actively recognize the many privileges we take for granted. Although those of us who stand *could* scrunch down all the time, we would not think this is really equitable or creates a just environment. The awkwardness and discomfort would be a barrier to our participation and contributions. Similarly, fully addressing ableism can't mean only "special" treatment such as offering to carry a wheelchair up the stairs of a restaurant: it needs to mean equitable and universal access that breaks down distinctions and stigma.

At the individual level, ability privilege can be seen in the many things that people without disabilities *don't* have to think about and the things that nondisabled people do that convey assumptions that the nondisabled way of being in the world is the only and "right" way. A major example of this is resistance to efforts toward universal design and access, such as feeling that having a sign language interpreter at a play is distracting, wanting to maintain cobblestones because they are quaint and "traditional," believing that students with learning disabilities will impede learning progress for other students in classrooms, or beliefs that counseling services in schools are "extras" that can be cut in tight budget times. Nondisabled people rarely think about how these stances reflect ability privilege. For many nondisabled people, the marginalization of people with disabilities is so normative and acceptable that we experience discomfort just by having disabled people around. It is difficult to imagine a different kind of world, where we would regularly see and interact with people with a wide range of abilities and experiences.

Reflection Questions

In considering the questions below, think about things that happen as well as things that don't happen (e.g., not being asked about your sexual partners when you go in for an annual physical). Think also about ways of thinking and feeling.

- What are some examples of oppression related to disability (condition + impairment, activity limitations, or participation restrictions) you have experienced or observed?
- What are some examples of privilege you have experienced or observed related to being nondisabled?
- What kinds of social messages have you received about your own abilities or disabilities? Where have you gotten these messages from? Have these messages conveyed that you are normal, healthy, and positive, or have they conveyed that you are not, because you are disabled? How have these messages made you feel about yourself?
- Have you had to deal with interpersonal or institutional discrimination related to disability? If so, what has that been like for you? Have you had to take time and energy to develop strategies to deal with these experiences of oppression? If not, what has that been like for you (and have you thought about this and about other privileges you have)?
- How have these experiences of oppression or privilege affected how you think and feel about yourself? How do they affect how you approach developing relationships with others?

In Chapter 2, we talked about the ways that oppression and privilege operate at individual (worldview and internal ideas), interpersonal, and institutional levels. How do your examples reflect these different levels?

The Americans with Disabilities Act (ADA) is an example of successful advocacy for legal reform. As in our discussion of advocacy and social change in other chapters, earlier organizations by and for people with disabilities contributed to support, community, identity, and advocacy to pave the way for the ADA, such as the Center for Independent Living, the Disability Rights Education and Defense Fund (DREDF), and ADAPT (Carmel, 2020). Although the ADA has contributed to substantial progress, equitable access continues to be denied in multiple ways, whether to transportation, education, employment, health care, leisure activities, parenting rights, or many other areas. Increasing use of universal design is one way to improve access and decrease activity limitations and participation restrictions. The UN Convention on the Rights of Persons with Disabilities defines universal design as "the design of products, environments, programs, and services to be usable by *all* people, to the greatest extent possible, without the need for adaptation or specialized design" (United Nations, 2006, Article 2, page 4, italics added). By "designing at the margins," we can more fully embrace the wide range of human experiences and abilities.

Prejudicial attitudes and erroneous beliefs about people with disabilities shape active discrimination, but a lack of basic awareness and understanding of disability, ability, and access contributes to widespread, ongoing, often unintentional discrimination. An example is the inclusion of work role criteria that are not actually necessary for the job, where the actual needs of the job are unrelated or could be met through accommodations. For example, does a reporter really need to be able to sit for eight hours continuously, lift 25 pounds, or type 50 words per minute (Lu, 2019)? An additional example is recent action by disability activists advocating against cuts in Medicare and changes to the Affordable Care Act: did Congress understand how these changes would differentially affect people with disabilities, in some cases threatening their very lives?

One way that current disability advocacy and activism is addressing this core issue is through centering the importance of "nothing about us (or for us) without us" (Charlton, 2000): this slogan captures the central importance of self-determination and resistance to both attitudes and access issues that maintain an idea or experience of disabled people as dependent. It also reflects awareness of the widespread ignorance of the actual lived experiences of people with disabilities: changes in social attitudes, interpersonal interactions, and institutional or legal reforms need to reflect the actual lived experiences, and the expert knowledge of people with disabilities. Unsurprisingly, people with disabilities highlight willingness to learn and communication skills as important characteristics of allies/accomplices, including the willingness to ask questions, be direct, and overcome fear of saying something "wrong" (Ostrove et al., 2019). Are these characteristics you see in yourself generally? Are they characteristics you bring to your interactions with people with disabilities?

Resources for Learning More about Disability and Ableism

Bogard, K. R., & Dunn, D. S. (Eds.) (2019). Ableism. *Journal of Social Issues*, 75(3), 650–664. https://doi.org/10.1111/josi.12354.
Davis, L. J. (2017). *The disability studies reader* (5th edition). Routledge.
Davis, L. J. (Ed.) (2018). *Beginning with disability: A primer* (1st edition). Routledge.
Nario-Redmond, M. R. (2020). *Ableism: The causes and consequences of disability prejudice*. Wiley.
Wong, A. (Ed.) (2020). *Disability visibility*. Penguin Books.
Also see the list of anthologies and readers in the Section Two Introduction. *These anthologies contain conceptual essays as well as personal narratives*, examples, stories, and poems.

9 Understanding Social Class and Classism

People often think about social class as the same as socioeconomic status (SES), which is typically measured as some combination of income, assets, education, and occupation. We are also socialized to believe that our SES is largely determined by meritocracy: that people have resources because they earn and deserve them and people who don't have resources have simply not worked hard enough to obtain them. This relates to our assumption that hard work is the primary determinant of upward social class mobility. Unraveling these assumptions involves understanding that social class is not only about how much money we have, or how many resources we can access, although these variables definitely shape both the social categories and our experiences of social class. Unraveling our assumptions also relates to understanding how social class works as a hierarchy of privilege and oppression that actively blocks upward mobility, and is highly intersectional, particularly in relation to race.

Defining Social Class and Classism

Social class is a social structure of hierarchical statuses involving different kinds of resources, or "capital," and access to those resources. Capital may include money, but also includes things such as education, cultural information or knowledge, social relationships and networks, prestige or reputation, and political influence.

Classism is the system of judgments, beliefs, actions, norms, and social/institutional practices that maintain a class hierarchy by limiting access to resources and maintaining belief in meritocracy.

Some Possible Responses to the Material in This Chapter

The idea that an individual's (or their parents, grandparents, and great grandparents') success is solely the result of personal effort and grit is such a gripping, dominant American story—you see it played out on screen, in books, on stage, even in video games. The flip side to this story is that an individual's (or their parents, grandparents, and great grandparents') struggle

DOI: 10.4324/9780429059599-12

is solely the result of lack of personal effort and lack of grit. The former is to be rewarded; the latter pitied or despised.

These myths, alongside silence around the social hierarchy of class, are a good part of why talking and learning about social class can feel dangerous. For example, if you're middle class or wealthy, or come from a family who is, you may experience identifying the privileges of social class as an attack on or a dismissal of your and your families' hard work. On the other hand, reading this chapter when you're in a place of financial struggle or come from a limited income family may cause feelings of shame or embarrassment or humiliation. It's also possible that the material in this chapter may cause you to question your previously held ideas about where you are on the social class hierarchy, which can be confusing or upsetting. For example, due to the flattening of middle-class ideas or the stigma associated with classism, some of our students have realized they are not middle class as they had perceived, but actually align more closely with another category that is "lower" on the class hierarchy (e.g., working class).

We ask that you pay close attention to whatever feelings come up for you, meeting them, if you can, with curiosity and compassion by asking yourself:

- What messages have I learned that might be contributing to the emotions I'm feeling or the thoughts I'm having right now?
- What ideas about myself and my ancestors would I have to let go of if I were to accept that social class was a hierarchy of privilege and oppression?
- What might I need right now in order to remain open to what I'm reading?

Before we move on, we do want to clarify one more thing that our students who are not affluent have objected to, that you might also find objectionable: the idea that challenging the system of classism means giving up aspects of your class culture you enjoy and value. Not so. We are not saying that everyone should be upper class or middle class in culture or values. On the contrary, challenging classism entails challenging a system that links worth and access to resources, to ways of thinking or being or relating, or to production and choices about work. More on this below.

Exploring Meanings of Social Class

Social Class as Social Construct

When we talk about **social class**, we often think first about financial resources such as money (income or assets) or things that relate to money such as owning your home or having lots of possessions. We might also think about educational level (educational capital) or occupation, which is related both to income and to education. In fact, income, education, and occupation are often used as the basis for measuring social class (as SES) or creating social class categories in research. But other kinds of resources also relate to social class, such as social capital, which is the network of relationships you have access to. For example, do you know many people who have a lot of influence? Do you or someone in your family know the mayor of your town, the governor of your state, or the president of the country? Information and knowledge, both abstract knowledge and skills, are also resources (cultural capital). For example, if your parents and grandparents went to college, they likely shared information with you about how to prepare a successful college application and essays; what financial aid is and how to apply (if you needed financial aid); what to expect from your classes and how professors expect you to act; the kinds of things that you might need in your dorm room to make life easier and less stressful for you; and how to plan your study so that you are most successful. If, on the other hand, you are the first in your family to go to college, you most likely had to actively seek out this information from teachers, advisors, mentors, or peers. There may be things you didn't know you didn't know and therefore didn't ask about, leading to missed opportunities, additional challenges, or even costly mistakes.

Social class hierarchies in the United States are related to the system of capitalism. Capitalism, as an economic system, is based on private and corporate ownership and control of trade, goods, and profit, rather than ownership or control by the people or the government. Capitalists aim to create more goods and profit, which benefits those who are the owners or bosses or who have capital to invest in the market. Owners and bosses not only have more capital to begin with, but they also have decision making power over things such as wages, who gets employed, or how the profits are distributed. This means they have more power to determine the economic system and how social class hierarchies are created or maintained, and how much social mobility is created or allowed. This is, of course, a tremendous over-simplification of capitalism: economic systems are complex and there are many types of capitalism or types of socialism and many arguments about the pros and cons of different systems and the specific ways they have been enacted in different countries and contexts.

One's social class within the United States is related to (but not wholly about) one's position within U.S. capitalism: the very affluent are the bosses and the owners, while the middle, working class, and limited income and economically marginalized people (LIEM) are workers. Wealthy people do not have to work to maintain basic necessities such as housing and food: they are not dependent on income (i.e., wages or salary). Instead, they have the option of living off wealth and assets. Consider what this might mean for daily life in relation to how one might spend one's time, things that one might think or worry about, ways that one might care for one's children or family, even values one might have about money and other resources. Considering these things helps us understand how capital, wealth, and social class shape our worldviews, perspectives, and experiences beyond simply having or not having money.

How Do I Say? There is not, unfortunately, a lot of consensus on what language we might best use to describe social class categories, particularly language for people with limited incomes and/or people experiencing poverty. The most recent guidelines from the American Psychological Association (2019) addressing social class issues recommends using the term Low-Income and Economic Marginalization (LIEM), which is what we will use in the rest of this chapter, unless we are explicating using language that reflects stereotypes or socially constructed ideas of inequity.

Questioning whether capitalism is good or whether it contributes to inequities often makes people uncomfortable, because capitalism is so engrained in the dominant U.S. culture. This relates to the ways in which we are socialized in the United States to perceive social class as related to meritocracy and the idea of the "American Dream" (McNamee & Miller, 2004). Within the idea of meritocracy, whether one is a boss or a worker is considered to be related to one's abilities and work-ethic: that is, to one's merit. The American Dream is the idea that anyone, regardless of their identities or statuses, can become affluent and influential, as long as they have enough drive and ability. However, it is definitely easier to become a boss if you are born at a higher status within the social class hierarchy, which is not related to individual merit and work, but to family history and intergenerational experiences of power, privilege, and oppression within the social categories we have been discussing (more on this below).

People in the United States born in the 1980s, 1990s, or the 21st century are increasingly critical of capitalism. Although some people in the U.S. view socialism quite negatively because of the ways that politicians, media, and education have highlighted the socialism that is tied to oppressive regimes in other countries, many people in the U.S. simultaneously regard some socialist countries (e.g., Sweden or Norway) quite positively and would like to have the benefits available in those countries such as affordable health care for all, free higher education, generous paid parental leave, and subsidized day care. In the U.S. capitalist society, the availability of many of these benefits depends on your social class.

We encourage critical thinking about the connections between the U.S. capitalist system and social class, classism, and other systems of inequity. This critical thinking is especially important given that the gap between rich people and those living in poverty has grown considerably in recent decades. Currently, the wealthiest 1% has more wealth than the bottom 90% *combined* (Board of Governors of the Federal Reserve, 2020). This expanding disparity between the wealthy and everyone else has made it increasingly difficult to move "up" in social class, regardless of how much personal merit you have. For example, about 90% of children born in 1940 earned more than their parents, while this was true for only 50% of children born in the 1980s. According to research, the unequal *distribution* of income growth is at the root of this decrease in income mobility and possibility of achievement (Chetty et al., 2017). Adding to the disparity is the changing nature of work due to the gig economy which comes with decreasing access to benefits that were previously associated with employment, such as health care, sick leave, and retirement benefits.

Thus far, we have explored social class in terms of resources and economic systems. But social class has both objective and subjective aspects. **Objective social class** relates to concrete and material resources and capital such as income, assets, or education. But social class also relates to how you see yourself and experience your own social class. In research, **subjective social class** is often measured comparatively by asking people to place themselves on a social class "ladder" in relation to others on a social class continuum or hierarchy. Subjective social class is often a stronger predictor of health compared to objective social class (Liu et al., 2004). Your experience of social class also relates to culture and identity based in contexts that you have been raised within and experiences of negotiating stereotypes or assumptions about your group membership (more on this below). However, because we often think that social class is primarily about resources, it's easy to overlook the influence of culture and identity. And our tendency to think mostly about resources interacts with our belief in meritocracy and social mobility. Said simply, our views of people are not often about social *categories* of social class, but about individuals' personal merit, personal choice, and personality characteristics such as being hard working. However, we do have socially constructed ideas about social class categories, and the people within them, based on how social class is a socially constructed structure of power with hierarchical categories associated with essentialized characteristics.

Reflection Questions

- What are some of the assumptions and stereotypes you have been exposed to in relation to social class categories? What might come to mind immediately are things that relate directly to resources (e.g., "upper class" people are rich, working-class people are less educated), but we encourage you to think beyond this. Consider whether we, as a society, have associations of values, personal characteristics, types of behavior, or ways of interacting with others associated with social class categories.
- What kinds of social messages have you received about what people in the following categories are like: "poor," "lower class," limited income, working class, middle class, upper class?

If social class were truly only about having or not having earned resources with open mobility between classes, it would be difficult to come up with socially constructed ideas about the values and characteristics of different social class categories. But we are exposed to many ideas about the personalities and values of people within different social classes, including ideas that limited income people are unemployed, on welfare, lazy, incompetent, stupid, coarse, bigoted, more animalistic, and interpersonally warm and that rich people are competent, intelligent, arrogant, and cold (Connor et al., 2021; Durante & Fiske, 2017). These ideas may not reflect your personal experiences or beliefs, but you are likely aware that these ideas exist as stereotypes. Research suggests the extent to which people endorse **social class stereotypes** is related to the severity of income inequality in their country (Durante et al., 2017). For example, more income inequality relates to stronger endorsement of limited income people as less competent and rich people as cold.

How Do I Say? One thing you may have noticed as you explored stereotypes is how language shapes our ideas. The language we use to describe social class statuses is emotionally loaded and often problematic. Issues with language are most problematic in relation to people who experience social class oppression because category language can reinforce classist ideas and discrimination. An example is the use of the label "poor." Although we may refer to people experiencing poverty, categorizing or labeling people as "poor" can reinforce classism because of the implication that the people rather than the economic circumstances are "poor." People experiencing poverty may be offended at the implication they are "less than"; or the lack of acknowledgement that they have "rich" relationships, emotions, skills, etc. We would recommend against using "lower class" or "poor" as category or status labels.

Even the basic language and idea of "class" reflects hierarchy. The word "class" is often used to mean having more valued characteristics, as in the saying "that's really classy" or "they have a lot of class." The language of class has also been historically comparative in ways that suggest more value (e.g., "upper class" and "lower class"). Language related to social class can also be difficult because it refers only or primarily to resources, rather than a more complicated understanding that class categories are not only about resources (e.g., affluent or underresourced). Class status labels are also notoriously unclear in terms of who or what defines the boundaries and whether people's personal class assignment or identity "matches" a particular social definition.

Many of our ideas about people in different social classes come from the ways we have created hierarchies and essentialized understandings about categorized people, as we discussed in Chapters 2 and 3 and as we have applied to other structural categories in this section. These stereotypes are imposed meanings that contribute to oppression for "lower" class statuses and maintain privilege for "upper" class status.

Although most students can come up with assumptions and stereotypes related to social class, many find it harder to consider what might be cultural differences between social classes. Differences in resources create social distance and segregation, and as we interact more with people within our shared social class, we develop worldviews of shared values and norms and ways of seeing ourselves and others. That is, we develop related **social class cultures**. Some cultural practices and values that researchers have demonstrated as general cultural differences between social classes within the United States include the following issues (see Carey & Markus, 2017; Jetten et al., 2017; Miyamoto, 2017; Piff & Robinson, 2017; Rucker & Galinsky, 2017; Stephens et al., 2014):

- child-rearing practices
- orientation towards self or others (individualism versus collectivism; independent versus interdependent self-view)
- attitudes toward and accepted rationales for seeking power
- contextual sensitivity/emphasis in cognition, explanations of behavior
- communication styles
- sympathy toward others and prosocial behavior (willingness to give to others)
- explanations for economic inequality.

Similar to our discussion of ethnic culture, we may not be aware of the ways in which our own worldviews or behaviors are class-cultured. However, people are generally able to differentiate patterns and make judgments of others based on those patterns. And people also tend to feel more comfortable with people who are "like them." Thus, we are likely to be more comfortable with people of our own class background, where subtle or unknown class cultural disconnections are less likely. This segregation contributes to maintaining class privilege and oppression, even if we believe we hold egalitarian values.

The development of the norms and values within different social class categories is related not only to differences in concrete resources, but also to the differences in privilege and oppression that relate to having greater resources. For example, a greater orientation towards others and increased sensitivity to context relates to the experience of being oppressed—of needing to be aware of others who are more privileged than you in order to mitigate discrimination, and needing to be more cooperative with others who share your oppression in order to increase survival and well-being (Miller, 1987) As we discussed in Chapter 3, structures of inequity such as social class are maintained through cultural imperialism: the ability of those with more power and privilege to shape our socialization and shared understandings. So, we are *socialized* to see some ways of being or behaving more positively because they are signals of social class. But the things themselves are not inherently better or worse. We can see this when we look at how some indicators mean different things now than in prior times. For example, being heavier in weight used to be seen as attractive and was associated with greater social class status, because it meant that one had more than enough to eat. Currently, however, being heavier in weight is seen less positively, and more associated with lower status within the social class hierarchy. We can also see this when we consider how characteristics or behavior associated with social class vary according to the dominant ethnic culture. For example, as a collectivistic society, Japan values a greater orientation toward others; higher social class status in Japan is associated with support for others and feelings of responsibility for others, but not in the United States (Miyamoto, 2017). This helps us understand how what is valued ethnoculturally interacts with what is valued in relation to social class, and how both relate to cultural imperialism.

Social Class Identity

Social class identity colloquially means how individuals label and understand themselves in relation to social class. Self-labeling or identity is a bit different than the subjective social class captured by a ladder, because it is not explicitly comparative. Categorical self-labeling in relation to social class does not consistently relate to objective social class and resources, or even to subjective and comparative social class on a continuum. You may see yourself as belonging to a social class (say middle class), even though "objectively" your access to resources places you among the working class or among the upper class. Evidence of this disconnect is reflected in research indicating that most Americans identify as "middle class," which means for example, that all of the following college students from an urban/suburban context may self-identify as "middle class" (Wenger & Zaber, 2021):

- Alex, a student whose parents work in food service at a university and as a retail worker, who make enough to maintain adequate food and housing for themselves and their two children. But they cannot afford restaurants, vacations away from home, or substantial contributions to college for their adult children. Alex and their siblings work full time in security, food services, and gig jobs in addition to having loans for tuition at a public university.
- Drew, a student whose parents work as a teacher and a nurse, who make enough for food and housing for themselves and their two children, occasional recreation and restaurants, and annual vacations to a rental cabin they can drive to. Drew's parents make some contributions to college for their children to supplement student loans and part-time income earned by Drew and Drew's siblings, who work for Instacart and TaskRabbit.
- Jaylen, a student whose parents work as a doctor and a lawyer, who travel internationally with their children for vacations, own a second home by the beach, and who are paying the majority of college tuition at a private university for their children, who are full time students who don't work during the academic year.

Reasons for the disconnect between one's social identity and one's access to resources are varied. They include the shifting salience of social class *identity* (as a claimed or labeled identity) or social class consciousness, which has become more complex, particularly in relation to creating a collective identity meaningful for collective political action (Eidlin, 2014). The shrinking middle class caused by the widening gap in income and wealth is also challenging some aspects of the traditional meanings of categorical distinctions.

All of these reasons don't mean that the actual influence of social class as a social construct and hierarchy has decreased. Even though the claimed identity may be less salient, both sociologists and psychologists have shown that subjective social class distinctions continue to affect individuals in a variety of ways and that individuals are aware of cultural class distinctions, that is, the ways that they are similar to or different from people with different class experiences. Importantly, psychologists have emphasized that coming to understand the meaning of one's personal social class status is often important to psychological development, particularly in relation to understanding differences in culture and worldview and in negotiating classism (Liu, 2012). So, although social class identity may not be as central to a sociological understanding of groups and social movements, social class status and identity continue to have major effects on life experiences and personal/interpersonal health (Thomas & Azmitia, 2014).

Reflection Questions

- What is your social class background? What makes you identify that way?
- How do you feel about the language used to describe your social class? What makes you use certain language for your own identity?
- What has it meant to you to belong to this class? What kinds of experiences have you had that relate to your social class? How has being of this social class shaped your values, behaviors, beliefs, worldview, social experiences? How are you similar to or different from the socially constructed stereotypes of people in your social class?
- Do you currently self-identify similarly or differently to your class background?
- How does your class interact with your race, and ethnicity? With other statuses of privilege and oppression? In a personal way? In relationships with others who are like or unlike you in relation to social class, race, ethnicity, other statuses?
- How would you and your life be different if you were from a different class background?

Exploring Classism

Classism is the system of judgments, beliefs, actions, norms, and social/ institutional practices that maintain a class hierarchy by limiting access to resources and maintaining belief in meritocracy. In our definition of classism, we include the belief in meritocracy because this belief locates differences in objective social class (e.g., in income, assets, educational or occupational achievement) within the individual, without consideration of the systems of power, privilege, and oppression that directly affect the ability to build different kinds of capital. The belief in meritocracy creates the idea that working-class people or limited income people have what they deserve, and do not have more because of some aspect of their character.

Most people *would* like to have enough resources to live comfortably, such as enough food, a safe and warm place to live, some "leisure" time for family and friends. However, this doesn't mean that people who do have those things are more deserving, or that the experiences, practices, or cultural aspects of "lower" social classes are less meaningful, rewarding, or desirable. It also doesn't mean that a lack of resources is because of some personal character deficit. Although people from working-class or LIEM class backgrounds work hard to develop the resources they need for their families to live comfortably, they are often stereotyped in ways that we described above. And they may not be able to obtain sufficient resources because they are unable to find a job that pays enough to enable this, even if they are working double or triple time. Stereotypes contribute to these challenges because when people are perceived as less wealthy, they are also perceived as less competent and intelligent (Durante & Fiske, 2017). Furthermore, it is easier to obtain more resources if one starts with resources. For example, the lending system in banks often requires collateral to get a loan, which inherently creates a barrier for those without assets, while those with assets can obtain a loan to increase their assets.

Some experiences of classism are direct and clear examples of **social class oppression**. At the institutional level, an example of direct and clearly oppressive classism is the early eugenics movement in the United States that included state practices and laws supporting forced sterilization, which was primarily aimed at the mentally ill and at LIEM or working-class women of color. At the individual and interpersonal levels, we have discussed several examples of how limited income people are stereotyped. The internalization of these stereotypes or interpersonal experiences in judgments of ourselves or others constitutes personal and interpersonal classism. Sometimes these are more obvious, such as judging a "poor" person as more like an animal, or bullying children who don't have the "right" kind of phone or who bring their own lunch rather than buy it (or who get school lunch rather than bring it), or seeing a person as less capable or worthy because of how they are dressed or because of a class-related accent or way of speaking.

However, most classism, at individual, interpersonal, and institutional levels, is more subtle and complicated because of an assumption of meritocracy and because classism is so institutionally embedded. An example of this complexity, at an individual or interpersonal level, is when some people (especially, but not only, more privileged people) view individuals who attend community or state colleges as less intelligent or capable as compared to individuals who attend Ivy League schools. They justify this belief by focusing on admission rates and competition, assuming that students at the Ivy League school are more intelligent or better qualified due to merit, without considering barriers and privileges related to social class. Even when people do consider these, they often discount them or only consider what is about direct financial resources (see Jost et al.'s 2004 review of "system justification"). For example, someone might say that Ivy League schools offer financial aid to less affluent students, and therefore these students should be able to attend if they are competitive applicants. But they might not consider how social class affects a wide range of resources prior to application to college. For example, how a student from an LIEM family might need to work as a teenager in order to contribute to food and rent for the family, while a more affluent teenager has the privilege of devoting all of their time to schoolwork and extracurriculars that demonstrate leadership and civic engagement which are more valued in the admissions process than working a minimum wage job. Or they might not consider how LIEM families might not be able to afford child care, so that older children or teens might be spending time caring for younger siblings. Or they might not consider the ways children of middle- and upper-class families have access to tutors, academically related summer programs, standardized test preparation courses, and other academic supports that contribute significantly to their children's academic achievement. Or they might not consider how Ivy League institutions have often engaged in "legacy" admissions, where children of alumni are given preference in admissions, maintaining intergenerational educational privilege.

Education is also a good example of how classism works at the institutional level. Historically, for example, people without significant resources were excluded from colleges and universities, regardless of their abilities. More recently, we can see the ways that institutionalized classism works by looking at public education. Public schools are not equally funded. In many areas of the country, public schools are partially funded (almost 50%) through local property taxes. This means that schools that are in affluent areas where property is more valuable have more resources, while schools that are in less affluent areas have fewer resources. Therefore, children from more affluent backgrounds attend schools with more resources, such as books, computers, air conditioning, arts and music programs, better paid teachers, etc., while children from limited income backgrounds attend poorly resourced schools.

Schools, and expectations within schools, are also structured differently in relation to their community location. Because social class mobility is actually quite challenging in the United States, educators in working-class communities often educate students to succeed in working-class jobs by socializing students into class-cultural norms (ways of thinking and acting) that are congruent with those jobs, but these norms may not be congruent with expectations in many higher education contexts or professional/managerial careers. For example, Stephens and colleagues (2014) talk about the ways that working-class schools are structured to foster "hard independence"—being strong and resilient, making do, and adjusting to other people and challenging situations rather than assuming these can be changed or challenged, whereas middle-class schools foster "expressive independence"—being self-assured and individually goal directed, believing one is equal with others, and emphasizing independent thinking, all of which relate to an assumption that one has the power to directly influence situations and other people. Both of these cultured value sets can be positive, but middle-class people and values are privileged in our society: those who are not familiar with those values will fit less well in settings that are gateways to greater resources and social class mobility. This is an example of how class privilege is maintained.

Understanding social class and classism is also complex because of the ways we do (or do not) differentiate issues of resources from culture. For example, an erroneous assumption commonly held in U.S. society is that everyone would want to be middle or upper class because we have the valid assumption that everyone would like to have sufficient basic resources (food, shelter) as middle-class people do. However, it is not true that everyone would like to be middle class or upper class in worldview, cultural attitudes, or behaviors; many working-class or LIEM people would not want to change their relationships or *values* or ways of thinking and behaving with which they have been brought up (such as the strength, "can do" approach, adaptability and resilience that characterize the hard independence that Stephens and colleagues (2014) describe). It is also not true that everyone would like to have white collar careers that are salaried (rather than hourly) but may be high pressure and stressful with extreme demands for time, travel, constant availability (although it is not only white collar careers that have these characteristics). Some people would prefer occupations that are skilled trades, such as plumber or deep sea pipe layer or glass blower, rather than a tech manager or office worker, despite the social class bias that associates white collar work with higher status. This raises the question of whether we can embrace differences in values and worldviews, in skills, or in work choices without creating hierarchies of privilege and oppression. And such a question relates to the ways our class structure and classism is maintained by the system of capitalism, which rewards production, and places less emphasis on the humanistic value of ensuring equal distribution of basic resources to care for people regardless of their capitalistic production.

The assumption that everyone would want to be middle or upper class in worldview and ways of living underscores how privilege works, in that the privileged group is seen as "normal," desirable, and positive. Similar to other social hierarchies, **social class privilege** includes the privilege of not recognizing that status shapes us, including our cultures and our access to power and resources. Those who have higher social class status with social class privilege are more likely to see their own success as relating to earned merit. If we are from more privileged class backgrounds, we may also be less affected by internalized stereotypes or negative views of those from less affluent and privileged backgrounds. Even if you are not seeking to personally enforce a social class hierarchy, because you are part of a social culture that creates hierarchy, you may do so nonetheless. Similar to our discussion of ethnic culture, you may not be aware of the ways in which your own worldviews or behaviors are class-cultured.

Reflection Questions

Reflecting on shared experiences:

- What are some examples of oppression related to having or not having resources? What are some of the judgments made about LIEM people and affluent or "upper" class people and their ways of being (class culture)? How do these judgments shape self-concept? How do they affect access to resources or opportunities that would open the door to obtaining better resources?
- What are some examples of privilege that relate to having resources or being raised in middle- or upper-class cultures and communities?
- In Chapter 2, we talked about the ways oppression and privilege operate at individual (worldview and internal ideas), interpersonal, and institutional levels. How do your examples reflect these different levels?

Reflecting on personal experiences:

- What are your personal experiences of oppression or privilege in relation to social class?
- Have you had to deal with interpersonal or institutional discrimination related to your social class background?
- If so, what has that been like for you? Have you had to take time and energy to develop strategies to cope with or resist these experiences of oppression and their negative effects?
- If not, what has that been like for you (and have you thought about this and about other privileges you have)?
- How have these experiences of oppression or of privilege affected how you think and feel about yourself? How do they affect how you approach developing relationships with others?

Inequities related to resources and social class interact strongly with other structural categories, such as race, ethnicity, gender, immigration, and disability. In Chapter 4, for example, we talked about the ways that chattel slavery related to economic exploitation of African labor, and the intergenerational effects on economic advancement of subsequent laws and practices aimed at maintaining the marginalization of African Americans such as redlining and segregated schools. Another example is how individuals from collectivistic ethnic cultures may understand their income not as individual resources but as family or community resources or how different ethnic or ethnoreligious cultures may have prohibitive attitudes toward loans. The setup of the U.S. economic system—including how income is calculated, expectations of how income or assets will be used, or institutional practices purportedly meant to enable advancement—reflects the values and norms of the dominant group.

There is increasing attention to social class and resource inequities in the United States. Young adults in the United States today are faced with increasing wage and wealth inequalities, rates of childhood poverty greater than in the vast majority of other rich nations, and decreasing or stagnant income mobility (Mather & Jarosz, 2014; Stanford Center for Poverty and Inequality, 2011). Recent and current attempts to address these inequities include movements such as Occupy Wall Street, which called attention to the widening gap between the richest 1% in the United States and the rest of the population; protests and movements to stop evictions and foreclosures; advocacy to raise the minimum wage, and to provide better and more equitable funding for public schools; new programs and laws to ensure affordable health care for all people; new programs to address housing instability inspired by research demonstrating that it is not only more humane but also less expensive to provide safe "no strings attached" housing for those people who lack housing or shelter than it is to ignore the issue; and increasing union organizing among workers, likely in response to increasing income and social class inequities, given that research demonstrates that labor unions reduce economic inequality (Ahlquist, 2017). These movements and initiatives have been fed by and contributed to a more active dialogue about income, resources, and classism that is also changing our understanding of class identity and culture, and the basis of class hierarchies.

Resources for Learning More about Social Class and Classism

Lareau, A. (2011). *Unequal childhoods: Class, race, and family life* (2nd edition). University of California Press.

Lareau, A., & Conley, D. (Eds.) (2008). *Social class: How does it work?* Russell Sage Foundation.

Markus, H., & Stephens, N. (Eds.) (2017). Inequality and social class: The psychological and behavioral consequences of inequality and social class: A theoretical integration. Special issue of *Current Opinion in Psychology*, 18, pp. 1–152. https://doi.org/10.1016/j.copsyc.2017.11.001.

Silva, J. M. (2013). *Coming up short: Working-class adulthood in an age of uncertainty.* Oxford University Press.

Also see the list of anthologies and readers in the Section Two Introduction. *These anthologies contain conceptual essays as well as personal narratives*, examples, stories, and poems.

Section Three

Resisting Oppression

The book's final chapter that makes up this section, "Understanding and Enacting Resistance to Oppression: Developing as an Ally and Advocate," focuses on how individuals develop as allies and advocates and take action to resist oppression. This chapter describes processes of developing critical consciousness and ways to resists oppression, particularly within relationships. It considers how these processes and actions are different depending on one's positionality, with attention to intersectionality. Our hope is that readers may develop greater confidence in their understanding and empowerment to apply that understanding to taking positive action to support the people and values that they care about.

DOI: 10.4324/9780429059599-13

10 Understanding and Enacting Resistance to Oppression

Developing as Allies and Advocates[1]

This chapter focuses on how people can resist oppression and contribute to a more socially just and equitable world. In prior chapters, we have tried to unravel the assumptions that we are socialized to believe about power, privilege, oppression, and some of the central structural hierarchies that are salient in U.S. society (race, ethnicity, gender, sexuality, disability, and social class). And we have encouraged you to reflect on how you, personally, have internalized assumptions, developed your own identities and perceptions of others in relation to these assumptions, and been affected by experiences of privilege and oppression.

This chapter starts to address the question "what can we do?" We say it "*starts* to address" this question because there is no easy answer, no straightforward prescription. There are actually hundreds of things (or thousands, or more) that people can do to resist enacting oppression or contributing to oppressive social constructs and hierarchies. And developing an ongoing praxis of resistance is a complicated and continuous process of (un)learning and trying out different ways of applying that (un)learning to our relationships and our actions. What each of us can do, individually and specifically, relates to our unique backgrounds, contexts, capacities, and access to people, organizations, policies, and so forth.

Some Possible Responses to the Material in This Chapter

Some readers might experience this chapter as illuminating and experience relief as they see their own struggles and develop an understanding of why taking action against oppression seems so hard. People who are caught in guilt about privilege, worried about enacting "microaggressions," fearful of hurting others or being judged by others, or those who feel like they just don't know how to interact across differences, are likely to find this chapter really

1   Citation for this chapter should be Hochman, A., Suyemoto, K. L., Donovan, R. A., and Kim, G. S. "Understanding and enacting resistance to oppression: Developing as an ally and advocate." In *Unraveling Assumptions: A Primer for Understanding Oppression and Privilege*. Routledge.

DOI: 10.4324/9780429059599-14

helpful. These readers may appreciate understanding the complexities of taking action against oppression and the guidance for considering how they can integrate understanding and action for resisting oppression in their daily lives. At the same time, these readers may continue to feel daunted by the size of the problem, and to feel like there is so much that needs to be addressed. The research on resisting oppression suggests it takes time to change the assumptions we have internalized from systemic oppression, but that it *is* possible to move forward, to take steps within ourselves and our relationships and our organizational contexts, even as we deepen our understanding and develop new skills to take action. So, remember that this is a journey, not a destination. And that steps forward are what matters, not being perfect, which is impossible.

On the other hand, some readers may feel impatient or frustrated with our focus on psychological experience and relationships and feel that it is more important to focus on how to take direct action to undermine structural oppression and change institutional policies and practices in our society and organizations (e.g., schools, housing, businesses, politics, policing, etc.). Currently, there is a lot of discussion about what is "genuine," or meaningful, or effective resistance to oppression. Some of this discussion criticizes those who are working to resist oppression at intrapsychic and interpersonal levels, calling attention to the need for more radical institutional changes if we are truly going to create a just society. We agree that changes in our major institutions are urgently needed to address oppression and inequity. Simultaneously, we believe that sustaining change as a society ultimately means changes in hearts and minds in both privileged and oppressed people. Our institutions are created and maintained by choices made by individuals and movements are built by individuals coming together to demand change. Also, as we move toward these structural changes (which will take some time), we need to be able to do so in ways that avoid causing further harm to those who are in oppressed positions. So, internal and relational understanding and skills are important.

Exploring Meanings of Resisting Oppression

Critical Consciousness + Action

When we talk about "resisting oppression" what do we mean? In Chapter 2, we talked about oppression as intrapsychic and internalized, as interpersonal, and as institutional. Just as people can experience oppression at these different levels, people can also resist oppression by working to change their ways of being at these different levels. What might this look like?

Addressing intrapsychic and internalized oppression is taking action to (un)learn and liberate our minds. The foundation of effective action to resist oppression is changing the ways we think, the ways we have internalized assumptions and biases about ourselves and others. Developing this critical **consciousness** contributes to motivation for promoting change. While changing our own worldviews, fostering good intentions, and developing skills create a vital foundation for other kinds of action, internal changes (especially from a privileged space) don't have a lot of effect on reducing the existence or impact of oppression for others, unless we build upon it through action. Thus, we have to *use* these personal understandings and motivations and bring them out into the world to take action to resist oppression at interpersonal and institutional levels. When we do this, we also expand our critical conscious- ness, and related understandings and awareness about ourselves, our world- views, and our views about other people. Resisting oppression is a complex, multifaceted, and iterative process of learning and action that unfolds again and again.

Considering Positionality and Solidarity

The experience of resisting oppression is different for people who are experi- encing that oppression (advocates) than for people who are privileged and therefore benefitting from the hierarchy of oppression (allies/accomplices). Let us start with what it means to be an **advocate**. Acting as an advocate means challenging oppression that you, yourself, experience. For example, this could apply to a queer person who is challenging heterosexism, or a person who is experiencing disability who is challenging ableism. Oppression is, at base, a dehumanizing process. Therefore, *experiencing* oppression means that one is *inherently* resisting oppression on an ongoing basis. The saying "existence is resistance" addresses the fact that continuing to exist, to thrive, to find joy in life, to maintain health and well-being in the face of oppression is, itself, an act of resistance. To be the target of oppression and to continue to center the humanity and worth of oneself and others in one's own oppressed group takes a significant amount of effort and energy that is often ignored or underestimated. This doesn't mean that all that an oppressed person does is right or just, or that we can't internalize our own oppression or contribute to the oppression of others. But it does recognize that thriving in the face of oppression takes real effort.

Starting with this understanding is vitally important because people often assume that those who experience oppression should be the only or primary people to resist oppression. Individuals who have this belief (including oppressed people) may judge oppressed people on whether they are being active *enough,* while completely overlooking the effort and energy that is being expended on existence *as* resistance. As oppressed people develop a stronger sense of conscientization, they may themselves feel that if they are not *always* educating, *always* advocating, *always* confronting, *always* protesting, then they are not resisting oppression. But this approach inevitably leads to burnout. Although there are many ways that oppressed peoples can (and do) engage in resisting oppression, the burden of social change should not be placed solely on them. Simultaneously, people who experience oppression also need to realize that their personal joy or success is unlikely to lead to systemic change.

People who are resisting or challenging oppression and oppressive systems from a place of privilege are **acting as an ally, or accomplice** (e.g., a White person who is engaging in anti-racist actions, or a man who is a feminist and engaging in anti-sexist actions). We say "acting as an ally/accomplice" rather than "being an ally/accomplice" to emphasize that ally is not a static identity or an achievement. Acting as an ally/accomplice involves supporting and uplifting those who experience oppression and/or challenging oppression enacted from privileged others and from systemic norms and practices (Suyemoto & Hochman, 2021). Acting as an ally/accomplice is different from "helping" a community, which can be paternalistic, based in asserting your own beliefs about what oppressed people want or need. Uplifting those who experience oppression means supporting the goals for justice identified by those who are oppressed. This means that it is important to listen to feedback. Ultimately, whether you are an effective ally is determined by the people whose oppression you are working to dismantle.

Acting as an ally/accomplice is about what you do and not who you are. Letting go of the ideas of ally/accomplice as an identity is helpful in maintaining engagement and avoiding defensiveness. If you recognize that resisting oppression is a process of continually trying out actions to resist oppression and thereby getting more effective, then making a mistake or receiving criticism about how to do it better will feel less like an attack on your character. Furthermore, an ally/accomplice takes action because it is the right thing to do for healing, well-being, and justice, not because one is seeking the approval of others, or wanting kudos from people who are oppressed (Suyemoto & Hochman, 2021).

Allies and accomplices mainly differ in the level of intervention or action in which they engage, and the risks and costs they are willing to take. Both allies and accomplices see how their own well-being is tied to others' well-being, recognize how their privilege protects them, and take actions to subvert or spend that privilege by working to dismantle oppression at the systemic level. Recently there has been criticism of the term "ally" because some people who claim they are allies are not engaging in any action beyond their own education and consciousness. But, in truth, if you are not taking action, then you are not really *acting* as an ally.

How Do I Say? Some people criticize the term "ally" because they see "ally" as synonymous with people who see themselves as allies and state that they value equity and justice but they don't act in ways that reflect this commitment. Ornamental, symbolic, or performative are terms for allies who express sympathy or support, but are unwilling to take action to challenge oppression, especially when taking action would result in negative appraisals from those in positions of power over them (e.g., supervisor) or those close to them (e.g., family, neighbors, friends). The terms also encompass those who are willing to challenge oppression from their position of privilege when it involves challenging others but who are unwilling to engage critiques about their own oppressive behaviors. In short, this is "allyship" in name only or when convenient and easy.

People who seek to be allies do engage in developing their own critical consciousness, but they also show up to actively support those experiencing oppression and push other people with privilege to do better. They take action at interpersonal and organizational levels. People who act as accomplices are more explicitly focused on directly challenging institutional and systemic oppression, which involves greater risk. This could mean taking actions that risk bodily harm or job loss, or that give up physical safety or economic stability, recognizing that the likely costs from these risks are lessened by their privilege. Because we are mostly talking about personal and relational processes in this chapter, we will generally use the language of "ally," but we want to be clear that allies take action.

As these definitions of advocate and ally/accomplice suggest, positionality matters in terms of the motivations, emotional experiences, and relational dynamics associated with resisting oppression. At the same time, advocates and allies are both taking action to promote social justice in the same oppressive systems. Both advocates and allies are caught in social constructs of oppression that are damaging to their own humanity and to values and desires to be a good person and respect and cherish others' humanity. People who experience oppression are clearly hurt *more* by oppressive systems, with greater consequence: they experience exclusion, stereotyping, interpersonal insults, invisibilization, and exploitation, as we have discussed throughout this book. But we have also unraveled the assumption that people with privilege are unaffected. Resisting oppression from both positionalities means negotiating imposed assumptions about our own and others' experiences, worth, deservingness, and humanity. Furthermore, most people are not wholly privileged or wholly oppressed. And we can't actually separate ourselves into discrete categories, and our intersectional experience affects our actions to resist oppression. For example, a White woman might face sexism when addressing systemic racism within her workplace and may need to consider how to resist her own oppressed experience from sexism and/or cissexism if she is interacting with male supervisors to promote changes in hiring policy to address racism, an area in which she holds privilege (Case, 2012). In addition, intersectionality is not only about an individual's multiple identities but also about how these social *systems* interact to reinforce each other (Warner et al., 2018). Effective resistance to oppression requires solidarity, as we discussed in earlier chapters. We invite you to engage and consider the ways you might resist oppression in relation to multiple hierarchies of race, ethnicity, gender, sexuality, social class, and disability. As Fannie Lou Hamer said: "nobody's free until everybody's free" (Hamer, 1971).

Foundations and Cycles of Learning and Action for Resisting Oppression

While a one-time action can be an *example* of resisting oppression, effective resistance to oppression involves a way of understanding the world and continuously acting from that understanding, rather than a discrete moment, experience, or action. An overview of this process is presented in Figure 10.1 (see also Dutt & Grabe, 2014; Rodriguez, 2011; Suyemoto & Hochman, 2021; see also Harro's [2000] Cycle of Liberation). Below, we unpack some of the complexities and try to address some assumptions and fears that might keep us from taking action to resist oppression or might make the action we take less effective.

Resisting Oppression at the Internal/Individual Level: Critical Consciousness and Cycles of Learning

Effective resistance from both privileged and oppressed positions builds upon critical consciousness, which involves understanding (a) how oppression is systemic (and not just related to individual motivations or actions) and the complexities of how it works in our social institutions; (b) developing awareness of others' experiences and the effects of oppression and privilege for

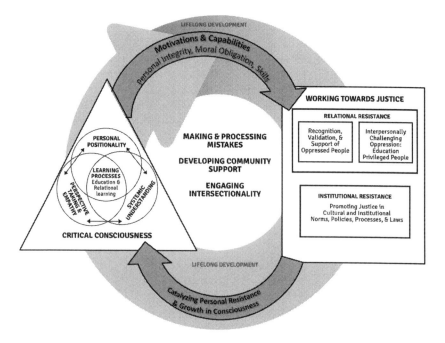

Figure 10.1 Ally and Advocate Cycles of Development
Source: Developed by Karen L. Suyemoto and Alissa L. Hochman. This work is licensed under a Creative Commons Attribution-NonCommercial-ShareAlike 4.0 International License. Used by permission.

others (perspective taking and empathy); and (c) developing awareness of one's own experiences and the personal effects of oppression and privilege (engaging and applying an analysis of positionality). Research suggests that this understanding, awareness, and empathy is related to both motivation and the ability to enact effective strategies for resisting oppression (Chavez-Dueñas et al., 2019; Mosley et al., 2021; Suyemoto & Hochman, 2021).

There are many ways that you can foster and deepen your critical consciousness (knowledge, awareness, empathy, and application to personal experience and positionality). Active methods for deepening your critical consciousness means continually *seeking out* new opportunities to expand understanding of how oppression is embedded in our society and its effects on different people, both similarly and differently privileged or oppressed in relation to you. This may include:

- Education such as reading books or blogs; seeking out movies or videos that focus on the experiences of oppressed peoples; choosing to take a non-required class that explores racism, sexism, ableism, classism, ageism, xenophobia, or heterosexism.
- Learning relationally from people might involve seeking out similarly privileged or oppressed role models, either in real life or through the media, developing affinity and support groups for accountability and processing, intentionally participating in events and activities hosted by people from a different background than you, and developing relationships across difference. Such experiences and relationships challenge our assumptions and deepen our awareness.
- Actively processing your learning and responses with attention to your positionality. For example, through mindfully observing your everyday experiences and automatic thoughts, checking your assumptions, critically analyzing the media you consume, and developing a practice of reflecting, such as journaling.

There are ways that the foundations of critical consciousness are similar for advocates and for allies/accomplices. Simultaneously, the processes of developing critical consciousness, and challenges to engaging in the process can be different depending on one's positionality.

Critical Consciousness for Advocates[2]

People who experience oppression are more likely to have some pieces of critical consciousness because they know from their lived experience what oppression looks and feels like. As we talked about in Chapter 3, experiences of oppression

---

2   When we speak of "you" in this section, we are speaking to readers who are taking action to resist oppression in areas that they personally experience oppression.

demand our attention, because of their detrimental effects, whereas people with privilege often are unaware of this privilege. Furthermore, the survival, well-being, and advancement of people who are oppressed often depends on understanding the privileged viewpoint. So, people who are oppressed also often have more experience taking the perspective of those who are privileged in relation to them. For decades, feminist researchers have examined the ways that women's "relationality" is associated with the dynamics of dominance and subordination, and the ways that women have needed to understand men's perspectives because of their imposed dependence on men (e.g., see Miller, 1987).

Although people who are oppressed may have experiences shaping personal and interpersonal awareness, they may not have the knowledge of how hierarchies of oppression are systemic and institutionalized (see also the discussion of racial identity in Chapter 4). This knowledge is vital to resisting internalization, and also to understanding the ways that people who are privileged are shaped by these systems, in order to understand why oppressed people are being treated the way that they are, and to develop more effective strategies for resilience and resistance.

Developing the kind of critical consciousness we describe above can be challenging for oppressed people. It is challenging to face the idea that no matter what you personally and individually do, you will not be able to completely avoid the pain and damage of oppression until there is structural change. Sometimes, people who are oppressed deal with the pain of oppression by denying that they (or their group) experience oppression or by trying to be more like the privileged group to decrease the oppression or to seem more "acceptable" to others. Psychologically, such responses make sense because they increase feelings of control, reduce conflict and interpersonal discrimination, and allow for distancing from the difficult emotions (e.g., pain, anger, despair, helplessness) that are inevitably related to facing the reality of living oppression. However, without critical consciousness of how oppression is systemic, these "strategies" of denial and attempts to "pass" or "cover" are generally associated with internalizing the idea that the problem is in the oppressed group.

How Do I Say? "Passing" means that you are assumed or accepted by others to be something you are not and you choose not to correct or challenge those assumptions. For example, when a gay man "passes" as heterosexual. Passing might include active deception such as lying about having a "girlfriend" or explicitly asserting that one is heterosexual, or might simply involve not correcting others' erroneous assumptions about identity.

"Covering" (Yoshino, 2006) means that others know your status or identity, but you act in ways that minimize the distinction and avoid calling attention to differences in status. For example, a person's heterosexual colleagues might know that a gay man is gay, but he might "cover" by not talking about his husband, not bringing his husband to work events, not discussing social events or media related to the gay community, avoiding political discussions about rights for sexual minority people, and so forth.

People often choose to pass or cover because it is less dangerous, or to avoid experiencing marginalization, stereotyping, or other harm from oppression. When a context consists of mostly privileged people with little discussion or awareness of dynamics or privilege and oppression, there are often cultural norms that reflect the dominant group. This creates an implicit demand and expectation that people will cover or pass. Although passing and covering may seem advantageous or comfortable, they take a toll on one's well-being and undermine the possibility of authentic relationships.

When you **internalize oppression**, you may believe that you or your group *deserves* this kind of treatment—that the oppression or barriers are because of some personal deficit. And internalization does its own damage, by eroding your sense of self-worth, of value, of humanity (David et al., 2019). This approach also denies the pain and effect of oppression experienced by others, which contributes to isolation. And this approach doesn't contribute to actually changing the problem of existing and ongoing oppression that does harm to you and to others. With critical consciousness, a person might *decide*, in a given moment, to pass or cover or to turn away from (or deny or deflect) experiences of oppression. But critical consciousness makes that a strategic choice, chosen for one's own well-being in light of one's own values and goals.

In sum, critical consciousness for oppressed people is about rooting out the damaging ideas and worldviews that invite them to self-blame, rooting out internalized oppression. However, this can be really hard because there is so much (un)learning to do, so much we have been told (implicitly or explicitly) that is not true or not wholly true, and so much we have not been told about the strengths and achievements of oppressed peoples. And because oppression is systemic, oppressive and biased messages are reinforced from everywhere, including media, educational institutions, and political policies. Developing critical consciousness is also hard for oppressed peoples because it means facing the reality of oppression, engaging the depth of pain and damage, letting go the idea of personal control (but not personal agency for resistance), and finding a way to channel the anger so that it is not self-damaging (Anzaldúa, 2002). There is a heavy emotional and energy toll in facing and engaging oppression.

Critical Consciousness for Allies/Accomplices[3]

People with privilege need to understand not just that they are privileged, but *how* that privilege manifests itself in their lives—how they have benefitted

---

3   When we speak of "you" in this section, we are speaking to readers who are taking action to resist oppression in areas that they are personally privileged.

from and are protected by privilege, and how privilege can act as a barrier to even seeing experiences of oppression (Suyemoto & Hochman, 2021). In areas of privilege, we have often been socialized to believe that privilege does not exist (an unfortunately good strategy for maintaining the status quo). It can be hard to hold that you both worked for what you have *and* were propped up by your privilege in certain ways in order to get it. For example, consider applying for jobs and the employers looking at the applicants' previous experiences. A person with social class privilege may have a number of experiences during high school or college, such as previous internships or volunteer activities related to the job. But a less financially privileged peer may not have been able to pursue those same experiences, because many internships are unpaid. Instead, the peers with less financial privilege may have had to hold jobs that paid, even if they were not necessarily related to what they wanted to do in the future and/or help their family with their family businesses or take care of people at home. While the person with social class privilege may have worked hard to obtain the internship and to pursue the volunteer work, their less privileged peers may have also worked very hard but may not have the same "credentials" or other experiences.

In their areas of privilege, allies also work to develop their understanding and empathy for the personal experiences of people with marginalized identities, which vary for each system of oppression and the specific identities or statuses within that system. This requires suspending your previously held assumptions about the world and really allowing yourself to step into someone else's shoes. Suspending your assumptions about the world from a place of privilege can be particularly challenging because an aspect of privilege is having your view align with the dominant view. In other words, society tells you that your worldview and experience is THE worldview and experience, rather than allowing you to develop the recognition that we each understand the world in very different ways based on how society has related to us, and we to it. It is common for people with privilege to question the experiences and perspectives of oppressed people: "Was that *really* racism?" or "Was that *really* sexism?" It is important to remember that people experiencing the oppression have had to ask and answer these questions for themselves throughout their lives, so if they think it was oppressive, it most likely was.

Critical Consciousness and Issues of Intersectionality

As we have talked about in prior chapters, hierarchies of oppression support each other, conceptually and practically. And most people are not wholly oppressed or wholly privileged. This means that developing critical consciousness, for most people, will involve engaging the processes and challenges that apply to *both* advocates and allies/accomplices. Unfortunately, most descriptions of critical consciousness and developing strategies to effectively resist oppression are framed as binaries of privileged *or* oppressed, rather than considering complex interactions. This kind of **binary framing** can, itself, be a challenge to developing critical consciousness. Binary framing can make it difficult to see complexities of systemic oppression, such as how different kinds of oppression reinforce each other. An example is the way sexism is used to support heterosexism, as when a gay man is denigrated as being too feminine, which is an insult because of the implicit assumption that being feminine makes someone "less than." Binary framing can also lead to assumptions that all people within a group are the same, leading us to be less open to learning about the experiences of diverse others within our group. For example, feminist activism in the 1960s and 1970s was strongly criticized for assuming that *all* women had the same experiences and challenges as White women, without considering how the experiences for women of color may differ, or how White feminists may also internalize and enact racism (e.g., Srivastava, 2005).

Binary framing can also contribute to struggles in seeing and engaging our own experiences of oppression and privilege. For example, José may be deeply invested in developing his understanding of his oppression as a Latine person, but may not be as open to exploring the ways that he personally benefits from social class privilege. He may be caught up in the pain of being oppressed, even as he also enacts oppressive judgmental assumptions against limited income and economically marginalized Latine people. Or Michelle may have done a lot of work to develop White racial consciousness and take action to resist racism but may resist exploring the ways that sexism has detrimentally shaped her worldview and expectations for herself and other women, because she would like to believe that all opportunities are open to her without others' negative assumptions or judgments. Michelle's racial privilege *does* mean that she will not encounter some of the particular racialized sexism that women of color encounter, but her internalization of sexism may contribute to difficulty making sense of experiences such as sexual harassment or not being promoted to leadership, and then contribute to psychological distress.

Historically, the oppressive status quo has been supported by the **"divide and conquer" strategy**, which pits oppressed people against each other, and demands that multiply oppressed peoples choose one primary oppression to resist (Lorde, 1995; Tran et al., 2018).

How Do I Say? What does "divide and conquer" mean, as a strategy to support systemic hierarchies? Divide and conquer refers to efforts aimed at preventing oppressed groups from coming together to build coalitions that could threaten the status and standing of the privileged group. These tactics serve as solidarity barriers among groups that have a shared identity in one area (e.g., social class) but not in another (e.g., race). Obvious examples of this tactic are the laws passed in Virginia during the 17th century that gave new rights and privileges to White indentured servants while removing rights and privileges from enslaved Black people to prevent both groups from joining forces against wealthy White landowners.

However, because oppressions support each other, and systems operate on oppressions remaining in their places, maintaining oppressive privilege in one area actually contributes to one's own oppression as well, emphasizing the need for solidarity (Lipsitz, 2001). José's liberation as a Latine person would be more fully realized if he (and all others) could see this connectedness. This doesn't mean that José has to entirely shift his focus of resistance or activism to social class issues. But it does mean that he will need to develop critical consciousness about his social class privilege in order to be most effective in resisting anti-Latine racism and ethnocentrism.

Reflection Questions

- How do you assess your own critical understanding or consciousness related to being an effective ally or an advocate?
- What kinds of things do you know more or less about? For example, knowledge about the U.S. history related to the experiences and sociopolitical contexts of various groups? Knowledge about the experiences and perspectives of people who experience oppression?
- How would you assess your awareness of your own and others' cultures, assumptions, values, emotional experiences, biases, privileges, lived experiences around oppression? For example, how self-aware are you about your own history, your family history, your own group's (racial, ethnic, cultural, sexuality, religious, ability, etc.) histories, and the legacies associated with power, privilege, and oppression?
- What areas would you consider as your growing edge? What aspects are challenging for you to explore from your positionality? What would you need to learn to build foundations about critical consciousness, intersectionality, and allyship?
- What can you do to start that learning process?

Resisting Oppression at the Interpersonal Level: Changing Dynamics and Fostering Resistance in Relationships

In this section we focus on how we can resist oppression through our interpersonal interactions by changing the ways we act with and toward others to reduce harm, by using relationships to foster critical consciousness and resistance action in others, and by relating in ways that support the power and self-determined resistance of people who experience oppression. Developing understanding and skills to resist oppression at the interpersonal level is vital for many reasons:

- Relationships are major influences on expanding and maintaining critical consciousness.
- Relationships are places where we enact or resist the enactment of oppression.
- Relationships are the heart of the coalitions and solidarity that are necessary for institutional change.

Moreover, relationships are central to resisting oppression because at the heart of liberation and justice is a vision of a world where people actively value, care, and respect each other, a world where people act with love and promote connection rather than act from or inflict pain and promote isolation (hooks, 2018).

Relational Resistance through Recognition, Validation, and Support

One approach to resistance at the interpersonal and relational level focuses on actions that support the power and self-determined liberation of people who experience oppression. Direct relational actions aim at resisting invalidation and invisibilization, marginalization, and exploitation through amplifying voices and contributions, validating experiences, and offering support in direct interpersonal interactions (Suyemoto et al., 2021; Suyemoto & Hochman, 2021). Some examples of direct interpersonal interactions include:

- Acknowledging the contributions of people who are oppressed, making sure that credit is given where it is due. The contributions of oppressed people are often ignored or co-opted by others.
- Actively making space for, inviting, and amplifying voices and perspectives of oppressed people. This includes your own active listening as well as explicit and public validation of voices and perspectives. The public part can be particularly important, as behind-the-scenes private validation (e.g., a private e-mail saying thank you for speaking up) may not affect organizational or institutional systemic bias.
- Sharing and validating voices, stories, art, news, and so forth about experiences of oppression, such as promoting art, music, or poetry created by oppressed people that is about race or racial discrimination. Often these experiences are ignored, minimized, or otherwise invalidated. One word of caution here is to remember the complexity and resilience of oppressed people. Often experiences of oppressed people are reduced to only suffering, pain, and discrimination. There is also resilience, achievements, and joys; make sure to consider these as you think about oppression.
- Sharing news articles and education resources that model or provide examples of resisting oppression.
- Offering relational or emotional support to people who experience oppression.

- Participating in and/or supporting activities and initiatives, organizing meetings, protests, or events that address issues of diversity and oppression. This might involve offering time, money, skills, and/or other resources.

Relational Resistance to Oppression as Advocates[4]

Many of the relational actions among similarly oppressed people focus on validating experiences and emotional responses. They may involve: sharing ways to promote self and community care; sharing strategies for **calling out/calling in** others who are engaging in interpersonal oppression; and sharing means to participate in or organize resistance actions aimed at the systemic level. These activities of validation and sharing strategies are often the easiest kinds of relational action to resist oppression because they can contribute to developing supportive and validating relationships, which can also support your ability to face your own oppression.

How Do I Say? What is the difference between calling in and calling out? Both are ways to let people know that they are enacting or maintaining oppression through their words or actions. For example, that they have done or said something microaggressive or offensive to people who experience oppression or marginalization, or that the policy they are supporting promotes or maintains inequity. Essentially, both calling in and calling out are ways to confront oppressive acts, requesting accountability. The difference between calling in and calling out is in how the confrontation takes place.

Calling in prioritizes relational care for the individual who has enacted the oppression. This approach is centered on an understanding that we are all caught in and hurt by oppressive systems. Calling in explicitly recognizes the good intentions of the agent, firmly but gently calls attention to the issue, and invites them to correct the problem. Calling out is more direct and is sometimes even angry. The emphasis is on confronting and calling attention to the error and the harm. "Cancel culture" is all about calling out.

Calling in takes a lot of emotional work, especially if one is in an oppressed space, because calling in means that you have to modulate the anger and pain from the oppression so that it does not come across as blaming. It means that you put greater priority on the other person's intentions and on relational care. Calling in can be a good strategy if you are aiming to build a relationship or have the capacity to foster another person's growth and motivation to be an ally or accomplice. Alternatively, calling out can be a good strategy when you are most interested in "speaking truth to power," when you don't see much potential

---

4   When we speak of "you" in this section, we are speaking to readers who are taking action to resist oppression in areas that they personally experience oppression.

to build a genuine relationship, or when you feel as if you have been banging your head against a wall. However, calling out can alienate other people (not only the agent) and may lead you to feel like you have not been the person you want to be. Sometimes anger and direct confrontation can be important to express, but not always. What is most important is that you are making an intentional choice, so that your action is in line with your values and your goals.

Relational Resistance to Oppression as Allies[5]

Acting as allies through validating and supporting people experiencing oppression can involve many of the general actions we have discussed so far. But one of the biggest challenges in doing supportive work from a position of privilege is ensuring one's efforts are experienced as supportive by those who experience oppression. Engaging in ally action challenges us to act differently in relation to our identity from how we are socialized, often requiring significant amounts of self-monitoring in support of people experiencing oppression and elsewhere. For example, people with privilege may need to check their inclination to speak first and/or often, to view their opinion as the right opinion, and to generally take up or dominate spaces. There may be moments where an ally's presence is not wanted, and a person who truly acts as an ally will respect this wish and withdraw. Remaining grounded in your values and sense of integrity may help guide you in moments where you feel drawn to assert yourself more. For example, when one of the authors of this chapter (Alissa), who is White, joined the protesters at Standing Rock, there were several moments when she felt sad or left out due to the requests or expectations of people coming to camp, but recognizing that her goal of supporting and respecting the Standing Rock Sioux tribe superseded her individual desires to feel included or personally connected helped her act accordingly in those moments. That included eating the food she had brought rather than a homemade camp meal so others who needed it more could have it (even though she really wanted to try the food) and not joining around the sacred fire while she was "on her moon" (even though no one would have known she violated this expectation). Remembering the damage and harm that has been caused by White people to Indigenous people throughout history and in current times served as an anchor in moving with the intention to only support and serve the community.

Although people often think about ally action in relation to supporting people experiencing oppression, a vital kind of taking action at the interpersonal level as an ally involves holding similarly privileged people accountable for their words and actions, and supporting similarly privileged people

---

5 When we speak of "you" in this section, we are speaking to readers who are taking action to resist oppression in areas where they are personally privileged.

in their critical consciousness and ally development. This includes identifying microaggressions and educating people about them, having discussions about privilege and oppression, and inviting people to join you in your actions to resist oppression. Often, this kind of relational action involves having difficult dialogues, also known as **brave conversations**.

> *How Do I Say?* What is the difference between "safe" space and "brave" space? Educators like Arao and Clemens (2013) have critiqued the safe space nomenclature because the word "safety" incorrectly suggests that the process of (un)learning will or should be comfortable and without risk. As a more accurate alternative, they and others have suggested using brave space (also known as brave conversations and courageous conversations) which highlights that change requires risk and the willingness to sit with discomfort and fear, all things that are inherent in resisting oppression.

Interpersonal Learning and Teaching: Difficult Dialogues

Difficult dialogues are difficult because of all the issues we have talked about throughout this book, including things we are differentially aware of, how we are socialized to not know or talk about systemic hierarchies, and the ways that issues of oppression are emotionally charged. If you experience oppression, these dialogues are often difficult because they are, themselves, moments of invalidation, invisibilization, and imposed assumptions. If you are privileged and being called out or called in, these dialogues are often difficult because they are revealing ways that you have likely been harming others which can contribute to feeling as if you are not a good person or are being judged on something you may not want to acknowledge.

Although in current times, people are aware that difficult dialogues are important, fear and anxiety about conflict can lead to avoiding these conversations. But there are things you can do to make these interactions more likely to contribute to learning and growth. First, you can realize that you don't have to be an expert in order to interrupt oppression. Even before you have deep knowledge and ability to discuss your understandings, you can interrupt oppressive behaviors and conversations. For example, you might say, "I am having a strong reaction to what you are saying" or "I don't agree with what you are saying" along with, "I need to think about why before I explain it to you." Rather than expecting yourself to get these conversations just right, you can acknowledge there is an issue and sort through the details of why in a follow-up conversation.

Second, we need to reframe our attitude towards these conversations. Given our socialization and different positionalities, we need to realize that working towards justice is going to inevitably involve these kinds of conversations. We are often socialized to avoid conflict and believe that mistakes are more about being bad as people than about opportunities to be better in our behavior. But if we recognize that we are socialized into harmful assumptions, then we are going to need to be open to (un)learning (for ourselves and for others), which inevitably means tolerating a certain level of discomfort and unpleasant emotions. Conflict doesn't have to be a bad thing if it is engaged with care and respect (with love, as bell hooks [2018] puts it). Conflict is an opportunity to explore differences, to grow in the ways in which we see ourselves, others, and the world around us. Difficult dialogues may create tensions and relational ruptures in the moment, but these ruptures don't have to be permanent or irreparable and they have the potential to create greater authenticity and intimacy in relationships.

We also need to be mindful about our own capacities and limitations, our goals and our values. One thing you can do is make active choices about when, whether, and how you want to have these dialogues. When someone else says or does something oppressive, you have a choice about whether or not to have a conversation, whether you want to ignore it, or whether you want to disengage from the interaction or person completely. When someone calls you in or out, you also have these choices. Research suggests that choosing to engage relates to having goals of promoting justice and resisting oppression and wanting a more authentic presence in the world or in the relationship at hand (Suyemoto et al., 2020; Suyemoto & Hochman, 2021).

At the same time, it may make sense to not engage these conversations if you are *sure* they won't go well, because they are often painful to participate in, especially if you're in the oppressed position. If you have tried repeatedly to have honest conversations with a person and they have never been willing to engage, then continuing to try is like banging your head against a wall—the wall remains but your head is painful and bloody.

On the other hand, you need to be careful about how you decide the conversation won't go well. We all sometimes make assumptions that other people are unwilling to hear us when they might be more open, especially if we are in a space where we have the capacity to emphasize their humanity, good intentions, hopes for authentic relationships, and the ways that they, too, have been caught in and damaged by the oppressive social system. We don't always have that capacity, though (e.g., to call in rather than call out or to check our own defensiveness). So even if you think there is openness, you might decide not to engage because your current capacity isn't enough to support the emotional energy the conversation might take or how much pain might be involved. Note, however, that just because you or others are not open or able to have a conversation in a given moment doesn't mean it will never happen. And sometimes you might find that an earlier conversation that you thought had no effect actually planted a seed that grew into greater consciousness over time. For example, sometimes students come to us at the end of the semester, or even months or years after a class has ended, and tell us that some idea or perspective they rejected during class now makes sense to them.

Difficult dialogues may also involve risks that go beyond the relationship with an individual, because you might be judged by others for introducing the conversation, or for the ways and the degree to which you choose to engage. The social rejection or judgments that may result from bringing up dynamics of oppression might be too costly, threatening your well-being, your job and ability to financially support yourself, or even your physical safety. It is okay to choose your battles with an eye towards promoting social justice as a long-term engagement. Simultaneously, within any cost/benefit analysis, consider your own responsibility for resisting oppression. Choosing not to act also has costs. Especially if you are privileged, it can be easy to avoid these conversations and simply allow oppressive dynamics to continue, undermining your intention to resist oppression and reinforcing your own privilege and the oppressive system. The bottom line is that whether you engage or disengage, there are personal and interpersonal risks, drawbacks, and benefits. There is no neutral choice, but there are choices.

The ways in which you experience or engage in difficult dialogues is also affected by your positionality, and the positionality of the person with whom you are interacting. We often think about difficult dialogues as occurring between people who are privileged (who are being called in or called out) and people who are oppressed (who are raising the issue and calling out or calling in the other person). But difficult dialogues can also take place between people who are similarly privileged or similarly oppressed. And they can take place in a group, not only between two individuals. Your responses and choices about responding relate not only to whether you are explicitly being challenged or raising an issue, but also to the context of the moment, the experiences you bring to hearing and being part of these conversations, and opportunities for growth and learning.

Difficult Dialogues from the Privileged Space

If you're privileged and being called out by a person who is oppressed, we encourage you to consider some of these central dynamics (Hardy & Lazloffy, 2002; Suyemoto et al., 2020):

- The importance of differentiating intention from effect. You may hold in your mind that you had good intentions, but you also need to widen your focus to include the impact that you had on the person. If a child is running around on a playground and accidently knocks over and hurts their friend, they still need to apologize and the fact that they did not intend harm does not change that the friend got hurt.
- Being "thick-skinned" and able to accept and endure the oppressed person's anger and hurt also means avoiding responses rooted in fragility and defensiveness, such as making the interaction about *your* hurt or about *your* dislike of how the person is responding. Reframing anger helps in this process. Many of us have been socialized to believe that anger is

not an okay emotion to express or will derail a relationship. In reality, when an oppressed person expresses anger about oppression, this can be a sign of trust and a sign that your relationship is meaningful. It can be helpful to recognize that someone approaching you about an issue and expressing anger shows trust and a belief that you can change and do better. We don't tend to take the time and energy to have these hard conversations with people who we know won't listen. So, try to hold on to the fact that being confronted with an issue is what Roxanne (one of the coauthors) calls "a gift of possible change." Avoiding conflict can lead to issues festering. Indeed, bell hooks (1995) identified that we cannot achieve a "beloved community" of justice without healthy conflict nor clear recognition of differences. Empathy is needed for the person who is naming the misstep, including the emotional labor of confronting you and the hurt or anger they may be experiencing, and self-compassion is needed for yourself, as you, too, are caught in the system and likely tolerating a lot of negative emotions in order to hear the feedback.

- Being cautious about conveying negation of oppression by, for example, minimizing the experience, questioning whether the oppressed person is overreacting, shifting the conversation to more universal experiences of oppression or one's own oppression, all of which suggest the specific experience is not truly important or worth being centered. A common example of this is the subtle negation within a seeming apology: "I'm sorry you feel that way." Such a statement locates the problem as the feeling that the other is experiencing, suggesting they misunderstood or are being overreactive, rather than locating the problem in the action that led to the dialogue. A true apology involves full accountability on your part without discussing intention, such as, "I'm very sorry I did X and I appreciate you bringing it to my attention. I am taking what you said to heart and will work to do better/make sure it does not happen again."

- Resisting emphasizing personal equality and thereby ignoring or mini-mizing structural inequity. It may be the case that you are interacting with a friend or colleague with whom you seek to have an equal relationship as unique and individual human beings. But it is *also* the case that the interaction you are having is about experiences related to systemic power and privilege that you differentially experience.

- Expect to feel uncomfortable and perhaps defensive in these conversa-tions, but do everything you can to avoid expressing that defensiveness, even if that means telling the person you appreciate them talking to you and you need to come back to the conversation after you think about what they have said. (Then you absolutely need to follow through on coming back once you've settled your defensiveness.) When defensiveness arises, it is likely because of underlying feelings of guilt and shame. We want to emphasize and normalize that missteps are inevitable because we are socialized into an oppressive norm: they do not make you "a bad person." That said, realizing you hurt someone or said something

problematic can be difficult. Remember that discomfort is just that and does not compare to the pain of oppression.
- Avoid apologizing in a way that is so profuse that you end up essentially asking the other person to reassure or center you and your feelings.

Many of these dynamics can occur between people who are similarly privileged. Such dialogues may also be intense and emotional, but the experience of causing oppressive damage from the dialogue itself is not present. This is one reason people acting as allies have a particular responsibility to engage difficult dialogues (calling in, calling out, and more general consciousness raising discussions) with people who also hold privilege and to relate to them with patience, doing the work so that people in the oppressed space don't have to. Sometimes this can seem very trying to people with privilege who have developed consciousness of how oppression works. It can be frustrating and painful to interact with others who are defending privilege, even if they are doing it unintentionally. Remembering that you did not always understand these concepts is one way to maintain empathy and patience.

Difficult Dialogues from the Oppressed Space

If you experience oppression and seek to resist imposed assumptions or oppression from privileged others through calling in or calling out, we encourage you to consider some of these central dynamics (Hardy & Lazloffy, 2002; Suyemoto et al., 2020).

- Resist internalized messages that minimize the experiences and effects of oppression. These might include thoughts that the issue wasn't "bad enough" to talk about it or make a fuss, or that naming oppression or calling people in or out is unreasonable or unacceptable. Oppressive experiences are harmful and it is reasonable and justifiable to object to being harmed. It is also reasonable to be angry, and justifiable to expect the privileged person to tolerate your anger. You don't need to justify your feelings and you especially don't need to justify them to yourself!
- At the same time, you must be prepared for the other person to not be able to tolerate your justifiable emotional responses. While we would *hope* that the privileged person could respond with empathy and openness, this is often not the case. So, it is important to be prepared for defensiveness, and to consider how you want to respond. For example, are you okay with an angry or defensive response? If this would be harmful to you, are there things you can do to better frame your perspective (calling in rather than calling out)? Are you willing to do these things or would having to do them be harmful to you (e.g., would you experience that as oppression)? Resisting internalized messages that your pain or anger is unreasonable doesn't mean that you have to express it all, but it does mean that you are making that decision based on *your* goals and values. And

there are strategies you can use that enable you to express your experience but put a boundary on it. For example, you can say something like "I don't really want to have a long conversation about this, but I'm upset/hurt/angry because you said/did X." Or, if someone responds defensively, you can back out of the conversation by saying something like "I don't want to talk about this further right now. Maybe you can think about it and see if you can see my perspective."

- Relatedly, avoid the pull to protect the other person from the pain of seeing their own privilege and the pain of seeing your oppression. You don't need to take care of them.
- Resist feeling responsible for educating or changing the other person. You don't have to know everything before sharing your experience. Sometimes it is enough to simply say "I just wanted you to know that I experienced it that way." It is up to the other person whether they want to develop a stronger relationship with you by working to hear your experience.

You can also have difficult dialogues with people who are similarly positioned to you in relation to oppression and privilege. Sometimes, these conversations might be about your shared oppression. People who are similarly oppressed can be in different places in their critical consciousness, particularly in understanding the systemic nature of oppression and resisting internalization. As we discussed in Chapter 4 in regards to racial identity development, a person of color who has understandings based in the integrative awareness and commitment status may, for example, take action to support and educate someone who is struggling with intense pain, anger, and anxiety that is characteristic of the awakening/dissonance status. The person in the awareness and commitment status may share strategies and actions they have taken to address their own internalized racism or ways they have developed systemic understandings that have enabled them to see possibilities of solidarity with other groups who are also marginalized. Sometimes such difficult dialogue is welcomed, but not always. Remembering that there is a process of development and conscientization that takes time and effort to engage can help you stay in a compassionate place for yourself and others.

There may also be times when people who are oppressed have difficult dialogues with those who are similarly oppressed, but who are enacting oppression from an area of privilege. For example, Dee (who is a trans person without disabilities) might engage in a difficult dialogue with Janet (who is also a trans person without disabilities) when Dee hears Janet using ableist language. This is an example of resisting oppression through promoting the growth of developing allies/accomplices from a place of intersectional oppression. One of the unique risks in these difficult dialogues is of damaging the support, connection, and community that sustains us in resisting one aspect of our own oppression. That is, Janet might be a person who Dee relies on a lot to support and validate them as a trans person. Dee might fear that calling out/in Janet might mean that Dee loses that support, making the damage from trans oppression much greater. Dee might end up deciding that resisting their own oppression as a trans person means, for the moment, not calling out or calling in Janet's ableism. But this is not a long-term solution for justice (and Dee's own integrity). There isn't a perfect solution for Dee as an individual caught in intersectional systems of oppression. But understanding reasons for possible inaction because of our own oppression can help us (and Dee) be more compassionate toward ourself and toward others.

Difficult Dialogues and Intersectionality: the Both/And Challenges of Authentic Loving Relationships within Oppressive Systems

Many of the points above relate to the fact that it is really challenging to have close, caring, and authentic relationships across differences in privilege within a society that is permeated by systemic oppression. Ideally, caring relationships would mean that we are able to see every individual's worth and humanity, and that we can expect that each person in the relationship wants to engage the other's unique and personal authenticity, including individual feelings, fears, tender spots, and so forth. And that each person in the relationship has an equally valid perspective, so that intimacy is advanced by bringing together these perspectives through equal openness and sharing. But systemic oppression has negatively shaped the foundations of our relationships so that we don't start out as equal: our perspectives and experiences are not equally informed or valid when it comes to discussing experiences and effects of oppression. People who experience oppression have more knowledge and insight and people who have more privilege have more responsibility and need to change in order to transform an oppressive system. However, in our relationships we are *also* not only our oppressed or privileged positionality. We are also individual people who care about individual people. If we treat each other only in relation to oppression or privilege, we are also reinforcing the system that we are trying to resist. So the question is, how can we interact in ways that simultaneously acknowledge and cherish each other's humanity and each other's positionality?

When we consider intersectional experiences, this becomes particularly evident. Given that most people have both privileged and oppressed positionalities, we will likely be negotiating all of the dynamics above at various moments. This can be helpful in grounding us in compassion and care for ourselves and each other, as we consider how we would like to be treated by the other in a difficult dialogue.

Reflection Questions

- How do you feel about difficult dialogues? How would/do you *react* if someone else says something that is oppressive, but does so unintentionally? By "react," we mean things about your immediate reaction, your feelings and internal thoughts.

- How are you likely to respond? By "respond," we mean things like what you would do or say. How would you like to respond? What is your intention in choosing your response?
- How would/do you react if YOU make a misstep and someone calls you out or in? What are you likely to think and feel? How would you ideally like to respond?

Major intersectional challenges in resisting oppression at the interpersonal level also relate to the ways the "divide and conquer" strategy has been used to undermine coalition building and solidarity among people who experience different kinds of oppression. One example of the divide and conquer strategy is the media's emphasis on heterosexism in communities of color, implicitly suggesting that the barriers to equality for sexual minority people (e.g., passing of gay marriage bills) was discrimination specifically from people of color, rather than holding accountable all people who engage in heterosexism. Other examples include the ways the KKK encouraged participation from limited income and economically marginalized White communities which divided possible solidarity among race and class (e.g., see C. P. Ellis's story in Terkel's *Race* [Terkel, 1992]); and the ways solidarity between Asian and Black Americans are undermined by the framing of Asian Americans as model minorities, which serves to maintain anti-Blackness, support White supremacy, and ultimately disenfranchises both Black and Asian Americans (Tawa et al., 2013). The consequences of divide and conquer are visible interpersonally in conversations characterized by "oppression Olympics" where individuals who are oppressed may discount the oppression experienced by others, and offer their own experiences of oppression as more valid or "worse." People who are oppressed may fall into this dynamic because they are overwhelmed by the pain of their own oppression, and the resources required to cope with this pain reduce the capacity to consider the pain of another and to consider the impact of associated or relative areas of personal privilege. For example, José, who we described above, may be ignorant of his social class privilege because he's caught in the pain of racism. If his classism is brought to his attention, his response might be, "How can I be privileged when I am so oppressed?" And yet, multiple kinds of privilege and oppression *do* exist simultaneously.

Another reason that oppressed people fall into the dynamic of "**oppression Olympics**" is because they feel that others who experience oppression don't support them, so why should they support others? So, for example, if Robert, a White person from a limited income and economically marginalized background (racially privileged, but oppressed in relation to social class), is talking to José about classism, José might become frustrated that Robert isn't addressing his racial privilege. And Robert might become frustrated that José isn't addressing his social class privilege. Both are seeing the other only through one lens, assuming that there is no common ground. It could be a very different conversation if both took up the challenge of engaging their privileged statuses as well as their oppressed experiences. Oppression Olympics simply pits oppressed people against each other, rather than against the oppression. While it is important to see how some oppressions may have a more severe consequence in a given moment and context (e.g., police brutality or rape rather than name calling or blocked job opportunities), it is also important to understand that oppression isn't a single moment or a single issue, and there are many kinds of detrimental effects. Because we are socialized so that histories and lived experiences of various marginalized groups are not taught or known easily, we also do not know others' pain in depth, and this could lead to not having empathy for other groups.

Reflection Questions

- Have you ever had a difficult dialogue with people who *share a similar oppression* with you (dialoguing as an advocate to an advocate)? By "difficult dialogue" we mean a conversation that encourages or confronts the other person with ways that they are contributing to oppression (their own or others).
- If you have, what was the conversation about and what made it a difficult dialogue? What internal reactions, reflections, and struggles did you have while engaging in this dialogue?
- What was beneficial about taking this step to engage in the dialogue? What was challenging about it?
- If you have not had a difficult dialogue with people who are similarly oppressed, what do you envision this would be like? What are the kinds of things that hold you back from having this kind of dialogue? What are the kinds of things that would invite you to do so?
- Have you ever had a difficult dialogue with people who *share similar privilege* with you (dialoguing as an ally to an ally)?
- If you have, what was the conversation about and what made it a difficult dialogue? What internal reactions, reflections, and struggles did you have while engaging in this dialogue?
- What was beneficial about taking this step to engage in the dialogue? What was challenging about it?
- If you have not had a difficult dialogue with people who are similarly privileged, what do you envision this would be like? What are the kinds of things that hold you back from having this kind of dialogue? What are the kinds of things that would invite you to do so?

Resisting Oppression at the Institutional Level

Most of this chapter has focused on individual and interpersonal actions to resist oppression. But resistance at the institutional level is needed for major change. Institutional level resistance aims to more directly challenge the structural policies and systems that create and maintain oppression. Ultimately, if we can change the institutionalized system of oppression and it's integration into our culture, then there would be no need for actions at other levels. Having just systems would mean being socialized in ways that foster individual and interpersonal justice, so personal and interpersonal discrimination would be quite rare. This level of change and vision of a truly just and caring society is difficult to imagine and will certainly not emerge all at once. Structural changes in laws, policies, and institutional procedures are the concrete changes that will build systemic change. These kinds of changes most directly result from participation in intentional and focused collective action, such as campaigns to raise the minimum wage, or to provide universally accessible high-quality education and health care to address known inequities. You can contribute to this activism in a variety of ways, through committing time, money, or skills to participate in or organize educational campaigns, protests, or efforts to develop or enact alternatives to oppressive institutions.

You can also participate in institutional change within your specific organizations, addressing inequities in policies, procedures, and cultural norms that are embedded within institutions or smaller social environments. For example, you can assess whether your own workplace has practices that discriminate against disabled people, people of color, or people who identify as women or trans by looking at policies and practices that either promote or create barriers to equity in hiring, pay, promotion, and the experience of a positive work environment. And if you do identify inequity, you can organize and advocate to change those policies and procedures.

If you are engaging in these actions as someone with privilege seeking to develop as an accomplice or co-conspirator, you will open yourself to more risk, including possible physical, psychological, or material repercussions for your actions. Participating in institutional change is seen as a deeper level of engagement than ally relational action because one is truly putting one's privilege on the line and taking on greater burdens so that those who are oppressed are protected or have less burden.

Standing Rock provides an example of the different risks or costs taken by someone acting as an ally versus an accomplice or co-conspirator. Showing up to support, bringing supplies, donating, etc., were all relational allied actions. But the ways that some White people engaged in protest at the request of Indigenous organizers exemplified acting as an accomplice/co-conspirator, such as when White protestors linked arms to became a physical barrier between the police outfitted in riot gear and the Indigenous protestors who were engaged in prayer and solidarity. Indigenous and other people of color had already experienced so much police violence, and there was evidence that even if the police acted against the protesters, White people would experience less severe police violence and face less serious charges if arrested.

Reflection Questions

• Consider an institution that you are part of, such as school, your place of employment, offices you work frequently with. Have you noticed any policies, procedures, or cultural norms that are not equitable? What are they?

• If you were to consider making systemic changes, what are some action steps you might want to take, either individually or as a group? In your own positionality, what might your actions look like, and how might they differ from others with different levels of privilege? What might you be willing to do? What risks might be present? And how do you feel about these risks?

Preparing for Activism as a Lifelong Process

Choosing Your Actions

There are so many ways that you can take action to resist oppression. You can make changes in your everyday experiences as well as taking action as part of intentional, planned campaigns for social change. Some examples of everyday changes include frequenting "minority"-owned businesses or boycotting businesses that fund anti-queer or anti-trans legislation, constantly inquiring about wheelchair access at restaurants, and redistributing your wealth through mutual aid funds. These small changes can be important not only in their direct effect (e.g., support for specific businesses or raising awareness in restaurant managers), but also in developing deeper commitments to resisting oppression for the individuals who are changing their lifestyles.

Thinking about how different actions might have different effects can help you match your own styles and skills to different kinds of action. And be honest and clear with yourself (and others) about what you are doing and how it may (or may not) be effective in resisting oppression. These different actions also relate to who you are working with in your resistance: are you working with and trying to affect the experience of those who experience oppression or are you working with and trying to affect the experience of those who are privileged?

Another way to think about your action choices relates to what aspect of oppression you are aiming to affect. Consider the analogy of experiencing oppression as akin to living in a burning house. What is the best way to address this issue? If you are privileged enough to live in a house that is not burning, one option is to ignore the houses that are burning (or even try to keep them burning). We hope this is not a choice you would make. But if you see the houses burning, and the people in them, what should you do? One type of action is to offer bandages and cream to the people in those houses, to try to help heal the burns or reduce the pain. But they still have to live in the house, because there is nowhere else to go. Another type of action is to offer fire-retardant coats to those people, to try to protect them from further harm. But they still have to live in the burning house, so their burns might be less severe, but they are still being burned. These kinds of individual helping actions are often the ones that people gravitate towards—assisting and supporting oppressed people and trying to protect them from the effects of oppression by providing resources or skills to decrease the harm. But the most effective action is to put out the fire. And ideally to put out *all* the fires from all different kinds of oppression. This is a much larger task, which will require collaboration and collective action, not just changes in individual or interpersonal behavior.

Our point here is not to dismiss the value of treating the harm from oppression or the importance of supporting people to protect themselves from oppression: until we put out the fire, people will be burned and care will be needed. But ultimately, that will not create justice. So, we invite you to think about how you might take action to resist oppression at multiple levels (intrapsychic, interpersonal, and institutional/structural), and in multiple ways (supporting people who experience oppression and actively working to change the system of oppression).

Reflection Questions

These questions are about building a plan for action, for taking your next step in resisting oppression.

- What issue will you focus on in your next step to resist oppression and contribute to social justice?
- What motivates you to do this work? (Checking in about this can be very helpful in deciding the best action to take.)
- What are the skills you might bring to this action?
- What are potential challenges to you, personally, moving forward toward this action?
- What do you need to know more about to be effective? What steps will you take to get that learning? Examples might include: read two articles, listen to a podcast, read a blog, talk to a peer, etc. By what date will you have gathered this knowledge?
- What is one *specific* action you will take as part of this next step? Examples might include: talk to one person with privilege, organize a discussion, call a number of representatives, write a letter, attend a protest. By what date will you take this action?
- Who are some supportive people and what are some restorative activities to help you sustain this work?

Taking Care of Yourself: Refilling Your Cup

Making activism a life-long commitment requires building sustainability for yourself—if you try to run a marathon the way you might run a sprint, you will burn out quickly and be unable to finish the race. Consider your reservoir of energy and wellness as a cup—when it's full, you have plenty to give to yourself, others, and the causes that matter to you. Doing things that are depleting drains your cup, and if you have nothing left, you have nothing to give. One way to avoid emptying the cup is choosing effective actions that match your strengths. Building sustainability includes considering your unique abilities and strengths, rather than expecting yourself to take on everything. Are you a people-person who is able to talk about privilege in ways others can hear? Perhaps you are good with data and can use your skill to show the negative impacts of oppression or the positive impacts of justice? Or maybe you are an excellent organizer or an artist or writer? On the other hand, expecting yourself to engage in work that you experience as highly stressful or toxic, or trying to get through every immovable wall will likely leave you feeling depleted. Sometimes you may decide to take actions that will be particularly depleting because they matter to you, but you can't do that all the time.

Another way to avoid burnout is to engage in activities that are restorative and/or energizing. Some of these activities may directly relate to our resistance actions. Perhaps calling out your colleagues at work about the ways that racism is manifesting in your organization is depleting and very risky for you, whereas going to or helping to organize a protest is something you find energizing. Paying attention to how different kinds of justice actions impact you and finding a balance between energizing and depleting experiences will help with sustainability. And, particularly for people with salient experiences of oppression, finding ways to be well and stay engaged is resistance in and of itself.

Knowing your needs and being protective of yourself can also mitigate depletion. Choosing how you consume information is one way to do this. For example, you may choose to read news rather than watch it, because visual media tend to sensationalize stories more; and pick sources that stick to the facts. You may also bookmark or follow specific pages on social media that are either energizing or provide information in ways that are, again, more fact-based and emotionally manageable. There also may be times when you are struggling and need to protect yourself by taking a step back to prioritize your wellness. Particularly when in a space of privilege, be careful to be intentional about your commitment to ultimately reengage.

While the term self-care has different, sometimes negative connotations (similar to the term ally), we still think in its true form it is a worthwhile concept. Some prefer to instead think in terms of community care. Community care, for example, involves shifting from caring for yourself to interpersonal acts of compassion and care, in which self-care and community care are connected (see Valerio, 2019). That is, the act of caring for others can itself be a form of self-care. Engaging in community care could involve cooking a meal for someone, running an errand, watching their children, or helping them get additional support. Be careful here, though, that the effort to care for others doesn't exacerbate exhaustion or burnout. When you are not doing well, it's okay to ask others to step up and care for you. Community care is reciprocal, and you are also part of the community.

Self-care that is effective is ultimately very personal to you—it requires paying close attention to how you feel and what provides incremental relief, restoration, and wholeness. This could include anything from making yourself a cup of tea and taking five minutes to quietly enjoy it, to taking a day away to engage in a favorite hobby, to prioritizing meeting your basic needs (sleep, food, moving your body), to being there for someone else. Peer groups or individual therapy can also be sources of additional support. People vary greatly in the time and money they can dedicate towards caring for themselves. It can help to be realistic with yourself about the options available to you, and to recognize that carving out even a few minutes for yourself in a day can have an impact. For example, 10–15 minutes of physical activity is shown to improve mood (Mayo Clinic, 2017). Other forms of self-care that are free, accessible, and research-backed include:

- Building a mindfulness practice: Taking time to engage in a mindful moment each day has been shown to reduce emotional reactivity and stress, and increase focus, flexible thinking, and relationship satisfaction (e.g., Davis & Hayes, 2012). Practicing can include listening to a guided meditation (there are many free apps and videos on YouTube) or engaging in an activity, like eating, without distraction and while using all of your senses.
- Connecting with nature: Getting outdoors for a bit of time each day is also effective for managing well-being (e.g., Tuyen & Torquati, 2019). This, again, does not need to be a huge endeavor where you drive to the mountains (although it could be). It could simply be going for a walk in your locality if it's safe to do so, while taking in the people, plants, and animals you may come across along the way.
- Practicing gratitude: When we feel helpless or hopeless, our mind zeroes in on the negativity and it becomes all-consuming. Practicing gratitude helps our minds and bodies expand to see that the difficulties we are experiencing exist within a larger context, which can ground us (Alkozei et al., 2018). You might take time at the beginning or end of each day to name three things *specific to you* that you are grateful for, including people in your life, positive moments from your day, or things you value about yourself.

Reflection Questions

In the previous reflection questions, we asked you to consider your next action step for contributing to resisting oppression. But resisting oppression is, as we say above, a life-long journey. These questions ask you to consider your long-term experience:

- How do you see yourself engaging in sustainable ally and advocate action?
- How do you care for yourself in order to avoid burnout? What will help you fill up your cup? Do you have specific self-care strategies that work for you?
- What relational support systems or community do you have who will uplift you? If you don't have support systems, what do you need in order to seek out more support?

Resources for Learning More about Resisting Oppression

Jobin Leeds, G., & AgitArte. (2016). *When we fight, we win: Twenty-first century social movements and the activists that are transforming our world*. New Press.

See also:

Sue, D. W., Calle, C. Z., Mendez, N., Alsaidi, S., & Glaeser, E. (2020). *Microintervention strategies: What you can do to disarm and dismantle individual and systemic racism and bias*. Wiley.

Toporek, R. L., & Ahluwalia, M. K. (2021). *Taking action: Creating social change through strength, solidarity, strategy, and sustainability*. Cognella.

whenwefightwewin.com.

References

Aboud, F. E., Mendelson, M. J., & Purdy, K. T. (2003). Cross-race peer relations and friendship quality. *International Journal of Behavioral Development, 27*(2), 165–173. https://doi.org/10.1080/01650250244000164.

Adams, M., Blumenfeld, W. J., Chase, D., Catalano, J., Dejong, K., Hackman, H. W., Hopkins, L. E., Love, B., Peters, M. L., Shlasko, D., & Zúñiga, X. (Eds.) (2018). *Readings for diversity and social justice: An anthology on racism, antisemitism, sexism, ableism, and classism* (4th edition). Routledge.

Ahlquist, J. S. (2017). Labor unions, political representation, and economic inequality. *Annual Review of Political Science, 20*, 409–432. https://doi.org/10.1146/annurev-polisci-051215-023225.

Akala, A. (2020, September 23). Cost of racism: U.S. economy lost $16 trillion because of discrimination, bank says. NPR. Retrieved October 7, 2021, from https://www.npr.org/sections/live-updates-protests-for-racial-justice/2020/09/23/916022472/cost-of-racism-u-s-economy-lost-16-trillion-because-of-discrimination-bank-says.

Alkozei, A., Smith, R., & Killgore, W. D. (2018). Gratitude and subjective well-being: A proposal of two causal frameworks. *Journal of Happiness Studies, 19*(5), 1519–1542. https://doi.org/10.1007/s10902-10017-9870-9871.

American Anthropological Association. (1998, May 17). AAA statement on race. https://www.americananthro.org/ConnectWithAAA/Content.aspx?ItemNumber=2583.

American Baby and Child Law Centers. (2018, November 6). Involuntary sterilization of disabled Americans: An historical overview. https://www.abclawcenters.com/blog/2018/11/06/involuntary-sterilization-of-disabled-americans-an-historical-overview/.

American Psychological Association. (2019). Guidelines for psychological practice for people with low-income and economic marginalization. Retrieved from www.apa.org/about/policy/guidelines-lowincome.pdf.

American Psychological Association, APA Task Force on Psychological Practice with Sexual Minority Persons. (2021). Guidelines for psychological practice with sexual minority persons. https://www.apa.org/about/policy/psychological-sexual-minority-persons.pdf.

American Sociological Association. (n.d.). Home page. Contexts: Sociology for the public. http://contexts.org.

Andersen, M. L., & Hill Collins, P. (Eds.) (2020). *Race, class, and gender: An anthology* (10th edition). Cengage Learning.

Anderson, S. K., & Middleton, V. A. (Eds.) (2018). *Explorations in diversity: Examining the complexities of privilege, discrimination, and oppression* (3rd edition). Oxford University Press.

Anzaldúa, G. E. (2002). Now let us shift … the path of conocimiento … inner work, public acts. In G. E. Anzaldúa & A. Keating (Eds.), *This bridge we call home: Radical visions for transformation* (pp. 540–578). Routledge.

Anzaldúa, G., & Keating, A. (Eds.) (2002). *This bridge we call home: Radical visions for transformation.* Routledge.

Arao, B., & Clemens, K. (2013). From safe space to brave spaces: A new way to frame dialogue around diversity and social justice. In L. M. Landreman (Ed.), *The art of effective facilitation: Reflections from social justice educators* (pp. 135–150). Stylus Publishing.

Arizona Humanities Council. (n.d.). Perils and perks of privilege: A workshop series. Arizona State University. https://projecthumanities.asu.edu/perils-and-perks-of-privilege.

Banaji, M. R., & Greenwald, A. G. (2016). *Blindspot: Hidden biases of good people.* Bantam Books.

Barroso, A., & Brown, A. (2021). *Gender pay gap in U.S. held steady in 2020.* Pew Research Center. https://www.pewresearch.org/fact-tank/2021/05/25/gender-pay-gap-facts/.

Bates, L. (2016). *Everyday sexism: The project that inspired a worldwide movement.* Macmillan.

Baumann, J. & the New York Public Library (Eds.) (2019). *The Stonewall reader.* Penguin Books.

Bayor, R. H. (Ed.) (2016). *The Oxford handbook of American immigration and ethnicity.* Oxford University Press.

Bhangal, N., & Poon, O. (2020, January 15). Are Asian Americans white? Or people of color? *Yes!* https://www.yesmagazine.org/social-justice/2020/01/15/asian-americans-people-of-color/?fbclid=IwAR3ObsXr2Vt9pN9zee2ZP36seT8ijpJ8pTWNeBQOJSjLmohzZ__GHLUoIBs.

Bigler, R. S., & Wright, Y. F. (2014). Reading, writing, arithmetic, and racism? Risks and benefits to teaching children about intergroup biases. *Child Development Perspectives*, 8, 18–23. https://doi.org/10.1111/cdep.12057.

Bizumic, B. (2019). *Ethnocentrism: Integrated perspectives.* Routledge.

Blashill, A. J., & Powlishta, K. K. (2009). Gay stereotypes: The use of sexual orientation as a cue for gender-related attributes. *Sex Roles*, 61(11–12), 783–793. https://doi.org/10.1007/s11199-009-9684-7.

Board of governors of the Federal Reserve. (2020, October 1). Distribution of Household wealth in the U.S. since 1989 [Data table]. Retrieved October 11, 2021, from https://www.federalreserve.gov/releases/z1/dataviz/dfa/distribute/table/#quarter:127;series:Net%20worth;demographic:networth;population:all;units:shares.

Bogard, K. R., & Dunn, D. S. (Eds.) (2019). Ableism. *Journal of Social Issues*, 75(3), 650–664. https://doi.org/10.1111/josi.12354.

Braverman (2011). Black–White disparities in birth outcomes: Is racism-related stress a missing piece of the puzzle? In A. J. Lemelle, W. Reed, & S. Taylor (Eds.), *Handbook of African American health: Social and behavioral interventions* (pp. 155–163). Springer.

Bronfenbrenner, U. (1979). *The ecology of human development: Experiments by nature and design.* Harvard University Press.

Broverman, I. K., Broverman, D. M., Clarkson, F. E., Rosenkrantz, P. S., & Vogel, S. R. (1970). Sex-role stereotypes and clinical judgments of mental health. *Journal of Consulting and Clinical Psychology*, 34(1), 1–7. https://doi.org/10.1037/h0028797.

Budiman, A., & Ruiz, N. G. (2021, April 29). Key facts about Asian Americans, a diverse and growing population. Pew Research Center. Retrieved October 7, 2021, from https://www.pewresearch.org/fact-tank/2021/04/29/key-facts-about-asian-americans/.

Carey, R. M., & Markus, H. R. (2017). Social class shapes the form and function of relationships and selves. *Current Opinions in Psychology*, 18, 123–130. http://dx.doi.org/10.1016/j.copsyc.2017.08.031.

Carmel, J. (2020, July 22). "Nothing about us without us": 16 moments in the fight for disability rights. *The New York Times*. https://www.nytimes.com/2020/07/22/us/ada-disabilities-act-history.html.

Carr, C. L. (2007). Where have all the tomboys gone? Women's accounts of gender in adolescence. *Sex Roles*, 56(7), 439–448. https://doi.org/10.1007/s11199-007-9183-7.

Carter, R. T., Johnson, V. E., Kirkinis, K., Roberson, K., Muchow, C., & Galgay, C. (2019). A meta-analytic review of racial discrimination: Relationships to health and culture. *Race and Social Problems*, 11(1), 15–32. https://doi.org/10.1007/s12552-018-9256-y.

Carter, R. T., Lau, M. Y., Johnson, V., & Kirkinis, K. (2017). Racial discrimination and health outcomes among racial/ethnic minorities: A meta-analytic review. *Journal of Multicultural Counseling and Development*, 45(4), 232–259. https://doi.org/10.1002/jmcd.12076.

Case, K. A. (2012). Discovering the privilege of whiteness: White women's reflections on anti-racist identity and ally behavior. *Journal of Social Issues*, 68(1), 78–96. https://doi.org/10.1111/j.1540-4560.2011.01737.x.

Centers for Disease Control and Prevention (2021, April 9). Working together to reduce Black maternal mortality. Retrieved October 5, 2021, from https://www.cdc.gov/healthequity/features/maternal-mortality/index.html.

Charlton, J. I. (2000). *Nothing about us without us: Disability, oppression, and empowerment.* University of California Press.

Chavez-Dueñas, N. Y., Adames, H. Y., Perez-Chavez, J. G., & Salas, S. P. (2019). Healing ethno-racial trauma in Latinx immigrant communities: Cultivating hope, resistance, and action. *American Psychologist*, 74(1), 49–62. http://dx.doi.org/10.1037/amp0000289.

Chetty, R., Grusky, D., Hell, M., Hendren, N., Manduca, R., & Narang, J. (2017). The fading American dream: Trends in absolute income mobility since 1940. *Science*, 356(6336), 398–405. https://doi.org/10.1126/science.aal4617.

Chopra, S. B. (2021). Healing from internalized racism for Asian Americans. *Professional Psychology: Research and Practice*. https://doi.org/10.1037/pro0000407.

Cole, E. R. (2009). Intersectionality and research in psychology. *American Psychologist*, 64(3), 170–180. https://doi.org/10.1037/a0014564.

Collins, F. S., & Mansoura, M. K. (2001). The human genome project: Revealing the shared inheritance of all humankind. *Cancer*, 91(S1), 221–225. https://doi.org/10.1002/1097-0142(20010101)91:1+<221::AID-CNCR8>3.0.CO;2-9.

Condon, J. C., & Yousef, F. S. (1974). *An introduction to intercultural communication.* Bobbs-Merrill.

Connor, P., Varney, J., Keltner, D., & Chen, S. (2021). Social class competence stereotypes are amplified by socially signaled economic inequality. *Personality and Social Psychology Bulletin*, 47(1), 89–105. https://doi.org/10.1177/0146167220916640.

Cowan, G. (2000). Women's hostility toward women and rape and sexual harassment myths. *Violence Against Women*, 6(3), 238–246. https://doi.org/10.1177/10778010022181822.

Cox, W. T. L., Devine, P. G., Bischmann, A. A., & Hyde, J. S. (2016). Inferences about sexual orientation: The roles of stereotypes, faces, and the gaydar myth. *The Journal of Sex Research*, 53(2), 157–171. https://doi.org/10.1080/00224499.2015. 1015714.

Cross, W. E., Jr. (1995). The psychology of nigrescence: Revising the Cross model. In J. G. Ponterotto, J. M. Casas, L. A. Suzuki, & C. M. Alexander (Eds.), *Handbook of multicultural counseling* (pp. 93–122). Sage.

D'Augelli, A. R. (1994). Identity development and sexual orientation: Toward a model of lesbian, gay, and bisexual development. In E. J. Trickett, R. J. Watts, & D. Birman (Eds.), *Human diversity: Perspectives on people in context* (pp. 312–333). Jossey-Bass.

David, E. J. R., Schroeder, T. M., & Fernandez, J. (2019). Internalized racism: A systematic review of the psychological literature on racism's most insidious consequence. *Journal of Social Issues*, 75(4), 1057–1086. https://doi.org/10.1111/josi. 12350.

Davis, D. M., & Hayes, J. A. (2012). What are the benefits of mindfulness? *Monitor on Psychology*, 43(7). www.apa.org/monitor/2012/07-08/ce-corner.

Davis, L. J. (2017). *The disability studies reader* (5th edition). Routledge.

Davis, L. J. (Ed.) (2018). *Beginning with disability: A primer* (1st edition). Routledge.

DiAngelo, R. (2018). *White fragility: Why it's so hard for White people to talk about racism*. Beacon Press.

Dillon, F. R., Worthington, R. L., & Moradi, B. (2011). Sexual identity as a universal process. In S. J. Schwartz, K. Luyckx, & V. L. Vignoles (Eds.), *Handbook of identity theory and research* (pp. 649–670). Springer.

Dirth, T. P., & Branscombe, N. R. (2018). The social identity approach to disability: Bridging disability studies and psychological science. *Psychological Bulletin*, 144(12), 1300–1324. https://doi.org/10.1037/bul0000156.

Donovan, R., Galban, D., Grace, R., Bennett, J., & Felicié, S. (2013). Impact of racial macro- and microaggressions in Black women's lives. *Journal of Black Psychology*, 39(2), 185–196. https://doi.org/10.1177/0095798412443259.

Donovan, R. A., & Ponce, A. N. (2009). Identification and measurement of core competencies in professional psychology. *Training and Education in Professional Psychology*, 3(4S), S46–S49. https://doi.org/10.1037/a0017302.

Dovidio, J. F., Gaertner, S. E., Kawakami, K., & Hodson, G. (2002). Why can't we just get along? Interpersonal biases and interracial distrust. *Cultural Diversity and Ethnic Minority Psychology*, 8(2), 88–102. https://doi.org/10.1037/1099-9809.8.2.88.

Dovidio, J. F., Gaertner, S. L., & Pearson, A. R. (2017). Aversive racism and contemporary bias. In C. G. Sibley & F. K. Barlow (Eds.), *The Cambridge handbook of the psychology of prejudice* (pp. 267–294). Cambridge University Press. https://doi.org/10. 1017/9781316161579.012.

Dovidio, J. F., Hewstone, M., Glick, P., & Esses, V. M. (Eds.) (2010). *The SAGE handbook of prejudice, stereotyping and discrimination* (pp. 3–27). Sage. https://dx.doi.org/10. 4135/9781446200919.

Dovidio, J. F., Hewstone, M., Glick, P., & Esses, V. M. (2010). Prejudice, stereotyping and discrimination: Theoretical and empirical overview. In J. F. Dovidio, M. Hewstone, P. Glick, & V. M. Esses (Eds.), *The SAGE handbook of prejudice, stereotyping and discrimination* (pp. 3–27). Sage. https://doi.org/10.4135/9781446200919.n1.

Dunn, D. S., & Andrews, E. E. (2015). Person-first and identity-first language: Developing psychologists' cultural competence using disability language. *American Psychologist*, 70(3), 255–264. https://doi.org/10.1037/a0038636.

Durante, F., & Fiske, S. T. (2017). How social-class stereotypes maintain inequality. *Current Opinion in Psychology*, 18, 43–48. https://doi.org/10.1016/j.copsyc.2017.07.033.

Durante, F., Tablante, C. B., & Fiske, S. T. (2017). Poor but warm, rich but cold (and competent): Social classes in the stereotype content model. *Journal of Social Issues*, 73(1), 138–157. https://doi.org/10.1111/josi.12208.

Dutt, A., & Grabe, S. (2014). Lifetime activism, marginality, and psychology: Narratives of lifelong feminist activists committed to social change. *Qualitative Psychology*, 1(2), 107–122. doi:10.1037/qup0000010.

Eagly, A. H., & Karau, S. J. (2002). Role congruity theory of prejudice toward female leaders. *Psychological Review*, 109(3), 573–598. https://doi.org/10.1037/0033-295X.109.3.573.

Eidlin, B. (2014). Class formation and class identity: Birth, death, and possibilities for renewal. *Sociology Compass*, 8(8), 1045–1062. https://doi.org/10.1111/soc4.12197.

El-Sayed, A. M., Paczkowski, M., Rutherford, C. G., Keyes, K. M., & Galea, S. (2015). Social environments, genetics, and Black–White disparities in infant mortality. *Pediatric and Perinatal Epidemiology*, 29(6), 546–551. https://doi.org/10.1111/ppe.12227.

Evans, M., Lorber, J., & Davis, K. (Eds.) (2012). *Handbook of gender and women's studies*. Sage.

Fausto-Sterling, A. (2020). *Sexing the body: Gender politics and the construction of sexuality* (Revised edition). Basic Books.

Fischer, Nancy L., & Seidman, S. (Eds.) (2016). *Introducing the new sexuality studies* (3rd edition). Routledge.

Forber-Pratt, A. J., Lyew, D. A., Mueller, C., & Samples, L. B. (2017). Disability identity development: A systematic review of the literature. *Rehabilitation Psychology*, 62(2), 198–207. https://doi.org/10.1037/rep0000134.

Ford, M. E., & Kelly, P. A. (2005). Conceptualizing and categorizing race and ethnicity in health services research. *Health Services Research*, 40(5 Pt 2), 1658–1675. https://doi.org/10.1111/j.1475-6773.2005.00449.x.

Fox, A. B., Smith, B. S., & Vogt, D. (2016). The relationship between anticipated stigma and work functioning for individuals with depression. *Journal of Social and Clinical Psychology*, 35(10), 883–897. https://doi.org/10.1521/jscp.2016.35.10.883.

Fredrickson, G. M. (2015). *Racism: A short history*. Princeton University Press.

Fuller, D. A., Lamb, H. R., Biasotti, M., & Snook, J. (2015). Overlooked in the undercounted: The role of mental illness in fatal law enforcement encounters. Treatment Advocacy Center. https://www.treatmentadvocacycenter.org/storage/documents/overlooked-in-the-undercounted.pdf.

Gaertner, S. L., & Dovidio, J. F. (2005). Understanding and addressing contemporary racism: From aversive racism to the common ingroup identity model. *Journal of Social Issues*, 61(3), 615–639. https://doi.org/10.1111/j.1540-4560.2005.00424.x.

Gannon, M. J., & Pillai, R. K. (2016). *Understanding global cultures: Metaphorical journeys through 34 nations, clusters of nations, continents, and diversity*. Sage.

Gans, H. J. (1979). Symbolic ethnicity: The future of ethnic groups and cultures in America. *Ethnic and Racial Studies*, 2(1), 1–20. https://doi.org/10.1080/01419870.1979.9993248.

Gara, M. A., Minsky, S., Silverstein, S. M., Miskimen, T., & Strakowski, S. M. (2019). A naturalistic study of racial disparities in diagnoses at an outpatient behavioral health clinic. *Psychiatric Services*, 70(2), 130. https://doi.org/10.1176/appi.ps.201800223.

Gee, G. C., Spencer, M. S., Chen, J., & Takeuchi, D. (2007). A nationwide study of discrimination and chronic health conditions among Asian Americans. *American Journal of Public Health*, 97(7), 1275–1282. https://doi.org/10.2105/AJPH.2006.091827.

Geronimus, A., Hicken, M., Keene, D., & Bound, J. (2006). "Weathering" and age patterns of allostatic load scores among Blacks and Whites in the United States. *American Journal of Public Health*, 96(5), 826–833. https://doi.org/10.2105/AJPH. 2004.060749.

Gerstner, D. A. (2006). *Routledge international encyclopedia of queer culture*. Routledge.

Glick, P., & Fiske, S. T. (2001). An ambivalent alliance: Hostile and benevolent sexism as complementary justifications for gender inequality. *American Psychologist*, 56(2), 109–118. https://doi.org/10.1037/0003–0066X.56.2.109.

Gobineau, H. C. (1853). *Essai sur l'inégalité des races humaines* [Essay on the inequality of the human races]. https://archive.org/details/inequalityofhuma00gobi.

Godon-Decoteau, D. (2018). Examining the moderating role of internalized racism on the relation between racism-related stress and mental health in Asian Americans. Doctoral dissertation, University of Massachusetts–Boston. ProQuest Dissertations & Theses Global. https://scholarworks.umb.edu/doctoral_dissertations/424/.

Golash-Boza, T. M. (2018). *Race and racisms: A critical approach* (Brief 2nd edition). Oxford University Press.

Goodman, A. H., Moses, Y. T., & Jones, J. L. (2020). *Race: Are we so different?* (2nd edition). John Wiley and American Anthropological Association.

Goodman, D. (2011). *Promoting diversity and social justice: Educating people from privileged groups* (2nd edition). Routledge.

Greenwald, A. G., Poehlman, T. A., Uhlmann, E. L., & Banaji, M. R. (2009). Understanding and using the implicit association test: III. Meta-analysis of predictive validity. *Journal of Personality and Social Psychology*, 97(1), 17–41. https://doi.org/10.1037/a0015575.

Grusky, D., & Hill, J. (Eds.) (2018). *Inequality in the 21st century: A reader*. Routledge.

Guest, K. J. (2020). *Essentials of cultural anthropology: A toolkit for a global age* (3rd edition). W. W. Norton.

Gunn, H. A. (2020). The experience of misgendering among trans and gender diverse people (28030114). Doctoral dissertation, University of Massachusetts Boston. Proquest.

Hall, D. E., & Jagosie, A. (Eds.) (2013). *The Routledge queer studies reader*. Routledge.

Hamer, F. L. (1971, July 10). Nobody's free until everybody's free. Speech delivered at the founding of the National Women's Political Caucus, Washington, D.C. https://muse.jhu.edu/chapter/25609/pdf.

Han, C. (2006). Geisha of a different kind: Gay Asian men and the gendering of sexual identity. *Sexuality and Culture*, 10, 3–28. https://doi.org/10.1007/s12119-006-1018-0.

Hardy, K. V., & Laszloffy, T. A. (2002). Couple therapy using a multicultural perspective. In A. S. Gurman & N. S. Jacobson (Eds.), *Clinical handbook of couple therapy* (pp. 569–593). Guilford Press.

Harmon, M. (2021). Blood quantum and the White gatekeeping of Native American identity. *California Law Review*. https://www.californialawreview.org/blood-quantum-and-the-white-gatekeeping-of-native-american-identity.

Harrell, S. P. (2000). A multidimensional conceptualization of racism-related stress: Implications for the well-being of people of color. *American Journal of Orthopsychiatry*, 70(1), 42–57. https://doi.org/10.1037/h0087722.

Harris, D. A. (2020). Racial profiling: Past, present, and future?American Bar Association. https://www.americanbar.org/groups/criminal_justice/publications/criminal-justice-magazine/2020/winter/racial-profiling-past-present-and-future/.

Harro, B. (2000). The cycle of liberation. In M. Adams, W. J. Blumenfeld, R. Castañeda, H. W. Hackman, M. L. Peters & X. Zúñiga (Eds.), *Readings for diversity and social justice: An anthology on racism, antisemitism, sexism, ableism, and classism* (pp. 463–469). Routledge.

Hauck, G. (2019, June 28). Anti-LGBT hate crimes are rising, the FBI says. But it gets worse. *USA Today*. Retrieved October 9, 2021, from https://www.usatoday.com/st ory/news/2019/06/28/anti-gay-hate-crimes-rise-fbi-says-and-they-likely-undercoun t/1582614001/.

Helms, J. E. (1995). An update of Helm's White and people of color racial identity models. In J. G. Ponterotto, J. M. Casas, L. A. Suzuki & C. M. Alexander (Eds.), *Handbook of multicultural counseling* (pp. 181–198). Sage.

Helms, J. E. (2019). *A race is a nice thing to have: A guide to being a White person or understanding White persons in your life* (3rd edition). Cognella.

Hoffman, K. M., Trawalter, S., Axt, J. R., & Oliver, M. N. (2016). Racial bias in pain assessment and treatment recommendations, and false beliefs about biological differences between blacks and whites. *PNAS*, 113(16), 4296–4301. https://doi.org/10.1073/pnas.1516047113.

hooks, b. (1995). *Killing rage: Ending racism* (1st edition). H. Holt.

hooks, b. (2018). *All about love: New visions*. William Morrow Paperbacks.

Hughes, D., Rodriguez, J., Smith, E. P., Johnson, D. J., Stevenson, H. C., & Spicer, P. (2006). Parents' ethnic-racial socialization practices: A review of research and directions for future study. *Developmental Psychology*, 42(5), 747–770. https://doi.org/10.1037/0012–1649.42.5.747.

Hughes, E. C. (1945). Dilemmas and contradictions of status. *American Journal of Sociology*, 50(5), 353–359. https://doi.org/10.1086/219652.

Institute for Policy Research. (2020, February 24). What drives Native American poverty? Northwestern University. Retrieved October 7, 2021, from https://www.ipr.northwestern.edu/news/2020/redbird-what-drives-native-american-poverty.html.

InterACT and Human Rights Watch. (2017). "I want to be like nature made me": Medically unnecessary surgeries on intersex children in the US. Human Rights Watch. https://www.hrw.org/report/2017/07/25/i-want-be-nature-made-me/m edically-unnecessary-surgeries-intersex-children-us.

Ip, K. I., Miller, A. L., Karasawa, M., Hirabayashi, H., Kazama, M., Wang, L., Olson, S. L., Kessler, D., & Tardif, T. (2021). Emotion expression and regulation in three cultures: Chinese, Japanese, and American preschoolers' reactions to disappointment. *Journal of Experimental Child Psychology*, 201, 104972. https://doi.org/10.1016/j.jecp.2020.104972.

Jetten, J., Wang, Z., Steffens, N. K., Mols, F., Peters, K., & Verkuyten, M. (2017). A social identity analysis of responses to economic inequality. *Current Opinion in Psychology*, 18, 1–5. https://doi.org/10.1016/j.copsyc.2017.05.011.

Jobin Leeds, G., & AgitArte. (2016). *When we fight, we win: Twenty-first century social movements and the activists that are transforming our world*. New Press.

Johnson, A. G. (2018). *Privilege, power, and difference* (3rd edition). McGraw-Hill.

Jones, C. P. (2000). Levels of racism: A theoretical framework and a gardener's tale. *American Journal of Public Health*, 90(8), 1212–1215. https://doi.org/10.2105/ajph.90.8.1212.

Jones, J. M., Dovidio, J. F., & Vietze, D. L. (2014). *The psychology of diversity: Beyond prejudice and racism*. Wiley.

Jost, J. T., Banaji, M. R., & Nosek, B. A. (2004). A decade of system justification theory: Accumulated evidence of conscious and unconscious bolstering of the status quo. *Political Psychology*, 25(6), 881–919. https://doi.org/10.1111/j.1467–9221.2004. 00402.x.

Kao, G., Joynwer, K., Balistreri, K. S. (2019). *The company we keep: Interracial friendships and romantic relationships from adolescence to adulthood*. Russell Sage Foundation.

Katz, P. (2003). Racists or tolerant multiculturalists? How do they begin? *The American Psychologist*, 58, 897–909. https://doi.org/10.1037/0003-066X.58.11.897b.

Kim, A. S., & del Prado, A. (2019). *It's time to talk (and listen): How to have constructive conversations about race, class, sexuality, ability, and gender in a polarized world*. New Harbinger Publications.

Kim, C. J. (1999). The racial triangulation of Asian Americans. *Politics and Society*, 27(1), 105–138. https://doi.org/10.1177/0032329299027001005.

Kim, G. S., Suyemoto, K. L., & Turner, C. B. (2010). Sense of belonging, sense of exclusion, and racial and ethnic identities in Korean transracial adoptees. *Cultural Diversity and Ethnic Minority Psychology*, 16(2), 179–190. https://doi.org/10.1037/a 0015727.

Kimmel, M. S., & Ferber, A. L. (Eds.) (2017). *Privilege: A reader* (4th edition). Routledge.

Kirk, G., & Okazawa-Rey, M. (2020). *Gendered lives: Intersectional perspectives* (7th edition). Oxford University Press.

Kluckhohn, F. R., & Strodtbeck, F. L. (1961). *Variations in value orientations*. Row Peterson.

Lareau, A. (2011). *Unequal childhoods: Class, race, and family life* (2nd edition). University of California Press.

Lareau, A., & Conley, D. (Eds.) (2008). *Social class: How does it work?* Russell Sage Foundation.

Leonardi, M., Bickenbach, J., Ustun, T. B., Kostanjsek, N., & Chatterji, S. (2006). The definition of disability: What is in a name? *The Lancet*, 368(9543), 1219–1221. https://doi.org/10.1016/S0140-6736(06)69498-1.

Levitt, H. M. (2019). A psychosocial genealogy of LGBTQ+ gender: An empirically based theory of gender and gender identity cultures. *Psychology of Women Quarterly*, 43(3), 275–297. https://doi.org/10.1177/0361684319834641.

Lipsitz, G. (2001). *American studies in a moment of danger*. University of Minnesota Press.

Liu, C. M., & Suyemoto, K. L. (2016). The effects of racism-related stress on Asian Americans: Anxiety and depression among different generational statuses. *Asian American Journal of Psychology*, 7(2), 137–146. https://doi.org/10.1037/aap0000046.

Liu, W. M. (2012). Developing a social class and classism consciousness. In E. M. Altmaier & J. I. C. Hansen (Eds.), *The Oxford handbook of counseling psychology* (pp. 326–345). Oxford University Press.

Liu, W. M., Ali, S., Soleck, G., Hopps, J., Dunston, K., & Pickett, T. (2004). Using social class in counseling psychology research. *Journal of Counseling Psychology*, 51(1), 3–18. https://doi.org/10.1037/0022-0167.51.1.3.

Loewen, J. W. (2018). *Lies my teacher told me: Everything your American history textbook got wrong*. New Press.

Lorde, Audre. (1983). There is no hierarchy of oppressions. *Bulletin: Homophobia and Education*. Council on Interracial Books for Children.

Lorde, A. (1995). Age, race, class, and sex: Women redefining difference. In B. Guy-Sheftal (Ed.), *Words of fire: An anthology of African American feminist thought* (pp. 284–291). New Press.

Losavio, J. (2020). What racism costs us all. International Monetary Fund. Retrieved October 7, 2021, from https://www.imf.org/external/pubs/ft/fandd/2020/09/the-economic-cost-of-racism-losavio.htm.

Lu, D., Huang, J., Seshagiri, A., Park, H., & Griggs, T. (2020, September 10). Faces of power: 80% are White, even as U.S. becomes more diverse. *The New York Times*. Retrieved October 5, 2021, from https://www.nytimes.com/interactive/2020/09/09/us/powerful-people-race-us.html.

Lu, W. (2019). This is how employers weed out disabled people from their hiring pools. *HuffPost*. https://www.huffpost.com/entry/employers-disability-discrimination-job-listings_l_5d003523e4b011df123c640a.

Marks, J. (1996). Science and race. *American Behavioral Scientist*, 40(2), 123–133. https://doi.org/10.1177/0002764296040002003.

Markus, H., & Stephens, N. (Eds.) (2017). Inequality and social class: The psychological and behavioral consequences of inequality and social class: A theoretical integration. Special issue of *Current Opinion in Psychology*, 18, pp. 1–152. https://doi.org/10.1016/j.copsyc.2017.11.001.

Markus, H. R. (2008). Pride, prejudice, and ambivalence: Toward a unified theory of race and ethnicity. *American Psychologist*, 63(8), 651–670. https://doi.org/10.1037/0003-0066X.63.8.651.

Markus, H. R., & Kitayama, S. (1991). Culture and the self: Implications for cognition, emotion, and motivation. *Psychological Review*, 98(2), 224–253. https://doi.org/10.1037/0033-295X.98.2.224.

Mather, M., & Jarosz, B. (2014). The demography of inequality in the United States. *Population Bulletin*, 69(2), 1–15. https://www.prb.org/wp-content/uploads/2014/11/united-states-inequality.pdf.

Matsumoto, D., & Juang, L. (2011). *Culture and psychology* (6th edition). Cengage Learning.

[The] Matthew Shepard and James Byrd, Jr., Hate Crimes Prevention Act of 2009, 18 U.S.C. § 249. https://www.justice.gov/crt/matthew-shepard-and-james-byrd-jr-hate-crimes-prevention-act-2009-0.

Mayo Clinic. (2017, September 27). Depression and anxiety: Exercise eases symptoms. https://www.mayoclinic.org/diseases-conditions/depression/in-depth/depression-and-exercise/art-20046495.

McDermott, M. (2006). *Working-class White: The making and unmaking of race*. University of California Press.

McIntosh, P. (1988). *White privilege: Unpacking the invisible knapsack. Excerpt from working paper 189: White privilege and male privilege: A personal account of coming to see correspondences through work in women's studies*. Wellesley College.

McNamee, S. J., & Miller, R. K. Jr. (2004). The meritocracy myth. *Sociation Today*, 2(1). www.ncsociology.org/sociationtoday/v21/merit.htm.

Miller, J. B. (1987). *Toward a new psychology of women* (2nd edition). Beacon Press.

Miller, J. M., & Garran, A. M. (2017). *Racism in the United States: Implications for the helping professions* (2nd edition). Springer.

Miller, S. M. (2011). The impact of the gender binary on gender nonconforming females' lives and psyches over time: an exploratory study. Master's thesis, Smith College. Smith ScholarWorks. https://scholarworks.smith.edu/theses/560.

Miyamoto, Y. (2017). Culture and social class. *Current Opinion in Psychology*, 18, 67–72. https://doi.org/10.1016/j.copsyc.2017.07.042.

Morden, N. E., Chyn, D., Wood, A., & Meara, E. (2021). Racial inequality in prescription of opioid receipt: Role of individual health systems. *New England Journal of Medicine*, 385, 342–351. https://doi.org/10.1056/NEJMsa2034159.

Mosley, D. V., Hargons, C. N., Meiller, C., Angyal, B., Wheeler, P., Davis, C., & Stevens-Watkins, D. (2021). Critical consciousness of anti-Black racism: A practical model to prevent and resist racial trauma. *Journal of Counseling Psychology*, 68(1), 1–16. https://doi.org/10.1037/cou0000430.

Mukhopadhyay, C. C., & Henze, R. (2014). *How real is race?: A sourcebook on race, culture, and biology* (2nd edition). Rowman & Littlefield.

Mukkamala, S., & Suyemoto, K. L. (2018). Racialized sexism/sexualized racism: A multimethod study of intersectional experiences of discrimination for Asian American women. *Asian American Journal of Psychology*, 9(1), 32–46. http://dx.doi.org/10.1037/aap0000104.

Nario-Redmond, M. R. (2020). *Ableism: The causes and consequences of disability prejudice*. Wiley.

Nario-Redmond, M. R., Kemerling, A. A., & Silverman, A. (2019). Hostile, benevolent, and ambivalent ableism: Contemporary manifestations. *Journal of Social Issues*, 75(3), 726–756. https://doi.org/10.1111/josi.12337.

National Association of the Deaf. (2021). Community and culture: Frequently asked questions. Retrieved October 11, 2021, from https://www.nad.org/resources/american-sign-language/community-and-culture-frequently-asked-questions/.

National Museum of African American History and Culture. (n.d.). Popular and pervasive stereotypes of African Americans. https://nmaahc.si.edu/blog-post/popular-and-pervasive-stereotypes-african-americans.

Neville, H. A., Awad, G. H., Brooks, J. E., Flores, M. P., & Bluemel, J. (2013). Color-blind racial ideology: Theory, training, and measurement implications in psychology. *American Psychologist*, 68(6), 455–466. https://doi.org/10.1037/a0033282.

Neville, H. A., Lilly, R. L., Duran, G., Lee, R. M., & Browne, L. (2000). Construction and initial validation of the color-blind racial attitudes scale (CoBRAS). *Journal of Counseling Psychology*, 47(1), 59–70. https://doi.org/10.1037/0022-0167.47.1.59.

Newcomb, M. E., & Mustanski, B. (2010). Internalized homophobia and internalizing mental health problems: A meta-analytic review. *Clinical Psychology Review*, 30(8), 1019–1029. https://doi.org/10.1016/j.cpr.2010.07.003.

New York Times. (2019). The 1619 project. https://www.nytimes.com/interactive/2019/08/14/magazine/1619-america-slavery.html.

Niemann, Y. F., Gutiérrez y Muhs, G., & González, C. G. (2020). *Presumed incompetent II: Race, class, power, and resistance of women in academia*. Utah State University Press.

Nosek, B. A., Banaji, M. R., & Greenwald, A. G. (2002). Harvesting implicit group attitudes and beliefs from a demonstration web site. *Group Dynamics: Theory, Research, and Practices*, 6(1), 101–115. https://doi.org/10.1037//1089-2699.6.1.101.

Omi, M., & Winant, H. (1994). *Racial formations in the United States*. Routledge.

Ostrove, J. M., Kornfeld, M., & Ibrahim, M. (2019). Actors against ableism? Qualities of nondisabled allies from the perspective of people with physical disabilities. *Journal of Social Issues*, 75(3), 924–942. https://doi.org/10.1111/josi.12346.

Oyserman, D., Coon, H. M., & Kemmelmeier, M. (2002). Rethinking individualism and collectivism: Evaluation of theoretical assumptions and meta-analyses. *Psychological Bulletin*, 128(1), 3–72. https://doi.org/10.1037/0033-2909.128.1.3.

Park, Y. S., & Kim, B. S. K. (2008). Asian and European American cultural values and communication styles among Asian American and European American college students. *Cultural Diversity and Ethnic Minority Psychology*, 14(1), 47–56. https://doi.org/10.1037/1099-9809.14.1.47.

Pascoe, E. A., & Smart Richman, L. (2009). Perceived discrimination and health: A meta-analytic review. *Psychological Bulletin*, 135(4), 531–554. https://doi.org/10.1037/a0016059.

Pastkey. (n.d.). Pastkey. Retrieved October 11, 2021, from https://pastkey.org/.

Pew Research Center. (2019). Attitudes on same-sex marriage. https://www.pew forum.org/fact-sheet/changing-attitudes-on-gay-marriage/.

Pew Research Center. (2020). What census calls us. https://www.pewsocialtrends.org/interactives/multiracial-timeline/.

Piff, P. K., & Robinson, A. R. (2017). Social class and prosocial behavior: Current evidence, caveats, and questions. *Current Opinion in Psychology*, 18, 6–10. https://doi.org/10.1016/j.copsyc.2017.06.003.

Plous, S. (2002). Home page. Understanding prejudice. https://secure.understandingprejudice.org/.

Pounder, C. C. H., Adelman, L., Cheng, J., Herbes-Sommers, C., Strain, T. H., Smith, L., Ragazzi, C., ... Corporation for Public Broadcasting. (2003). *Race: The power of an illusion*.

Raifman, J., Moscoe, E., Austin, S. B., & McConnell, M. (2017). Difference-in-differences analysis of the association between state same-sex marriage policies and adolescent suicide attempts. *JAMA Pediatrics*, 171(4), 350–356. https://doi.org/10.1001/jamapediatrics.2016.4529.

Ramsey, P. G. (2008). Children's responses to differences. *NHSA Dialog*, 11(4), 225–237. https://doi.org/ 10.1080/15240750802432607.

Reiter & Walsh, P.C. (2018, November 6). Involuntary sterilization of disabled Americans: A historical overview. American Baby & Child Law Centers. https://www.abclawcenters.com/blog/2018/11/06/involuntary-sterilization-of-disabled-americans-an-historical-overview/.

Rice, D. R., Hudson, S. T. J., & Noll, N. E. (2021). Gay = STIs? Exploring gay and lesbian sexual health stereotypes and their implications for prejudice and discrimination. *European Journal of Social Psychology*. https://doi.org/10.1002/ejsp.2793.

Robinson, M. (2020). Two-spirit identity in a time of gender fluidity. *Journal of Homosexuality*, 67(12), 1675–1690. https://doi.org/10.1080/00918369.2019.1613853.

Rodriguez, D. (2011). Silent rage and the politics of resistance: Countering seductions of Whiteness and the road to politicization and empowerment. *Qualitative Inquiry*, 17(7), 589–598. doi:10.1177/1077800411413994.

Rosenblum, K. E., & Travis, T. C. (Eds.) (2016). *The meaning of difference: American constructions of race and ethnicity, sex and gender, social class, sexuality, and disability* (7th edition). McGraw-Hill.

Rothenberg, P. S., & Accomando, C. H. (Eds.) (2020). *Race, class, and gender in the United States: An integrated study* (11th edition). Macmillan.

Rucker, D. D., & Galinsky, A. D. (2017). Social power and social class: Conceptualization, consequences, and current challenges. *Current Opinion in Psychology*, 18, 26–30. https://doi.org/10.1016/j.copsyc.2017.07.028.

Savin-Williams, R. C. (2011). Identity development among sexual-minority youth. In S. J. Schwartz, K. Luyckx, & V. L. Vignoles (Eds.), *Handbook of identity theory and research* (pp. 671–689). Springer.

Sawchuk, S. (2021, May 18). What is critical race theory, and why is it under attack? *Education Week*. Retrieved October 7, 2021, from https://www.edweek.org/leadership/what-is-critical-race-theory-and-why-is-it-under-attack/2021/05.

Schmidt, R. W. (2011). American Indian identity and blood quantum in the 21st century: A critical review. *Journal of Anthropology*, 2011, 1–10. https://doi.org/10.1155/2011/549521.

Schwartz, G. L., & Jahn, J. L. (2020). Mapping fatal police violence across U.S. metropolitan areas: Overall rates and racial/ethnic inequities, 2013–2017. *PLOS ONE*, 15(6), e0229686. https://doi.org/10.1371/journal.pone.0229686.

Schwartz, S. J., Luyckx, K., & Vignoles, V. L. (2011). *Handbook of identity theory and research* (1st edition). Springer. https://doi.org/10.1007/978-1-4419-7988-9.

Semuels, A. (2015, July 30). White flight never ended: Today's cities may be more diverse overall, but people of different races still don't live near each other. *The Atlantic*. https://www.theatlantic.com/business/archive/2015/07/white-flight-alive-and-well/399980/.

Serano, J. (2016). *Whipping girl: A transsexual woman on sexism and the scapegoating of femininity*. Seal Press.

Shultz, J. W. (2015). *Trans/portraits: Voices from transgender communities*. Dartmouth College Press.

Silva, J. M. (2013). *Coming up short: Working-class adulthood in an age of uncertainty*. Oxford University Press.

Smedley, A., & Smedley, B. D. (2005). Race as biology is fiction, racism as a social problem is real: Anthropological and historical perspectives on the social construction of race. *American Psychologist*, 60, 16–26. https://doi.org/10.1037/0003-066X.60.1.16.

Smedley, A., & Smedley, B. (2012). *Race in North America*. Routledge.

Smedley, A., & Smedley, B. (2018). *Race in North America: Origin and evolution of a worldview* (4th edition). Routledge.

Smith, K., & Hall, M. R. (2018). *Uncommon bonds: Women reflect on race and friendship*. Peter Lang.

Spruhan, P. (2006). Legal history of blood quantum in federal Indian law to 1935. *South Dakota Law Review*, 51(1), 1–50. https://nnigovernance.arizona.edu/legal-history-blood-quantum-federal-indian-law-1935.

Srivastava, S. (2005). "You're calling me a racist?" The moral and emotional regulation of antiracism and feminism. *Signs*, 31(1), 29–62. https://doi.org/10.1086/432738.

Stanford Center for Poverty and Inequality. (2011). 20 facts about U.S. inequality that everyone should know. Stanford Center on Poverty and Inequality. Retrieved October 11, 2021, from https://inequality.stanford.edu/publications/20-facts-about-us-inequality-everyone-should-know.

Statista. (2021, March 9). U.S. unemployment rate, by ethnicity 2020. Retrieved October 7, 2021, from https://www.statista.com/statistics/237917/us-unemployment-rate-by-race-and-ethnicity/.

Stephens, N. M., Markus, H. R., & Phillips, L. T. (2014). Social class culture cycles: How three gateway contexts shape selves and fuel inequality. *Annual Review of Psychology*, 65(1), 611–634. https://doi.org/10.1146/annurev-psych-010213-115143.

Sue, D. W. (2004). Whiteness and ethnocentric monoculturalism: Making the "invisible" visible. *American Psychologist*, 59, 761–769. https://doi.org/10.1037/0003-066X.59.8.761.

Sue, D. W. (2010). *Microaggressions in everyday life: Race, gender, and sexual orientation*. Wiley.

Sue, D. W. (2015). *Race talk and the conspiracy of silence: Understanding and facilitating difficult dialogues on race*. Wiley.

Sue, D. W., Calle, C. Z., Mendez, N., Alsaidi, S., & Glaeser, E. (2020). *Microintervention strategies: What you can do to disarm and dismantle individual and systemic racism and bias*. Wiley.

Sue, D. W., Sue, D., Neville, H. A., & Smith, L. (2019). *Counseling the culturally diverse: Theory and practice* (8th edition). Wiley.

Sutherland, G., & Supreme Court of The United States (1922a). *U.S. Reports: Ozawa v. United States, 260 U.S. 178* [Periodical]. Retrieved from the Library of Congress, https://www.loc.gov/item/usrep260178/.

Sutherland, G., & Supreme Court of The United States (1922b). *U.S. Reports: United States v. Thind, 261 U.S. 204* [Periodical]. Retrieved from the Library of Congress, https://www.loc.gov/item/usrep261204/.

Suyemoto, K. L., Abdullah, T., Godon-Decoteau, D., Tahirkheli, N. N., Arbid, N., & Frye, A. A. (2021). Development of the resistance and empowerment against racism (REAR) scale. *Cultural Diversity and Ethnic Minority Psychology*. Advance online publication. https://doi.org/10.1037/cdp0000353.

Suyemoto, K., & Donovan, R. A. (2015). Exploring intersections of privilege and oppression for Black and Asian immigrant and U.S. born women: Reaching across the imposed divide. In O. M. Espin & A. L. Dottolo (Eds.), *Gendered journeys: Women and migration through a feminist psychology lens*. Palgrave Macmillan.

Suyemoto, K. L., & Hochman, A. L. (2021). "Taking the empathy to an activist state": Ally development as continuous cycles of critical understanding and action. *Research in Human Development*, 37(3–4), 293–301. https://doi.org/10.1080/15427609.2021.1928453.

Suyemoto, K. L., Hochman, A. L., Donovan, R. A., & Roemer, L. (2020). Becoming and fostering allies and accomplices through authentic relationships: Choosing justice over comfort. *Research in Human Development*, 18(1), 1–28. https://doi.org/10.1080/15427609.2020.1825905.

Tatum, B. (2017). *Why are all the black kids sitting together in the cafeteria? And other conversations about race* (3rd edition). Basic Books.

Tawa, J., Suyemoto, K. L., & Tauriac, J. J. (2013). Triangulated threat: A model of Black and Asian race relations in a context of White dominance. In S. O. Pinder (Ed.), *American multicultural studies: Diversity of race, ethnicity, gender and sexuality* (pp. 229–247). Sage.

Taylor, K., Frankenberg, E., & Siegel-Hawley, G. (2019). Racial segregation in the southern schools, school districts, and counties where districts have seceded. *AERA Open*, 5(3). https://doi.org/10.1177/2332858419860152.

Terkel, S. (1992). *Race: How Blacks and Whites think and feel about the American obsession* (pp. 271–279). Anchor Books.

The Everyday Sexism Project. (n.d.). The everyday sexism project. https://everydaysexism.com/.

Thomann, C., & Suyemoto, K. (2018). Developing an antiracist stance: How White youth understand structural racism. *The Journal of Early Adolescence*, 38(6), 745–771. https://doi.org/10.1177/0272431617692443.

Thomas, V., & Azmitia, M. (2014). Does class matter? The centrality and meaning of social class identity in emerging adulthood. *Identity*, 14(3), 195–213. https://doi.org/10.1080/15283488.2014.921171.

Tolman, D. L., Diamond, L. M., Bauermeister, J. A., George, W. H., Pfaus, J. G., & Ward, L. M. (Eds.) (2014a). *APA handbook of sexuality and psychology*. Vol. 1: *Person-based approaches*. American Psychological Association. https://doi.org/10.1037/14193-000.

Tolman, D. L., Diamond, L. M., Bauermeister, J. A., George, W. H., Pfaus, J. G., & Ward, L. M. (Eds.) (2014b). *APA handbook of sexuality and psychology*. Vol. 2: *Contextual approaches*. American Psychological Association. https://doi.org/10.1037/14194-000.

Toporek, R. L., & Ahluwalia, M. K. (2021). *Taking action: Creating social change through strength, solidarity, strategy, and sustainability*. Cognella.

Tran, N., Nakamura, N., Kim, G. S., Khera, G. S., & Ahn Allen, J. M. (2018). #APIsforBlackLives: Unpacking the interracial discourse on the Asian American Pacific Islander and Black communities. *Community Psychology in Global Perspective*, 4(2), 73–84. https://psycnet.apa.org/record/2019-24875-006.

Tucker, W. H. (2004). "Inharmoniously adapted to each other": Science and racial crosses. In A. S. Winston (Ed.), *Defining difference: Race and racism in the history of psychology* (pp. 109–133). American Psychological Association. https://doi.org/10.1037/10625-005.

Tuyen, H., & Torquati, J. C. (2019). Examining connection to nature and mindfulness at promoting psychological well-being. *Journal of Environmental Psychology*, 66, 101370. https://doi.org/10.1016/j.jenvp.2019.101370.

Umaña-Taylor, A. J., & Hill, N. E. (2020). Ethnic-racial socialization in the family: A decade's advance on precursors and outcomes. *Journal of Marriage and Family*, 82(1), 244–271. https://doi.org/10.111/jomf.12622.

Umaña-Taylor, A. J., Quintana, S. M., Lee, R. M., Cross, W. E., Rivas-Drake, D., Schwartz, S. J., Syed, M., Yip, T., & Seaton, E. (2014). Ethnic and racial identity during adolescence and into young adulthood: An integrated conceptualization. *Child Development*, 85(1), S21–39. https://doi.org/ 10.1111/cdev.12196.

United Nations, Department of Economics and Social Affairs. (2006). Convention on the rights of persons with disabilities (CRPD). United Nations. Retrieved October 11, 2021, from https://www.un.org/development/desa/disabilities/convention-on-the-rights-of-persons-with-disabilities.html.

U.S. Census Bureau. (2021). Current population survey, 2020 and 2021 [data table]. https://www.census.gov/content/dam/Census/library/visualizations/2021/demo/p60-273/Figure1.Pdf.

U.S. Census Bureau. (2020). Health insurance coverage in the United States: 2019. https://www.census.gov/content/dam/Census/library/publications/2020/demo/p60-271.pdf.

U.S. Department of Housing and Urban Development. (2021, March 22). Closing the African American homeownership gap: HUD user. Retrieved November 1, 2021, from https://www.huduser.gov/portal/pdredge/pdr-edge-featd-article-032221.html.

U.S. Department of Justice. (n.d.). Information and technical assistance on the Americans with Disabilities Act. Retrieved October 11, 2021, from https://www.ada.gov/ada_intro.htm.

U.S. Department of Labor, Women's Bureau. (2020). Median annual earnings by sex, race, and Hispanic ethnicity [Interactive data file]. Retrieved October 9, 2021, from https://www.dol.gov/agencies/wb/data/earnings/median-annual-sex-race-hispanic-ethnicity.

Valerio, N. (2019, April 16). This viral Facebook post urges people to rethink self-care. *Fashion*. https://fashionmagazine.com/flare/self-care-new-zealand-muslim-attack/.

Violence Against Women Act of 1994, Title IV of the Violent Crime Control and Law Enforcement Act, H.R. 3355 (1994). https://www.congress.gov/bill/103rd-congress/house-bill/3355.

Wang, L., Lin, H. C, & Wong, Y. J. (2021). Perceived racial discrimination on the change of suicide risk among ethnic minorities in the United States. *Ethnicity & Health*, 26(5), 631–645. https://doi.org/10.1080/13557858.2018.1557117.

Wang, V. O., & Sue, S. (2005). In the eye of the storm: Race and genomics in research and practice. *American Psychologist*, 60(1), 37–45. https://doi.org/10.1037/0003-066X.60.1.37.

Warner, L. R., Settles, I. H., & Shields, S. A. (2018). Intersectionality theory in the psychology of women. In S. L. Cook, A. Rutherford, C. B. Travis, J. W. White, W. S. Williams & K. F. Wyche (Eds.), *APA handbook of the psychology of women: History, theory and battlegrounds* (pp. 521–539). American Psychological Association. http://dx.doi.org/10.1037/0000059-027.

Wenger, J. B., & Zaber, M. A. (2021, February). Who is middle class? RAND Corporation. https://www.rand.org/pubs/perspectives/PEA1141-3.html.

West, L. M., Donovan, R. A., & Daniel, A. (2016). The price of strength: Black female college students' perspectives on the strong Black woman stereotype. *Women & Therapy*, 39(3–4), 390–412. https://doi.org/10.1080/02703149.2016.1116871.

Whaley, A. L. (2001). Cultural mistrust: An important psychological construct for diagnosis and treatment of African Americans. *Professional Psychology: Research and Practice*, 32(6), 555–562. https://doi.org/10.1037//0735-7028.32.6.555.

When We Fight, We Win. (n.d.) Home page. https://www.whenwefightwewin.com/.

Wirth, L. (1945). The problem of minority groups. In R. Linton (Ed.), *The science of man in the world crisis*. Columbia University Press.

Wong, A. (Ed.) (2020). *Disability visibility*. Penguin Books.

World Health Organization. (2011). *World report on disability*. https://www.who.int/publications/i/item/9789241564182.

Worthen, M. G. F. (2013). An argument for separate analyses of attitudes toward lesbian, gay, bisexual men, bisexual women, MtF and FtM transgender individuals. *Sex Roles*, 68(11), 703–723. https://doi.org/10.1007/s11199-012-0155-1.

Wu, E. (2014). *The color of success: Asian Americans and the origin of the model minority*. Princeton University Press.

Yarber, W., & Sayad, B. (2019). *Human sexuality: Diversity in contemporary society* (11th edition). McGraw-Hill.

Yoshino, K. (2006). *Covering: The hidden assault on our civil rights*. Random House.

Young, I. M. (1990). Five faces of oppression. In Iris Marion Young (Ed.), *Justice and the politics of differences* (pp. 39–65). Princeton University Press.

Zhang, X., Carabello, M., Hill, T., Bell, S. A., Stephenson, R., & Mahajan, P. (2020). Trends of racial/ethnic differences in emergency department care outcomes among adults in the United States from 2005 to 2016. *Frontiers in Medicine*, 7, 300. https://doi.org/10.3389/fmed.2020.00300.

Zinn, H. (2015). *A people's history of the United States: 1492–present* (3rd edition). HarperCollins.

Zivony, A., & Lobel, T. (2014). The invisible stereotypes of bisexual men. *Archives of Sexual Behavior*, 43(6), 1165–1176. https://doi.org/10.1007/s10508-014-0263-9.

Author Index

Subject Index

Page numbers in *italics* refer to figures. Page numbers in **bold** refer to tables.

self-compassion 11, 86, 189
self-construal 101
self-determinism of meritocracy 6
self-labeling, in relation to social class 161
self-segregation, issue of 61
self-worth, sense of 179
sex 113–116: assigned at birth 113; biological characteristics 114; chromosomes 113; continuum 114; definition of 111; diversity of 113; meanings of 112–113; non-binary construction 113–115; as social construct 113–116
sexism 121–125: benevolent 121–122; cissexism, definition of 112, 122–123; definition of 111–112; institutional 121–122; internalized 50; interpersonal 121–122; misogyny 121
sexual assault 50, 125, 136
sexual arousal, 129
sexual attraction 129, 133
sexual desires 129
sexual diversity 113–114
sexual harassment 123, 181
sexual identity 129, 133, 134–136
sexuality: 127–139; concept of 40–41; definition of 127; factors influencing 128–129; identity 134–136; privilege 137; as separate from gender 131–133; as social construct 128–134; terminology 130; *see also* heterosexism
sexual minorities 128, 130, 136; barriers to equality for 193; homophobia 136; Nazis' persecution of 136; oppression against 136; rights for 179; social attitudes toward 138; social constructions of 132
sexual minority culture 129, 134, 135
sexual orientation 40, 127–128, 129, 130, 133–134; definition of 128
sexual preference 130
sissy 123; *see also* cissexism, transmisogyny
slavery, issue of 42, 56
social acceptance 30
social capital 156
social categories 30; common factors among 33–36; culture within 33; determination of 26; differentiating influences from personal identity 31–33; hierarchical nature 34; intersectionality of 35; meaning of 30, 49; and positionality 12; related to oppression and privilege 29–36;

statuses (subcategories), creation of 33
social change, burden of 173
social class 135; 154–167; assumptions 165; capitalism, system of 156, categories 157; culture 155, 158, 160–161, 165–166; definition of 154; hierarchies in the United States 156–157; identity 161–162; implicit bias about 49; low-income and economically marginalized people (LIEM) 156–157, 163; mobility 154; norms and values 160; objective 158; people's attitudes about 50; privilege of 165–166, 182, 193; SES 155; related to dominant ethnic culture 161; self-labeling in relation to 161; as social construct 155–161; stereotypes 157; subjective 158, 161; *see also* classism
social connection, loss of 144
social construct 20, 25–26: culture and 26–29, 43; definition of 20; disability as 142–148; ethnicity and ethnoculture as 99–103; gender as 32, 116–118; idea of money 26; inequity 157; of oppression 175; of race 32, 75–82; sex as 113–116; sexuality as 128–134; social class as 155–161
social cost, of oppression for White people **62**
social cultures, in association with statuses 33
social distancing 61
social exclusion 32
social hierarchies 30, 69; as intersectional 35; invisible influence of 7–8; of power 3, 26; and prejudice 47
social identifications 30
social identities 30; models of 32; in relation to social groups and categories 32
social inequities and privilege 37
socialization, process of 25, 27–28, 49, 74, 95, 97, 105, 117, 131
social justice 1, 37, 44, 64, 141, 175, 186, 188, 197
social categories, of oppression 29–30
socially constructed categories: racial categories 79; systemic hierarchies of 48
social science 1, 21, 32, 63, 71–72, 77–78, 128
social stigma 130
social systems 30

Made in the USA
Las Vegas, NV
27 January 2023